John F. Kennedy
on Leadership

The Lessons and Legacy of a President

JOHN A. BARNES

AMACOM
American Management Association

NEW YORK • ATLANTA • BRUSSELS • CHICAGO • MEXICO CITY • SAN FRANCISCO
SHANGHAI • TOKYO • TORONTO • WASHINGTON, D. C.

This publication is designed to provide accurate and authoritative information in regard to the subject matter covered. It is sold with the understanding that the publisher is not engaged in rendering legal, accounting, or other professional service. If legal advice or other expert assistance is required, the services of a competent professional person should be sought.

Library of Congress Cataloging-in-Publication Data

Barnes, John A., 1960–
    John F. Kennedy on leadership : the lessons and legacy of a president / John A. Barnes.
       p. cm.
    Includes index.
    ISBN 0-8144-0834-6
    1. Leadership—Case studies.   2. Communication in management—Case studies.
   3. Teams in the workplace—Case studies.   4. Decision making—Case studies.
   5. Crisis management—Case studies.   6. Kennedy, John F. (John Fitzgerald), 1917–1963.   I. Title.

HM1261.B37 2005
658.4'092—dc22

2004030980

Printing number

10 9 8 7 6 5 4 3 2 1

For Mary Elisabeth
Our Mimi

Contents

Preface

Another book on John F. Kennedy? What is there left to be studied that hasn't been studied already?

His leadership. Remarkably, given the spate of "leadership" books that have been published in the decade since Donald Phillips's *Lincoln on Leadership* created the genre, no one has attempted a book examining the leadership style of the modern American president who is probably most closely identified with the term.

You don't have to look far for the evidence of the imprint Kennedy has left on American life and politics. From the day of his death, virtually every president and presidential candidate since has, to varying degrees, sought to portray himself as the heir to the Kennedy legacy. Lyndon Johnson was obsessed with living in Kennedy's shadow. Richard Nixon was immensely jealous of the man he also thought of as his friend. Jimmy Carter reveled in being described by *Time* magazine as "Kennedyesque" during his 1976 campaign. Ronald Reagan invoked Kennedy's tough stance toward the Soviet Union and his tax-cutting economic strategy to buttress his own efforts in these realms. A sixteen-year-old Bill Clinton famously was photographed—with a beatific look on his face—shaking Kennedy's hand in the Rose Garden. John F. Kerry (with the same initials and from the same state) took the comparisons to extremes at times, windsurfing off Nantucket Island in seemingly conscious emulation of Kennedy sailing off Hyannis.

Perhaps the politicians sense something that the political science professors—who have tended not to rate Kennedy's presidency very highly—don't: Even four decades after his death, JFK remains extraordinarily popular. An ABC News poll taken over President's Day weekend in 2003 listed JFK as the second-greatest president of all time. A Zogby poll showed an almost identical result. Although recentness and nostalgia no doubt play a major role in such results, the fact is that at the time of his death, Kennedy had the highest average approval rating of any president ever measured by the Gallup polling organization: 70 percent.

Cynics have looked back at Kennedy's career and proclaimed that he was the spoiled son of a wealthy father whose success was inevitable. Such a conclusion sells Kennedy seriously short. There were plenty of talented, handsome, well-off, and politically ambitious young men in America in the 1950s and they did not all become president, much less an icon of the age for millions of their fellow citizens. Advantages JFK certainly enjoyed, but they were offset by considerable disadvantages that he had to labor mightily to overcome. *John F. Kennedy on Leadership,* I believe, will demonstrate how the modern executive—or merely the interested reader—can profit from learning how Kennedy went about this process of leadership development.

Kennedy, for example, gave us the "look" of the modern presidency. If Franklin D. Roosevelt created the "imperial presidency," it was Kennedy who gave it its royal trappings. Kennedy took the boxy, functional presidential aircraft; hired a top industrial designer to repaint it; and christened the result Air Force One, to descend majestically from the skies as the very symbol of presidential power. No longer would American presidents greet their foreign visitors prosaically at the airport. Instead, the visitor would be whisked to the White House for a grand "welcoming ceremony" on the South Lawn. State dinners, which had been fairly staid affairs for decades, were transformed into spectacular events with men in white ties and women in evening dresses. The White House itself, after being a fairly down-at-the-heels mansion from one administration to the next, would now glitter in grand style. And the supposedly plebeian American public loved it.

Kennedy was also, in the words of biographer Geoffrey Perret, the first "celebrity president." This may be a good or bad thing, but starting with Kennedy, Pennsylvania Avenue intersected with Sunset Boulevard and has never looked back.

Kennedy had other notable leadership accomplishments to his credit:

➡ *He made his own rules.* When he ran for Congress in 1946 without having held any previous office, old-line Boston pols grumbled that he was cutting the line. Kennedy didn't care. He just built his own organization, a practice he would retain throughout his career. Today, virtually all ambitious politicians rely on their own organizations, rather than on party organizations, to win elections.

➡ *He started early.* In 1951, he began laying the groundwork to take on the wealthy, handsome, and popular Republican incumbent U.S. senator from Massachusetts, Henry Cabot Lodge Jr., in what was certain to be the Republican year of 1952. Kennedy traveled the state, never taking a single vote for granted. He began running for president in 1958 and declared his candidacy in January 1960, both of which were considered absurdly early at the time. Now, the early start is standard operating procedure.

➡ *He mastered TV.* The political debate form had all but died by the early 1950s. But Kennedy thought that if he could hold his own in a televised debate, it would help him. His theory proved correct against both Lodge and Nixon. Today, entire cable television networks are devoted to nothing but political debate.

➡ *He made friends of the press corps.* Kennedy was the first president to answer questions from journalists on live television. ("The dumbest idea since the hula hoop," groused *New York Times* columnist James Reston at the time.) The live presidential press conference, of course, is now an institution.

➡ *He made policy makers of the White House staff.* Under the Kennedy administration, the cabinet was eclipsed as a major decision-making body by the White House staff, which moved to the fore as the chief executive's primary advisers and instruments.

And all the while, Kennedy made it look effortless.

However, although the public saw the finished product, it did not see the hard work—as well as real pain and discomfort—that lay behind the polished image. Neither did Kennedy's opponents—to their cost.

Conventional wisdom, for example, has it that Kennedy was a "natural" on TV, but he was not. His early appearances before the camera were nervous, hesitant, halting. Kennedy worked extensively on his television presence. Those "spontaneous" press conference appearances as president, in which Kennedy affected the manner of someone who had almost incidentally dropped by, were preceded by hours of rehearsal. Kennedy won his famous first debate with Nixon in 1960 because he prepped hard and steered the debate toward his own strengths. Nixon, in spite of his own positive experiences with television (most notably the 1952 "Checkers Speech"), oddly, did not prepare.

Nor did the outside world see Kennedy's extensive health problems. A persistent back injury from before World War II, which was exacerbated by the PT-109 incident, often caused him to hobble around on crutches in private. Addison's disease nearly killed him three times and would plague him to the end of his life. It has been said that Kennedy should have been more up-front about these problems. No doubt he concealed these issues partly for political reasons, but a strong element of pride entered into the matter as well. Like Franklin Roosevelt, who suffered from polio, Kennedy didn't want anyone's pity.

Kennedy's brief yet action-packed career can be studied with profit by business executives. He knew what he wanted, but he wasn't wedded to particular ways of getting it. When he wasn't getting the economic growth rates he wanted (i.e., "Getting the country moving again"), he shocked observers by calling for a large tax cut. He dismantled the rigid chain-of-command style of the Eisenhower White House—which he thought stifled creativity—in favor of a more freewheeling approach. At the same time, he centralized policy making in the White House to ensure the administration spoke with a single voice.

That much, and far more, combined to make John F. Kennedy one of the stellar leaders of the twentieth century. You may not be aiming to become president, but any executive looking to improve himself or herself can profit by studying JFK's leadership lessons.

Acknowledgments

The precise origins of a book are sometimes murky, but I vividly recall the origin of this one. It was at the Princeton Club in the fall of 2001 when I attended a party for a book on Ronald Reagan by my friend Steve Hayward. Another attendee, Larry Kudlow, co-host of CNBC's *Kudlow & Cramer* show, spoke with passion about how John F. Kennedy's leadership, particularly in the economic realm, had been generally overlooked. That got me thinking there might be a book on Kennedy's leadership.

The project kicked into higher gear when I heard a lecture by Geoffrey Perret, author of *Jack: A Life Like No Other*, the first single-volume biography of JFK. Perret emphasized how much learning went into creating the "JFK" of folk memory. Researching the subject further, I discovered that like many people, I had been fooled into believing that because Kennedy made his leadership *look* effortless, that it in fact *was* effortless. Nothing could be further from the truth. Kennedy had to work hard at becoming a "natural leader." There were lessons to be learned from that experience.

I'd also like to thank Christina McLaughlin Parisi, who acquired this book for AMACOM on the basis of my proposal. She and the rest of the staff at AMACOM, including Jim Bessent and Barry Richardson—who really pulled it together for publication—could not have been more courteous and helpful.

The staff at the John F. Kennedy Library in Boston was unfailingly polite in putting up with my numerous inquiries. The Society Library of New York, a great institution, was a terrific place to write as well as do research.

Thanks also go to my colleagues at Pfizer, Inc.: Chairman and CEO Hank McKinnell, Corporate Affairs Senior Vice President Chuck Hardwick, John Santoro, Jeanne Ammermuller, and Loretta McKenzie.

Thanks also to Lucianne Goldberg, who worked as a literary agent before finding fame as a pundit, and who graciously agreed to read my contract for this book and offer her advice.

Last but certainly not least, I thank my wife, Mary, our daughter Mary Elisabeth, and the rest of our extended families, who encouraged and pushed me to finish this book. I could not have done it without them.

John F. Kennedy on Leadership

Prelude:
June 11, 1963

The Oval Office, just before 8 P.M., EDT.

It was a frustrating end to a very long day.

President John F. Kennedy was seated behind his desk in the Oval Office. Tension was rising because, in just a few moments, the president was scheduled to give a nationally televised address on the emotionally and politically charged subject of civil rights for black Americans (who were then known as Negroes). And he didn't even have a fully prepared text.

This was his own fault. Early that afternoon, he simply declared his desire to address the nation that very night on civil rights, catching his team flat-footed. Not only was there no final text; there wasn't even a rough draft. As soon as the president made his desire known, however, Attorney General Robert Kennedy, his brother's closest confidant; Burke Marshall, the assistant attorney general for civil rights; and Theodore Sorensen, the president's chief speechwriter, closeted themselves in the Cabinet Room to start hashing out exactly what he would say.

The civil rights issue was, in many ways, a distraction the president thought he didn't need. Never very partial to domestic policy, he had devoted a single, ambiguous phrase to the entire subject in his inaugural address, stating that Americans were "unwilling to witness or permit the slow undoing of those human rights to which this Nation has always been committed, and to which we are committed today *at home* and around the world." Kennedy strongly believed his main business was overseas. Just that afternoon, he had met with Averell Harriman, the diplomat and former governor of New York, who was about to depart for Moscow to begin negotiations on a treaty for a limited ban on nuclear testing. A successful conclusion to those negotiations, Kennedy believed, would give the hawkish president strong momentum as a "peace candidate" going into the all-important 1964 elections.

The situation was also heating up in a place most Americans were only vaguely aware: Vietnam. That morning, Kennedy had been shocked by a front-page newspaper photograph of a Buddhist monk burning himself to death in the streets of Saigon, the capital of America's ally, South Vietnam. The Buddhists were protesting the policies of the American-backed government of Ngo Dinh Diem, who, like Kennedy, was a Roman Catholic presiding over a mostly non-Catholic country. From Kennedy's perspective, Diem's regime was fast becoming a liability. It was just repressive enough to cause the United States international embarrassment, and seemingly unable to build either a stable domestic order or defeat the increasingly bold communist Vietcong guerrillas. Some sort of firm action appeared to be needed there soon.

Whatever the news from abroad, however, the pressure of events at home was forcing the issue of civil rights to the fore.

Shortly after Kennedy's election, the Supreme Court had declared segregated buses, trains, and the stations that served them unconstitutional. To test the new ruling, a small group of northern blacks and whites who called themselves "freedom riders" expressed their intent in May 1961 to board a bus and head south. Sensing the coming confrontation, Kennedy tried to have the effort called off by his civil rights aide, Harris Wofford. The riders were not to be deterred, however, and they ran into a near-riot in Anniston, Alabama, where the bus they were riding was burned.

Though no one knew it at the time, 1961 was the beginning of what was later to be termed "the long, hot summers" of the 1960s. More freedom rides, along with sit-ins at segregated lunch counters and street marches, erupted across the South as an increasingly affluent and self-confident black population—many of whom were World War II or Korean War veterans—proved unwilling to accept the second-class citizenship that had been imposed on their forebears. Led by charismatic preachers such as Martin Luther

King Jr. and Ralph Shuttlesworth, their tactics of nonviolent resistance were met by the frequently violent response of the forces of the status quo.

The president was personally sympathetic to the plight of black Americans. Despite his own affluent circumstances, Kennedy knew enough about "no Irish need apply" signs and the reality of anti-Catholic prejudice to empathize with those experiencing discrimination. He was also concerned about how the image of denying civil rights to black Americans would play in the international arena of newly emerging African and Asian countries. The Soviet Union rarely missed an opportunity to play up its own supposed racial enlightenment in order to win support from such countries in the United Nations and other world forums.

Kennedy was also not blind to the political benefits of siding with black Americans' struggle. His telephone call to King's wife while the civil rights leader was jailed late in the 1960 campaign—while Republican Richard Nixon remained aloof—was credited with helping tip some key states into Kennedy's column in that close-fought election.

As president, however, Kennedy knew the potential political downside of the issue loomed large. The House and Senate committees he needed to pass his program were chaired mostly by Southern Democrats, who were all segregationists. A too-aggressive stance on civil rights risked alienating them, as well as Southern voters who, in 1964, might be susceptible to another Dixiecrat revolt similar to the one that had rocked the Democratic party in 1948.

Caught on the horns of this dilemma, Kennedy had bobbed and weaved on the issue for more than three years. Seeking to keep his options open, he held back from endorsing the idea of using the federal government to guarantee equal rights and opportunities for blacks. Instead, he signed executive orders outlawing discrimination in most federally funded facilities, such as airports. He also signed an order demanding that the federal government adopt "affirmative action" to reach out and hire more black employees. (With the surly assent of J. Edgar Hoover, the first black FBI agents were hired under the Kennedy administration.)

But even in this limited realm, Kennedy held back from committing himself fully. During the 1960 campaign, he had promised to end discrimination in public housing "with the stroke of a pen," yet once in office, he kept finding reasons to delay such action. (Outraged blacks mailed him hundreds of pens; eventually, though, he did sign the order.) When it came to federal judicial appointments in the South, he could not find the courage to nominate even a few racially liberal whites, let alone blacks. Also, the undeniable presence of communists and former communists in the civil rights movement made the president leery of being too closely identified with it.

Black votes, Kennedy and his brother Robert believed, were the ultimate solution to the problem. A sizable bloc of black voters in Southern states, they reasoned, would compel the segregationist politicians of the South to change their tune. But in the absence of federal legislation, the Kennedy Justice Department never moved to protect those trying to register the voters, or the voters themselves, who sometimes lost their farm tenancies or welfare benefits when they weren't physically threatened or attacked. There was a deep and growing sense of betrayal on the part of blacks and Democratic party liberals.

As the administration entered its second year, it was clear that events on the ground weren't taking much account of the president's finely calibrated sense of what was politically possible. In September 1962, a black veteran named James Meredith—who, ironically, had been inspired by the ringing rhetoric of Kennedy's inaugural address—expressed his determination to enroll in the University of Mississippi. Equipped with a court order requiring the university to enroll him, Meredith arrived at the campus accompanied by U.S. marshals and Justice Department officials. Kennedy wanted the federal presence to remain low key, hoping that Governor Ross Barnett could be relied on to keep order. It was to be a forlorn hope.

Once Meredith and the federal officials were inside the university administration building, Barnett ordered the state troopers who were holding back the crowds to withdraw. Rioters swarmed around the marshals surrounding the building, swinging iron bars and throwing Molotov cocktails. Pistol shots rang out and some of the marshals were wounded. But they obeyed orders and kept their side arms holstered, responding only with tear gas and nightsticks. Kennedy went on television to assure the nation that the situation in Mississippi was under control, a fact that was not at all obvious to the federal officials present at the scene, who were comparing their situation to the Alamo.

Federal military police, who had driven pell-mell from Memphis all night, arrived on the scene just before daybreak and dispersed the crowd. Meredith was finally able to register. But two people lay dead, and many others were injured. The deadly melee had exploded on worldwide television.

A similar crisis was teed up for the succeeding June in neighboring Alabama, where Governor George C. Wallace had declared his intention to "stand in the schoolhouse door" to prevent two black students from registering at the University of Alabama. In the meantime, Martin Luther King had organized more demonstrations, including a "children's protest" in Birmingham, Alabama, where hundreds of black youngsters were attacked by police dogs and mowed down with fire hoses.

Kennedy's "voting rights" strategy had manifestly failed, so in February 1963, he warily proposed a bill limited to securing voting rights. But a meeting in Alabama on May 17 with an intransigent Governor Wallace convinced Kennedy that more serious action would probably be needed. The governor had refused to provide any kind of assurances about establishing peace on the University of Alabama campus, or a more enlightened attitude generally on civil rights. "I think we can't duck this one," Kennedy told an aide.

So, on the morning of June 11, with the two black students preparing to register, Kennedy didn't wait on events. He acted to federalize the Alabama National Guard. In the event the guardsmen chose to shirk their duty, he ordered troops at Fort Benning, Georgia, to stand by aboard helicopters and be ready to fly to Tuscaloosa to take control. Kennedy called Republican congressional leaders to the White House that same day and sounded them out on how far they thought he could go on civil rights.

The Kennedy White House held its breath in anticipation of bad news from down south. But the show of resolve in Washington had its intended effect. After a flourish of rhetoric about abusive federal power, Wallace, who was standing at the schoolhouse door, stepped into his car and was driven away. The two black students, Vivian Malone and James Hood, registered peacefully for classes. Wallace and Kennedy had gone eyeball-to-eyeball—and Wallace had blinked.

By that evening, Kennedy felt he had to say something. All afternoon, drafts had been passed back and forth between the president, the attorney general, and the staff involved in preparing the speech. When the red light finally illuminated atop the camera in the Oval Office, the president still held an incomplete draft in his hand.

While his team had been laboring away, Kennedy had roughed out some of his own ideas to help fill the gaps. Contrary to what many critics believed—that JFK was a mere ventriloquist's dummy who only mouthed the eloquent platitudes written for him by others—he was in fact his own best speechwriter. This was a skill he had honed during his seventeen years in public life, and one that would serve him well in this, probably his greatest single act of public leadership.

The speech could not have been more different from the one he had delivered the previous September at the height of the University of Mississippi crisis. At that time, still in thrall to a romanticized image of the Old South (also evident in his book *Profiles in Courage*), he recalled (white) Mississippians' martial and even football prowess while avoiding any mention of James Meredith's courage. The speech had deeply disappointed civil rights leaders and had precious little effect on the campus in Oxford, Mississippi. But now, nine months later, Kennedy decided he had given the white South enough breaks. It was time to choose sides.

Following a brief review of the events in Alabama that morning, Kennedy adopted a more philosophical tone and invited Americans to do something that few presidents had ever asked of them before: to examine their consciences.

"This nation was founded by men of many nations and backgrounds," Kennedy said. "It was founded on the principle that all men are created equal, and that the rights of every man are diminished when the rights of one man are threatened."

Reminding Americans that the eyes of the world were upon them, he underlined the unsustainable contradiction of defending freedom abroad while denying it at home. "Today, we are committed to a worldwide struggle to promote and protect the rights of all who wish to be free," he said. "When Americans are sent to Vietnam or West Berlin, we do not ask for whites only. It ought to be possible, therefore, for American students of any color to attend any public institution they select without having to be backed up by troops."

He spoke of the poor educational opportunities available to blacks, and how their employment prospects and life expectancy were considerably below that of whites. Then, his voice rising, he cut to the nub of the matter:

> We are confronted primarily with a moral issue. It is as old as the Scriptures and is as clear as the American Constitution.

The heart of the question is whether all Americans are to be afforded equal rights and equal opportunities, whether we are going to treat our fellow Americans as we want to be treated. If an American, because his skin is dark, cannot eat lunch in a restaurant open to the public, if he cannot send his children to the best public school available, if he cannot vote for the public officials who represent him, if, in short, he cannot enjoy the full and free life which all of us want, then who among us would be content to have the color of his skin changed and stand in his place? Who among us would be content with the counsels of patience and delay?

All of this was buildup to the centerpiece of the address: a call for federal civil rights legislation far more sweeping than what he had proposed a few months earlier, legislation that would ensure equal access to public accommodations such as hotels, restaurants, movie theaters, stores, and schools, as well as the right to vote. He then moved to the conclusion he had written himself:

This is one country. It has become one country because all the people who came here had an equal chance to develop their talents. . . .

We have a right to expect that the Negro community will be responsible and will uphold the law; but they have a right to expect that the law will be fair, that the constitution will be colorblind, as Justice [John Marshall] Harlan said at the turn of the century.

This is what we are talking about. This is a matter which concerns this country and what it stands for, and in meeting it, I ask the support of all our citizens.

The address had lasted barely eighteen minutes. It was not his most polished or eloquent—given the circumstances surrounding its preparation, it could hardly have been otherwise. But it was almost certainly his most important. No president before him, not even Abraham Lincoln, had dared call for a "color-blind" society. In one breathtaking leap, Kennedy had left behind the measured rhetoric about "maintaining law and order" and "compliance with the courts," on which he and previous presidents had relied in racially charged circumstances, and he seized the mantle of ensuring the legal equality of all Americans.

Once spoken, these words could not be taken back. JFK had committed himself—and the nation—to a course on which no other country had ever embarked successfully: the full and complete integration of a racial minority into a nation's life. The road ahead would be rocky, and considerable violence still lay in the future. (In an exceptionally tragic and ironic twist of fate, Mississippi NAACP leader Medgar Evers was assassinated in his front yard on the very night of the president's speech. His killer, a white supremacist named Byron De la Beckwith, would not be convicted for the crime until 1994.)

It was a course not many would have expected of John F. Kennedy, who throughout his career had been branded by many as an idle rich kid, a dilettante playboy who owed whatever success he enjoyed to the machinations of his wealthy and politically ambitious father. There were many who no doubt still thought that way.

But not African-Americans. Once doubters, they now believed. It may have been Kennedy's successor, Lyndon B. Johnson, who eventually passed the Civil Rights Act and the Voting Rights Act into law, but it was Kennedy who at long last had finally spoken the words they had longed to hear. And it was JFK's portrait, along with Martin Luther King's, that would eventually grace the walls of millions of black homes and businesses across America.

CHAPTER 1

Vision:
Let the Word Go Forth

"We need leaders of inspired idealism, leaders to whom are granted great visions, who dream greatly and strive to make their dreams come true; who can kindle the people with the fire from their own burning souls."

—THEODORE ROOSEVELT

"For I know what happens to a nation that sleeps too long. I saw the British deceive themselves before World War II, as Winston Churchill tried in vain to awaken them and while England slept, Hitler armed; and if we sleep too long in the sixties, Mr. Khrushchev will 'bury' us yet. That is why the next president . . . must be commander in chief of the grand alliance for freedom."

—JOHN F. KENNEDY, NOVEMBER 5, 1960

"Vision" is a word often used in leadership studies. Some people swear by it; others think it a waste of time. What is it, precisely, and how should it be employed?

Vision, quite simply, is a way of spelling out for your listeners "the big picture," to help them understand the effort in which they are engaged and win their "buy in." That some vision statements are poorly crafted or restate the obvious does not invalidate the concept. Properly employed, vision is indispensable to serious leadership. Those who think they can do without it—the first President George Bush, who derided "the vision thing," comes to mind—usually discover their error too late.

Often overlooked is the power of vision to motivate your listeners. Vision provides the essential "spark" that makes the difference between people who are just going through the motions and people who are really trying to achieve something. Vision appeals to their higher self, something above and beyond the mundane and the everyday. The ideal vision is elevating. Consider Henry Ford's vision for his company, which was used in a television advertising campaign as recently as the late 1990s:

> I will build a motorcar for the great multitude. It will be large enough for the family, but small enough for the individual to run and care for. It will be constructed of the best materials, by the best men to be hired, after the simplest designs that modern engineering can devise. But it will be so low in price that no man making a good salary will be unable to own one and enjoy with his family the blessing of hours of pleasure in God's great open spaces.

A vision presents an idealized view of what the future can be. It looks beyond the immediate future to what an organization—or a nation—can be. It gives employees, or citizens, something to strive for. Vision becomes particularly important in times of crisis.

Kennedy's Vision: The Twilight Struggle and the New Frontier

In retrospect, the early 1960s seem an almost idyllic period, with peace abroad and prosperity at home. To many Americans at the time, however, the dawn of the 1960s seemed threatening, if not actually terrifying.

The hopes, perhaps naive, of the early postwar period—for a peaceful world overseen by the World War II allies, including the Soviet Union—had long since turned to ashes. In their place had risen a "Cold War." (George Orwell was first into print with the term in 1947.) Not only was the alliance gone, so was the nuclear monopoly on which the United States had planned to stake its postwar national security. Assisted by Soviet spies within the Manhattan Project, the first Russian atomic bomb was exploded in 1949, far earlier than U.S. experts predicted. It was followed just four years later by the first Soviet hydrogen bomb, which overnight massively multiplied the Kremlin's firepower. The threat of Soviet nuclear weapons was a major reason the bloody Korean War, which killed more than 33,000 Americans, ground on for three long years.

True, Joseph Stalin was gone, having died in 1953. A period of unstable "collective" leadership followed until, in Stalin's place, a new Soviet chieftain rose who, in many ways, loomed even more menacingly because he appeared to be so unpredictable: Nikita Sergeyevich Khrushchev. A coarse, rough-hewn peasant, Khrushchev was fond of issuing grandiloquent pronouncements, such as his prediction that the Soviet Union would "bury" the West. "Your grandchildren will live under communism!" he snarled to Vice President Richard Nixon in Moscow in 1959.

Worse, Khrushchev increasingly seemed to have the wherewithal he needed to make good on his threats. In 1957, he startled the world with the launch of Sputnik, the first artificial Earth-orbiting satellite whose nighttime passes over the United States were visible from the ground with the naked eye. The steady "beep-beep-beep" radio beacon that it emitted, which was picked up by ham radio operators worldwide, seemed to mock the problem-plagued U.S. space program.

National prestige, though, seemed almost the least of the problem. It didn't take much imagination to conclude that if the Soviet Union could use powerful rockets to loft a satellite into orbit, it would be child's play to mount a nuclear weapon on one and aim it at the United States. Memories were still fresh of the damage wrought on London by the conventionally armed and short-range V-weapons that Hitler had launched against Britain in the last year of World War II. What could long-range, nuclear-tipped missiles achieve?

And despite his World War II experience, President Dwight Eisenhower seemed to be putting all his eggs in the nuclear basket. Concerned about budget deficits, he emphasized relatively cheap nuclear weapons ("bigger bang for the buck"), over more expensive conventional forces. Even so, some critics, especially Massachusetts Senator John F. Kennedy, charged that a "missile gap" favoring the Soviet Union was opening up.

Tensions eased somewhat in late 1959 with Khrushchev's visit to the United States for ten days in September, which ended with the Soviet chieftain extending an invitation to the American president to visit the Kremlin. But relations were plunged back into deep freeze in early May 1960 when a U-2 spy plane piloted by CIA agent Francis Gary Powers was shot down over the Soviet Union and Powers was captured. Although Eisenhower initially claimed the flight was not an espionage mission, he was soon proved wrong by Powers's confession. It was probably the most embarrassing moment of Eisenhower's administration. No wonder that, as the 1960s dawned, polls showed foreign policy to be Americans' top concern.

Was the United States in danger of falling behind the Soviet Union, economically as well as, it seemed, militarily? With hindsight, the question itself seems absurd. But it didn't seem so at the time. Respected American economists estimated the Soviet economy to be growing at a 10 percent annual clip, while the U.S. economy plugged along at 2 to 3 percent yearly growth. A deep recession in 1958 had sent the unemployment rate shooting up so far and so quickly that memories of the Great Depression were briefly rekindled. As Kennedy prepared to take office, the unemployment rate hovered worrisomely near 7 percent.

The incoming president was particularly concerned about how this state of affairs was being perceived overseas, particularly in the area that French demographer Alfred Sauvy had, in 1952, dubbed "the Third World." The answer did not seem promising. Communists had seized power in China in 1949, a shocking development to Americans who had business and missionary ties in the country dating back more than a century. Cuba, a country for which the United States had gone to war to free from Spanish colonial rule in 1898, had fallen under the spell of a new communist dictator named Fidel Castro. He openly pledged to "export" his Soviet-style revolution throughout Latin America in coming years and dared the "Yanquis" to try to stop him.

Elsewhere, the British and French empires were in their terminal stages, with nineteen new African and Asian nations winning their independence in 1960 alone. Each of those countries would have a vote in the United Nations. Centrally planned socialism seemed to offer new world leaders the prospect of faster economic progress than free markets and democracy.

Worse, the Soviet Union perceived such sentiments as well and was showing every sign of moving to exploit them.

At home, the consumerism and prosperity of the 1950s had led to a widespread questioning of whether Americans had gone "soft." The generation that had coped with the Great Depression and then world war was left wondering, "Is this all there is?" Books such as *The Man in the Grey Flannel Suit* and *The Organization Man,* which chronicled the rat race of postwar corporate life, shot up the best-seller lists. Eisenhower actually appointed a commission to look into the issue of "the national purpose." The children of the war generation, dubbed the baby boom, were just coming of age as Kennedy took office. What would be their challenge?

Kennedy and Churchill

Almost all leaders have heroes and role models, and Kennedy was no exception. His hero was the man who had taken office in Great Britain twenty years earlier at a moment of supreme crisis in that nation's life: Winston S. Churchill.

The similarities between Churchill and Kennedy are striking. Both were the sons of famous and politically active fathers. Both were born into their respective nation's aristocracies and received elite educations (though Churchill never attended university). Both used their family connections to get into—rather than avoid—combat and made their reputations as war heroes, Churchill in South Africa and Kennedy in the South Pacific. Both launched themselves almost immediately into politics upon returning home. Both were facile with words and worked as newspaper correspondents. And both were able to convert seeming forensic handicaps into assets (in Churchill's case a lisp, and in Kennedy's case a pronounced regional accent) that made them electrifying public speakers. They even married at somewhat advanced ages, Churchill at thirty-four and Kennedy at thirty-six.

Churchill also lived the kind of life Kennedy himself found attractive. At the center of public life for more than fifty years, Churchill carved out a position for himself as a historian and public intellectual. Kennedy would come to prominence in a remarkably similar way.

If nature made JFK the son of Joseph P. Kennedy Sr., choice made him the son of Churchill, a man his father couldn't stand. It was a crucial decision, because had young Jack (like his brother Joe Jr.) embraced his father's crabbed, pessimistic, isolationist politics rather than Churchill's optimistic internationalism, he almost certainly could never have become president of the United States. Kennedy later implicitly acknowledged his debt to the British leader by naming him only the second person in history to receive honorary citizenship of the United States. (The Marquis de Lafayette was the other.)

Proclaiming His Vision: JFK's Inaugural Address

The United States was not at war in 1960, nor was there any desire on the part of the American people for another world war so soon after ending the second one, especially when there was a strong likelihood of any such conflict quickly becoming nuclear in scope. Still, Kennedy thought the dangers great. In his first book, *Why England Slept* (the title was a play on the title of Churchill's book, *While England Slept*), published in 1940, Kennedy expressed his belief that democracies were at a disadvantage when pitted against totalitarian dictatorships because the people of the former were more peace loving than the governments of the latter, which did not need to consult their own people. If the United States was to avoid the dire circumstances in which Britain found herself in 1940, Kennedy wrote, her political leaders would have to step up to their responsibilities:

> Any person will awaken when the house is burning down. What
> we need is an armed guard that will wake up when the fire first
> starts, or, better yet, one that will not permit a fire to start at all.

It is hard to avoid the conclusion that Kennedy saw himself in the role of that armed guard. The new president, however, would need to walk a fine line between conveying the need for military preparedness, and perhaps action, while preventing nuclear Armageddon.

Between the election and the inauguration, he spent much time working with Ted Sorensen, his chief speechwriter, whom Kennedy told to study such memorable presidential orations as the Gettysburg Address in an effort to determine why they were so successful. He solicited ideas from family, friends, and advisers, both formal and informal.

Kennedy's experience shows that your vision does not have to spring full blown from your own head. Talk to your team and members of your organization. Do research and use your own intuition and experience.

The final product, however, was very much Kennedy's own. As Thurston Clarke demonstrates in *Ask Not,* his history of the Kennedy inaugural address, "[H]e was too proud of his demonstrated literary talents . . . to risk relying too heavily on others for a work that would be scrutinized by generations of historians and critics."

Picking up the black binder containing the "reading text" of his address on that frigid January morning, Kennedy set forth his vision:

> Let the word go forth from this time and place, to friend and foe alike, that the torch has been passed to a new generation of Americans, born in this century, tempered by war, disciplined by a hard and bitter peace, proud of our ancient heritage, and unwilling to witness or permit the slow undoing of those human rights to which this Nation has always been committed, and to which we are committed today at home and around the world. . . .
>
> Let every nation know, whether it wishes us well or ill, that we shall pay any price, bear any burden, meet any hardship, support any friend, oppose any foe, in order to assure the survival and the success of liberty. . . .
>
> To those new states whom we welcome to the ranks of the free, we pledge our word that one form of colonial control shall not have passed away merely to be replaced by a far more iron tyranny. We shall not always expect to find them supporting our view. But we shall always hope to find them strongly supporting their own freedom—and to remember that, in the past, those who foolishly sought power by riding the back of the tiger ended up inside.
>
> To those people in the huts and villages of half the globe struggling to break the bonds of mass misery, we pledge our best efforts to help them help themselves, for whatever period is required—not because the communists may be doing it, not because we seek their votes, but because it is right. If a free society cannot help the many who are poor, it cannot save the few who are rich.
>
> To our sister republics south of our border, we offer a special pledge—to convert our good words into good deeds—in a new alliance for progress—to assist free men and free governments in

casting off the chains of poverty. But this peaceful revolution of hope cannot become the prey of hostile powers. Let all our neighbors know that we shall join with them to oppose aggression or subversion anywhere in the Americas. And let every other power know that this Hemisphere intends to remain the master of its own house.

But neither can two great and powerful groups of nations take comfort from our present course, both sides overburdened by the cost of modern weapons, both rightly alarmed by the steady spread of the deadly atom, yet both racing to alter that uncertain balance of terror that stays the hand of mankind's final war. . . .

So let us begin anew, remembering on both sides that civility is not a sign of weakness, and sincerity is always subject to proof. Let us never negotiate out of fear. But let us never fear to negotiate. . . .

Now the trumpet summons us again, not as a call to bear arms, though arms we need; not as a call to battle, though embattled we are, but a call to bear the burden of a long twilight struggle, year in and year out. . . .

In the long history of the world, only a few generations have been granted the role of defending freedom in its hour of maximum danger. I do not shrink from this responsibility—I welcome it.

The speech was short, just 1,355 words delivered in only fourteen minutes in Kennedy's distinctive Boston twang. For all the perils that Kennedy saw in the world situation, his vision was not fundamentally pessimistic. Like Churchill, who invoked the "broad, sunlit uplands" of human freedom in the midst of his grim "finest hour" speech of June 18, 1940, Kennedy held out the spread of freedom, not merely for America and her allies, but throughout the world, as the best guarantor of America's ultimate security.

Making this vision a reality would require effort and some sacrifice on the part of the American people as well as the people of the world. So just as Churchill had summoned his fellow Britons to "brace ourselves to our duties" in the interest of achieving victory, Kennedy concluded with a ringing call to service on the part of his own countrymen and people everywhere:

And so, my fellow Americans: Ask not what your country can do for you; ask what you can do for your country.

My fellow citizens of the world: Ask not what America will do for you, but what together we can do for the freedom of man.

Kennedy was tapping into something deep with this call to service, which is why it is undoubtedly the speech's most memorable line. This is especially true for those who heard the speech as teenagers or young adults (such as the young Bill Clinton). They had heard from their parents tales of deprivation during the Great Depression, followed by the challenge of the greatest conflict in human history. They had missed out on all of that. Was there anything great left to be done?

Finding a New Challenge

Theodore Roosevelt, another youthful peacetime president who had to contend with unprecedented challenges abroad and the need for reform at home, faced a not dissimilar set of circumstances early in the twentieth century. In keeping with his own Rough Rider image, Roosevelt's 1905 inaugural parade had featured the aging veterans of General George Armstrong Custer's cavalry, along with the dignified figure of Geronimo. Twelve years earlier, historian Frederick Jackson Turner had declared the frontier closed, and the overall atmosphere of Roosevelt's celebration was one of homage to an era that was passing. The West had been won; the Civil War was long over. What was the challenge of the new century?

In the pages of *The Strenuous Life,* Roosevelt answered by invoking the greatness of America's achievements as a standard that had to be met by future generations:

There was scant room for the coward and the weakling in the ranks of the adventurous frontiersmen—the pioneer settlers who first broke up the wild prairie soil, who first hewed their way into the primeval forest, who guided their white-topped wagons across the endless leagues of Indian-haunted desolation and explored every remote mountain-chain in the restless quest for metal wealth. Behind them came the men who completed the work they had roughly begun: who drove the great railroad systems over plain and desert and mountain pass. . . . Such is the record of which we are so proud. It is a record of men who greatly dared and greatly did. . . .

Roosevelt's mission for the next generation was one of service to the public good. "Unless Democracy is based on the principle of service by everybody who claims the enjoyment of any right, it is not true democracy at all," Roosevelt said.

In his book *The Code of Man,* Waller Newell sums up the Rooseveltian ethos as one replacing the outward conquest of the frontier with a new frontier of the spirit, "an inner struggle to purify and ennoble the American character through a dedication to the common good."

Kennedy struck this theme several times in his public career. He returned to it again the summer before the inauguration, with his speech in Los Angeles accepting the Democratic party's nomination for president:

> [T]he problems are not all solved and the battles are not all won—and we stand today on the edge of a New Frontier—the frontier of the 1960s—a frontier of unknown opportunities and perils—a frontier of unfulfilled hopes and threats.
>
> Woodrow Wilson's New Freedom promised our nation a new political and economic framework. Franklin Roosevelt's New Deal promised security and succor to those in need. But the New Frontier of which I speak is not a set of promises—it is a set of challenges. It sums up not what I intend to offer the American people, but what I intend to ask of them. It appeals to their pride, not to their pocketbook—it holds out the promise of more sacrifice instead of more security.

It wasn't the first time he had used the phrase. In 1950, he had called Southeast Asia "the New Frontier" in the struggle against communism, and he had borrowed the phrase from one of his Harvard professors. But it came to stand for the renewed dedication to public service that, for many, came to symbolize what John F. Kennedy ultimately stood for.

But I tell you the New Frontier is here, whether we seek it or not. Beyond that frontier are the uncharted areas of science and space, unsolved problems of peace and war, unconquered pockets of ignorance and prejudice, unanswered questions of poverty and surplus. It would be easier to shrink back from that frontier, to look to the safe mediocrity of the past, to be lulled by good intentions and high rhetoric—and those who prefer that course should not cast their votes for me, regardless of party.

But I believe the times demand new invention, innovation, imagination, decision. I am asking each of you to be pioneers on that New Frontier. My call is to the young in heart, regardless of age—to all who respond to the Scriptural call: "Be strong and of a good courage; be not afraid, neither be thou dismayed."

Evaluating Kennedy's Vision

Leadership consultant James M. Strock has identified the elements composing a successful vision. It must be simple and direct, so as to be memorable. It must be flexible, so as to accommodate differing ways of making the vision a reality. It has to be consistent with the intended audience's values. It has to be inclusive and optimistic, and ideally, the leader himself must personify the vision.

Kennedy's vision succeeded on all counts. Indeed, better than even he found comfortable at times. Early in his administration, when the "freedom riders" sought to test the desegregation of bus routes in the South, a move that provoked violence on the part of segregationists, Kennedy upbraided some of them for moving too quickly. They responded by stating they were only doing something for their country.

Idealistic

In calling for sacrifice on the part of the American people as the price of "manning the ramparts of freedom," Kennedy displayed another Churchillian insight into human psychology. Normally, a political leader is advised to flatter his audience by telling them all is well, when he (and they) know darn well it isn't really. Kennedy, like Churchill, realized that people can feel good about themselves if they see their sacrifice as serving a higher, more worthy goal than their own comfort. Thus, the higher defense budgets and increased draft calls of the Kennedy years were not resented by the mass of Americans.

Flexible and Inclusive

The flexibility and inclusiveness of Kennedy's vision could accommodate both the civilian Peace Corps, which Kennedy established only three months after taking office, as well as the U.S. Army Special Forces, or Green Berets, which he also founded. And this flexibility and inclusiveness allowed new visions within the vision, such as his declaration, in May 1961, that "this nation should commit itself to achieving the goal, before this decade is out, of landing a man on the moon and returning him safely to earth."

Memorable

To call Kennedy's vision memorable would be putting it mildly. The sheer power of his forward-looking rhetoric and imagery can be grasped by the simple fact that, four decades later, JFK's motivational speeches remain the "gold standard" by which presidential rhetoric is judged. It is instructive that every president since Kennedy—and many presidential candidates of both parties—have in some way or another sought to portray themselves as heirs to Kennedy's vision.

The power of Kennedy's unshakable belief in America's determination in the face of a global challenge to freedom endured in spite of the disillusion that set in over the Vietnam War and other American defeats and setbacks in the decades to come. Later leaders, especially Ronald Reagan, would invoke Kennedy's vision to offer encouragement during the difficult times. JFK helped put the rhetorical steel in America's spine to see the course through until the rapid and, for most, unexpected end to the Cold War in 1989.

Through a combination of action and superior communication skills—painfully acquired over a lifetime of physical illness and considerable adversity—Kennedy turned himself into that rarest of leaders, one who was able to personify his vision, endowing it with enduring force.

How to Create Your Own Vision

➡ *Craft an inspiring vision.* If you aspire to leadership, your ability to inspire people is not optional; it is essential. A properly formulated vision will not only motivate your people to support your organization's goals; it will inspire them to pull the organization through crises.

➡ *Don't think you have to come up with a vision all by yourself.* Look for role models, and consult widely. Start with the history of your organization to discover the roots of its spirit. Think of how Kennedy and Teddy Roosevelt before him appealed to the spirit of the American frontier. There was a driving force that once sparked the imaginations of your employees and inspired them. Tapping into the organization's memory is key to creating a vision that resonates and rekindles passion.

➡ *Keep it simple and direct—and make it memorable.* CNN, for example, was a bold idea in the early 1980s. It aimed to be not only the first twenty-four-hour news network, but also the network of record worldwide, seen in every nation on the planet. This vision is easily understood by all and ambitious enough to be memorable.

➡ *Don't be boxed in by your vision.* Keep it flexible in order to accommodate unforeseen circumstances or a changing marketplace. Jeff Bezos started out with the vision of creating the "earth's biggest bookstore" by selling books on the Internet. Had he stuck to books only, he would have been overwhelmed by the competition that cropped up in response to his success. Bezos refocused his vision, thinking larger each step of the way. Today Amazon.com stands as "earth's biggest anything store."

➡ *Make your vision inclusive.* If there are divisions or departments that cannot relate to or support the vision, they will not be inspired to reach their goals. Worse, some may feel left out and actually be demotivated by the vision. Include people from different parts of your organization in the process of creating a vision. Use focus groups to discover what inspires them. Why do they work for your company?

➡ *Be optimistic.* Demonstrate how implementing the vision will lead to a brighter future. Consider Apple Computer's vision, for example. Steve Jobs and Steve Wozniak set out not to simply make computers, but to have Apple computers change the world. That higher mission appeals to our vision of the future where our lives are significantly improved by technology.

CHAPTER 2

Breaking the Rules:
Question the Status Quo

"Courage is rightly esteemed the first of human qualities, because it is the quality which guarantees all others."
—WINSTON CHURCHILL

"Conformity is the jailer of freedom, and the enemy of growth."
—JOHN F. KENNEDY

Part of being a leader is not to follow blindly. A leader is someone who evaluates the "way things are done" and determines whether they are the way things should be done. Leaders are not afraid to challenge the status quo if necessary or to strike out on a new path. John Kennedy was encouraged to question authority and stir things up even as a child, and he carried this trait with him throughout his life. He was not afraid to challenge authority or to break the rules, and this confidence originating in his childhood was able to help him make significant changes as president.

At Choate, the elite boarding school JFK attended in Connecticut, Jack's older brother, Joe Jr., was a standout athlete and good student, winning praise from George St. John, the school's intimidating headmaster. Jack's grades were middling (though he did well in English and history), and he didn't play sports. And for the school's many rules and regulations, he had little use.

One day at chapel, St. John stood up and denounced ill-disciplined boys he dubbed "muckers," and he threatened to expel any he could identify. The young Kennedy, knowing that St. John probably already considered him a mucker, reacted to this threat with a challenge: He gathered a group of about a dozen other like-minded boys together in what he dubbed a "Muckers Club," dedicated to raising hell on campus.

When one of the Muckers' pranks got out of hand, however, St. John identified young Kennedy as one of the ringleaders and summoned Joseph P. Kennedy Sr. from his post as chairman of the Securities and Exchange Commission in Washington, D.C. to hear a stern lecture about his son's conduct. St. John compared Jack unfavorably with his brother Joe and said he couldn't believe the two boys were from the same family. Jack's future at Choate seemed in doubt.

But when St. John stepped out of the office briefly, Joe Sr. made it clear he didn't entirely disapprove of his son's ways.

"If that Muckers Club had been mine," the elder Kennedy growled, "it wouldn't have started with an 'M.'"

Jack Kennedy was not expelled. But through this incident he learned from his father not to be afraid of challenging authority or of answering a threat with a challenge: He would remain a mucker all his life. As author Christopher Matthews pointed out in his study *Kennedy and Nixon,* many institutions—the Democratic party, organized labor, big business, Southern segregationists, and the Washington establishment among them—would all discover that in due course.

Mucking Is Not Just for Children

Leaders who leave their mark are all "muckers" to some extent or another. Kennedy's political model, Winston S. Churchill, was a world-class bull in a china shop. As first lord of the admiralty before the First World War, Churchill turned the world of naval construction upside down when he declared that all new British battleships should be powered by oil rather than coal. This was a radical notion at the time, given Britain's abundance of coal and lack of oil. Yet, because oil offered improved steaming radius and ease of refueling, Churchill thought it was worth the risk. Leaders need to be able to be critical of their organization's decisions to determine whether they are the right decisions. If they are not, they need to have the courage and stamina to shake things up and refocus the organization in the right direction.

Established organizations are almost inherently resistant to change. The not-invented-here syndrome and the natural pressures to make people "wait their turn" stand in the way of changes in leadership and innovation. Overcoming institutional resistance requires the full measure of a leader's attention.

John F. Kennedy rose to prominence and power in a way wholly dissimilar to any of his predecessors. His main political rivals—notably Lyndon B. Johnson and Richard M. Nixon—were alternately baffled and infuriated by Kennedy's success. They had generally followed the traditional route to political upward mobility through the accumulation of power and influence in legislative bodies and among major interest groups (although both Johnson and Nixon were innovators within this tradition). Kennedy took a different path that brought him to the pinnacle of political success much earlier than either of his rivals.

A Different Way of Running for Office

When John F. Kennedy decided to run for Congress in 1946, Massachusetts Democratic politics was about as spontaneous as a Japanese kabuki dance.

A young man who wanted to make his way in politics started at the bottom as a neighborhood organizer. (Women candidates were all but unheard of.) If he showed energy and loyalty, he might in time expect to become a precinct captain and then a ward leader. Eventually, his work would be recognized with the party's nomination to run for city council or the state legislature. In that event, the party would take care of everything. He might be expected to give some speeches at organized rallies with his fellow candidates for other offices, but by and large, actual campaigning was superfluous. The organization would deliver the votes on Election Day.

This was the system that twenty-eight-year-old John F. Kennedy confronted when he sought nomination (which was tantamount to election) in the eleventh district. There was no question of his doing things the old-fashioned way. Even if he were by nature and disposition inclined to go along and get along, which he wasn't, there was no guarantee that accepting the world as it was would lead to bigger things politically. Many toiled anonymously in the political vineyards for years. Others achieved only limited success. Still others never got a chance at all.

But just because the rules or the status quo makes progression seem impossible doesn't mean that you should accept that situation. You should not think yourself under any obligation to accept a lower position than one to which you believe you are suited by your talent and drive, nor should you accept mediocrity in your organization. Kennedy may not have followed the normal course of political progression, but that did not stop him from becoming president of the United States. The country he inherited as a president was considered by some to be less than ideal, but he was not afraid to question those shortcomings or to insist that Americans were capable of more. He was personally ambitious and had ambitions for his country.

Plenty of people were put off by young Kennedy's ambition (among them, Thomas P. "Tip" O'Neill, the future speaker of the U.S. House of Representatives). Many people thought Kennedy had no chance and told him so up front. In January 1946, he met with Dan O'Brian, an aide to former Cambridge Mayor Mike Neville, Kennedy's main rival. As Kennedy later recalled the conversation, O'Brian "says I'll get murdered. . . . He is the first man to . . . bet me *I can't win.*"

Kennedy was unimpressed. O'Brian, he wrote, "is an honest Irishman but a mistaken one."

Critics have been quick to point to his father's money as the prime factor in young Kennedy's political success. Joseph P. Kennedy Sr., it was charged, simply bought the seat for his son, not unlike the way eighteenth-century British lords secured "rotten borough" seats in Parliament for their offspring. But Joe Sr. was not some anonymous millionaire. His money came with heavy baggage because of his reputation as an isolationist appeaser in his foreign policy and an unscrupulous businessman in his private dealings.

Money *was* certainly indispensable to Kennedy's success. His father went so far as to effectively purchase a failing Boston newspaper solely for the purpose of keeping it alive to promote Jack's candidacy. And he successfully offered to underwrite James Michael Curley's run for another term as mayor of Boston if he would vacate his seat in Congress to make way for Jack.

But in politics or business, money simply isn't everything. Wealthy and famous men such as Henry Ford and William Randolph Hearst (among many others) had lost in their attempts to gain political office by liberal deployment of money and publicity. Similarly, many are the business projects that have simply eaten up money to no purpose. To be effective, money has to be channeled in the right direction. Fortunately for Jack, he had the raw brains, energy, and talent to make the investment worthwhile. His father's money and name, therefore, were mixed blessings.

Jack Kennedy had some distinct liabilities, too. There was his youth and political inexperience. His roots in the district were shallow. (He had only ever lived in the eleventh district while an undergraduate at Harvard.) He faced several tough, well-known, and experienced competitors for the seat. With a sole exception, not a single Democratic officeholder or official endorsed Kennedy. (Even Curley, after accepting Joe Sr.'s money, insisted on maintaining his "neutrality.") The animosity of the local Democratic organization meant Kennedy was barred from campaigning in police stations, firehouses, and other public buildings. All of the district's newspapers, save for the one his father controlled, were aligned with his opponents. And although the public didn't fully appreciate it, there was also the fragile state of Kennedy's health. (Kennedy has often been criticized for not being more forthcoming about his poor health. He wasn't the only one in the race concealing his true medical condition, however. Kennedy's opponent, Mike Neville, was sick with diabetes during the campaign and actually died before the November election.)

Jack Kennedy had some clear advantages as well. The Kennedy and Fitzgerald names were well known in Boston politics. He was a fresh face among veteran political wheelhorses. His boyish good looks, quick wit, and winning smile were a hit, especially with female voters.

To compete successfully, though, he would need more than just charm and a name advantage. Ultimately, he would come up with five essential steps for winning, and they became the roadmap for every subsequent Kennedy political campaign.

Kennedy's Five Steps for Successfully Challenging the Status Quo

1. *Organization's against you? Create your own.* Instead of working through the party organization, Kennedy would build his own. As Kennedy

biographer Geoffrey Perret put it, Jack would conquer the eleventh district "one hand at a time."

Thus, the twenty-eight-year-old war veteran "hit the streets." It was an act of will for him, a naturally reserved man, to wade into the pool halls, taverns, and factories of Cambridge, Charlestown, the North End, and Somerville. "I'm Jack Kennedy. I'm running for Congress," he said over and over again to bewildered passersby, who thought the unnaturally skinny and pale young man before them looked scarcely old enough to shave, let alone run for office.

An indifferent public speaker, Kennedy kept his talks short and left plenty of time for questions and answers. It was markedly different from the florid forensic fireworks that Boston-area residents had come to expect from politicians such as James Michael Curley.

Kennedy was a strong believer in the power of the personal touch. He accepted as many invitations to as many events as he could cram into his schedule. In the service of increasing personal contact with voters, he had neighborhood house parties. A volunteer would open his house to his neighbors, free food and drink would be available, and the candidate would drop by to chat and shake hands. Since the Kennedy campaign budget could afford it, the comestibles were of the highest quality. And the volunteer would receive $100 for the use of his house—nearly two weeks' wages for a working man in 1946.

Then were the "teas." Tapping the vast reservoir of female family talent, Kennedy enlisted his mother and sisters to host semiformal "teas" for female voters. Kennedy's opponents initially thought the idea ridiculous, but then they were amazed at the sight of the wives of truck drivers and stevedores dressing up in their best clothes and donning white gloves for the opportunity to rub shoulders with the famous Kennedys.

Needless to say, the names and addresses of all attendees of house parties and teas were noted and many were recruited as volunteers. Follow-up notes of appreciation also went out soon thereafter.

Kennedy used the same formula in his winning 1952 Senate race against Henry Cabot Lodge. When asked afterward why he thought he had lost, Lodge snarled, "It was those damned tea parties!"

2. *Start early, work late.* Before John F. Kennedy, political campaigns were short, compressed affairs, often lasting no more than a couple of months. But Kennedy realized that if he was to run without—indeed, against—the established organization, he had to start much, much earlier. He began running for Congress in the fall of 1945, a full year before the general election and eight months before the primary. Never known as an early riser, Kennedy nevertheless compelled himself to get up before dawn each day of the campaign in order to be at factory gates when the first shift arrived. He rarely quit before late in the evening.

This would have been a punishing schedule for someone in top physical condition, which Kennedy certainly was not. His problematic back, the effects of malaria and Addison's disease (a wasting of the adrenal glands that could be controlled by cortisone), and other maladies gnawed at him incessantly. After marching in ninety-degree heat in the Bunker Hill Day parade, for example, Kennedy nearly passed out from heat prostration.

Still, he pushed on. The early start would become a hallmark of Kennedy campaigns. He began running hard for the Senate two years before the 1952 election, visiting towns and cities throughout Massachusetts to shake hands and give speeches. When he ran for president, he followed the same game plan, but on a larger scale, campaigning more or less full-time following his reelection to the Senate in 1958. He followed the risky course of entering political primaries in order to prove he had popular appeal.

When Lyndon Johnson and Hubert Humphrey began running for president in 1960, they were stunned to discover that Kennedy had been there long before them, sewing up the support of just about everyone who mattered.

Today, of course, the early start is standard operating procedure in American politics. But even outside of politics, working hard (not necessarily just working long, which is not the same thing) will give you a leg up on your competition.

3. *Hire local "Sherpas."* When mountaineers began arriving in the wilds of the Himalayas in the late nineteenth and early twentieth centuries, intent on conquering the world's highest peaks, they would hire local

men, known as Sherpas, to guide the way and help carry the supplies. The sheer indispensability of these men and their local knowledge was vividly illustrated when Sir Edmund Hillary brought his Sherpa guide, Tenzing Norgay, with him to the summit of Mt. Everest in 1953.

A virtual stranger in the Massachusetts eleventh district, John F. Kennedy needed political "Sherpas" in 1946 like no one else. And like many of the Sherpas who climbed with the great mountaineers in Tibet, Kennedy's aides became devoted to him for the rest of his life and long thereafter.

The first was Joe Sr.'s cousin Joe Kane. A hard-bitten Boston political veteran, Kane dissuaded Jack from seeking the lieutenant governorship—a dead-end job—in favor of a run for Congress.

Kane brought on board Dave Powers, an elflike air force veteran. Kenneth O'Donnell, another war veteran and a Harvard football friend of brother Bobby, joined the Kennedy organization as well, as did Ted Reardon, who played football with Joe Jr. at Harvard.

Together, these men guided the well-born Kennedy into places he never would have ventured otherwise: up the long flights of tenement stairs overlooking the Boston Navy Yard, to the crowded flats where several families shared a single toilet. Kennedy's willingness to visit such places, where politicians were rarely seen, proved to be worth many votes.

4. *Disarm opponents with wit.* Kennedy was always among the first to perceive the comedy or irony in any situation, even when he himself was involved. He used this facility to devastating effect throughout his public life.

Superficially, Kennedy appeared vulnerable on the issue of his family's great wealth. The eleventh district was the poorest in the state, and few of its residents could be expected to identify with Kennedy's monied background. His opponents hammered away at this fact. One even took out a mock newspaper "wanted" ad:

CONGRESS SEAT FOR SALE
NO EXPERIENCE NECESSARY
APPLICANT MUST LIVE IN NEW YORK OR FLORIDA
ONLY MILLIONAIRES NEED APPLY

In candidate forums, Kennedy's opponents sought to outdo one another with tales of childhood poverty and deprivation, seeking to identify with similarly situated voters and embarrass Kennedy at the same time. The newcomer, however, refused to take the bait. "I do seem to be the only one here," he said when it came his turn at the microphone, "who did not come up the hard way."

Another story Kennedy enjoyed telling may have been apocryphal, but it still illustrates the point. Supposedly, the candidate was once confronted by a grizzled factory worker.

"Is it true, Mr. Kennedy," the worker asked, "that your father is one of the richest men in America?"

Kennedy admitted that was indeed the case.

"Is it also true," the assembly line worker continued, "that you never wanted for anything in your whole life?"

Kennedy conceded that such a description was probably accurate.

Boring in, the candidate's questioner finally asked, "Would it be fair to say that you've never worked a day in your life?"

Somewhat sheepishly, Kennedy admitted the man was probably more right than wrong.

"Well, Mr. Kennedy," he finally said, "let me tell you something. You ain't missed a thing."

The anecdote never failed to bring down the house, as did his famous quip about his rich father refusing "to pay for a landslide."

Funny as they are, these remarks display an insight into human character that Kennedy's opponents missed. For all of America's supposed love of Horatio Alger "rags to riches" tales, people are actually far less likely to be put off by inherited wealth than those who make it themselves. Individuals don't choose their parents, after all, but self-made millionaires (not excluding Joe Sr.) are open to suspicion about how they made their money and might even inspire jealousy. "At least he won't steal," is a phrase often heard with regard to wealthy candidates.

5. *Find issues that resonate with your audience.* "Boss"-style politics were mostly about personal relationships and favor trading. Issues took a distinctly secondary position. Kennedy turned that around by finding issues that would resonate with the district's voters. Specifically, he focused on one issue: returning veterans.

"A new generation offers a leader," was Kennedy's slogan, and it spoke implicitly to the sense of change prevailing in the country after the war. With its working-class profile, the eleventh district had sent more men into the armed forces during the war than any other in the state. By the spring of 1946, an estimated 100,000 of them had returned home. As the only veteran in the race, Kennedy saw an opening and never looked back.

His advisers urged him to play up his war record in speeches. Kennedy, however, was uncomfortable with such an approach. Two of his PT-109 crew had died, after all, and it might seem their former commander was taking advantage of their deaths to promote himself. Instead, he took to referring to the valor of one of his PT-109 crewmen who had refused a medical discharge even after being badly burned in the collision that sank the boat. Kennedy thus accomplished the goal of reminding voters of his own heroism while giving the credit to others. (Notwithstanding, the campaign mailed tens of thousands of reprints of a *Reader's Digest* article on the PT-109 to homes throughout the district.)

Kennedy stuck to specific issues of interest to these men and their families, such as the shortage of housing and the need for jobs. Above all, he didn't want to be stereotyped as a *liberal,* a word he associated with a somewhat effete way of thinking and acting and a misplaced sympathy for the Soviet Union. He made it clear he favored a robust American presence in the world to forestall any possibility of a third world war. (This was a major area of difference he had with his isolationist father.) A profile in *Look* magazine actually described young Kennedy as "a fighting conservative," a description Kennedy never repudiated.

Not only was Kennedy himself a veteran, but the fact that his elder brother had been killed in the war added to his credibility when he discussed these issues. Mothers who had lost sons in the war placed large gold stars in the window of their homes as a sign to the world of the household's sacrifice. Meeting with a group of these Gold Star Mothers during the campaign, Kennedy noted, "You know, my mother is a Gold Star mother, too."

Kennedy won far and away, garnering almost as many votes as the rest of the field put together. He had taken his biggest perceived weakness—his status as a rich, political gate-crasher—and converted it into his biggest asset.

Choosing LBJ

The most important decision a presidential candidate makes immediately upon securing his party's presidential nomination is his choice of a running mate. Most of the time, however, the choice will have little impact on the outcome of the race. Voters select presidents, not vice presidents. Occasionally, a poor choice can actually hurt the ticket, such as George McGovern's selection of Missouri Democratic Senator Thomas F. Eagleton in 1972.

John F. Kennedy's stunning choice of Lyndon B. Johnson as his running mate in 1960 was the rare circumstance where the number-two person actually helped the ticket in November. Indeed, Johnson might well have been responsible for winning Kennedy the White House. And Kennedy did it against the advice of his brother and his other closest political advisers.

Kennedy and Johnson were not personally close, which is hardly surprising given their differences in background and temperament. Nine years older than Kennedy, Johnson had come to the House of Representatives a decade earlier than the Massachusetts man. Although he was also the son of a politically active father, Johnson grew up in the Texas Hill Country in circumstances far more straitened than those of Hyannis, Massachusetts, and Palm Beach, Florida. Whereas Kennedy was reserved in his interpersonal relations and disliked touching anyone or being touched in turn, Johnson was noted (some would say notorious) for his "treatment," which sometimes amounted to semimanhandling those he was trying to convince to see things his way.

The men also had an uneasy personal relationship. Johnson simply couldn't fathom Kennedy's success, and Kennedy saw Johnson as an old-school pol unsuited to the new media age. Early on, Johnson developed an exceptionally strong dislike for Robert Kennedy, whom he saw as far too big for his britches. (RFK returned the favor.) But Jack gave him pause, too. Johnson even told President Dwight Eisenhower during a private conversation in 1959 that he considered John Kennedy "a dangerous man."

But Johnson and Kennedy had things in common, too. Neither man saw the House of Representatives as the summit of his ambition, and both plotted their respective moves to the Senate as soon as possible. Each had his eye on the White House, too, though both suffered from accidents of birth that placed significant obstacles in the way. For Kennedy, it was his Catholic faith; for Johnson, it was his Southern birth.

The Texan sought to overcome his roots in the segregationist South by identifying himself with the Western, rather than the Southern, aspects of the Texas tradition. When his colleagues from the Old Confederacy issued the so-called Southern Manifesto, proclaiming resistance to the Supreme Court's 1954 *Brown* v. *Board of Education* decision ordering the desegregation of public schools, Johnson conspicuously refused to sign. After some hesitation, he also helped shepherd the 1957 Civil Rights Act through a skeptical Senate. Although more progressive than that of his Southern colleagues, Johnson's overall stance on civil rights remained cautious.

So, unlike a northern liberal like Minnesota's Hubert Humphrey, Johnson as vice president was unlikely to set off alarm bells in the South, where voters were still almost all white. Northern liberals would be upset, but would they really vote for Richard Nixon? Eisenhower and Nixon had made inroads in Texas and the South in 1952 and 1956. Johnson's selection would ensure that those states would be in Kennedy's column. The only question was, would Johnson take the job if Kennedy offered it?

There seemed reason to doubt that he would. For his part, Johnson repeatedly declined interest in the number-two spot, continuing his own hopeless presidential quest right up to the 1960 Democratic convention in Los Angeles. "I wouldn't want to trade a vote for a gavel," Johnson declared. JFK told Washington lobbyist Tommy Corcoran, who was urging him to pick the Texan, "Stop kidding, Tommy. Johnson will turn me down."

But the fact was Johnson wanted the job. There were several reasons. The elections of 1958 had brought seven new, mostly liberal, members into the Senate. These members (such as Wisconsin's William Proxmire) made it clear they had no use for Johnson's authoritarian style as Senate majority leader. In addition to the erosion of his authority within the Senate Democratic caucus, Johnson faced the prospect, if Kennedy won, of simply being the new president's water boy in the Senate. If Nixon won, he was far less likely to work with Johnson as smoothly as LBJ had worked with Dwight Eisenhower. Also, if Johnson ran for vice president and Kennedy lost, the Texan would be well positioned to make his own race in 1964.

The precise sequence of events surrounding the offer of the post to Johnson in Los Angeles remain clouded in a fog of conflicting memories even four decades later. What is clear, however, is that many of the people closest to JFK were bitterly opposed. Kenneth O'Donnell, who had actually spoken to labor and civil rights leaders and all but promised them there was no possibility of a Johnson candidacy, was furious with Kennedy.

In the bathroom of Jack's convention suite, the only place to which they could retreat for a private conversation, O'Donnell swore that "this is the worst mistake you ever made" and that a Johnson candidacy would go against "all the people who supported you." When liberals in the labor movement got wind of the proposed Johnson pick, they reared up on their collective hind legs and went after Kennedy hammer and tong, threatening to block Johnson on the convention floor.

But cooler heads soon prevailed. The logic of the Johnson pick was compelling, and more realistic liberals realized that dividing the party and potentially electing Nixon was a greater threat than Johnson could ever be. Jack had made a decision against the grain and was not afraid to stick it through.

Changing the Way Presidents Communicate

Television was fast displacing newspapers and radio as the public's primary source of news in 1960. (Nightly television network newscasts expanded from fifteen minutes to thirty minutes during the Kennedy administration.) Kennedy was among the first political leaders to perceive the potential power and reach of television, which would allow him to "go over the heads" of the Washington media and Congressional establishments. (He sought out training at the CBS television school in the early 1950s in an effort to overcome the stiff self-consciousness evident in his early appearances before cameras.)

The live press conferences that Kennedy initiated soon after taking office quickly became a showcase for Kennedy's wit and charm. For instance, when May Craig, a reporter known for her tough questions, rose to ask Kennedy what he had done to promote women's rights in accord with the party platform, Kennedy said, to general laughter, "Well, I'm sure we haven't done enough, Mrs. Craig."

And the public loved it. An incredible 91 percent of Americans said they approved of Kennedy's performances. Reporters quickly warmed to the format as well. "We were props in a show," said Peter Lisagor of the *Chicago Daily News*. "We should have joined Actors' Equity." Many print reporters found themselves having the unfamiliar and generally welcome experience of being stopped on the street or recognized in airports.

What the public did not see, however, was the president's meticulous preparation for each session. Although JFK would affect a relaxed, almost detached demeanor during these sessions in the State Department auditorium, he would in fact spend most of the day huddled with his advisers, working out answers in advance to likely questions. (Sometimes, Press Secretary Pierre Salinger would plant questions with friendly reporters.) Once the session was over, Kennedy and his staff would watch a playback, critiquing his performance, noting mistakes and areas for improvement.

Kennedy's use of television fundamentally reshaped how Americans view their government. If Franklin D. Roosevelt's radio "fireside chats" began the process of moving the presidency to the center of American public life, Kennedy's televised presidency cemented it there for all time. Although the press conference has fallen into disfavor in the twenty-first century, other forums have been opened up. President Bill Clinton played his saxophone on Arsenio Hall's talk show and submitted himself to (sometimes embarrassing) questions on MTV. Arnold Schwarzenegger announced his candidacy for governor of California on Jay Leno's *The Tonight Show*.

"We couldn't survive without TV," Kennedy said at one point during his presidency. Few of us can expect to master the medium the way President Kennedy ultimately did. But for anyone who aspires to a serious leadership position in business, politics, or even religion (as Pope John Paul II has demonstrated), television is a fact of life. If you don't know how to use it effectively, you must learn.

The Mucker's Way

"The greatest managers in the world do not have much in common," write Marcus Buckingham and Curt Coffman in their book *First, Break All the Rules*. "They are of different sexes, races, and ages. They employ vastly different styles and focus on different goals. But despite their differences, these great managers do share one thing: Before they do anything else, they first break all the rules of conventional wisdom."

There isn't much that's very wise in conventional wisdom. In the instances cited in this chapter, "conventional wisdom" was against Kennedy. Yet instead of putting his ideas on hold or giving up on them altogether, he found a way around the conventional wisdom and, in the process, created a new one.

Make no mistake, however—the way of the mucker is not for the faint of heart. Kennedy was nearly expelled from school when he formed his Muckers Club. He had legions of critics and second-guessers. It should be no surprise, however, that one of the traits Kennedy valued most highly, in himself as well as others, was courage.

A certain independence of mind is a necessary characteristic of someone aspiring to a position of successful leadership. Leadership involves, almost by definition, doing things differently and questioning how they have been done before. Imitators rarely get a chance to lead, and those who do usually fail. Paradoxically, independent thought can be especially crucial when it comes to patrons or mentors.

Helmuth von Moltke, for example, lived his entire career in the Imperial German Army in the shadow of his uncle and namesake, who had won Germany's wars of unification in the 1860s and 1870s. The younger von Moltke imitated his illustrious uncle's ways of doing things to the point of slavishness. But when he was army chief of staff in the opening days of World War I, that was no longer enough. He suffered a nervous breakdown barely a month after the start of hostilities and was forcibly retired. Less than two years later, he was dead.

Good mentors understand the need for independent thinking and encourage it among their subordinates.

Often, it takes more than a little bit of courage to speak up. One risks looking "wrong" and potentially foolish. Occasionally, that might indeed be the case. More often, though, the person who asks the "dumb" question is asking the same question that is in everyone's mind. It is a way of standing out from the crowd, which is indispensable for anyone who aspires to leadership.

John F. Kennedy had courage in spades and admired it in others. At Harvard University in the prewar years, courage of an almost reckless sort was not only encouraged; it was something of a requirement for those who aspired to be thought of as "manly" by their fellows. Thus, Kennedy competed in sports such as football and swimming, in spite of his physically weak and sickly constitution. While in Europe in 1937, he was photographed scaling the walls of a French chateau, far above the ground, giving his traveling companion some anxious moments. During World War II, he used his family connections to get *into* action, rather than avoid it, as another similarly privileged youth might have done.

Kennedy made much of his reputation by using that courage to carve out an identity for himself independent of his family background and contemporary political orthodoxy.

How, When Necessary, to Break the Rules and Be a Mucker

➡ *Be bold.* The temptation, in almost any environment, is to go along with the consensus. It is very difficult to stand out while blending in. Look for opportunities to stand out that others may have neglected. You might be surprised at how far a few bold ideas might take you. One of the oldest rules in retailing was to place your stores in cities and towns where people go to shop. Convinced that discounting was the future of the retail business, Sam Walton started putting his Wal-Mart discount stores outside of population centers. This helped him keep his costs down and offer better prices. The "experts" shook their heads and said no one would travel out of the way to shop. However, the discount prices Walton was able to offer on name-brand merchandise more than made up for a little inconvenience.

➡ *Stand your ground.* If you are confident of your position, don't crumple in the face of adversity. In the late 1980s, the founder of Qualcomm, Inc., Irwin Jacobs, was so certain that his digital wireless technology (known as CDMA) and products would prove superior to the TDMA systems already almost universally adopted throughout the cellular phone industry. After years of struggle, Jacobs finally won out. Today, nearly all new wireless technology is CDMA based, and Qualcomm is a multibillion-dollar company.

➡ *Don't be afraid to revise your position.* This is not being wishy-washy. It's staying on top of new and relevant information to make the best decision. You count on your key people to keep you informed in their areas of expertise, but you should also keep an eye on the latest trends and developments for yourself. JFK scanned through four newspapers each day, concentrating on the front pages and the important columnists and editorials, to stay on top of the latest events and current opinion. He also read newsmagazines and watched the news broadcasts on television. Today, there are even more sources of valuable information available to you, from cable news and financial stations to the Internet.

➡ *Follow Kennedy's five steps for challenging the status quo.* Starting with his very first campaign for Congress, JFK adopted methods that flew in the face of conventional wisdom. He determined for himself what he wanted to follow because he had the confidence and the determination to think for himself. The fact that he was successful at such a young age in each of his campaigns is powerful proof that his break-the-rules system worked.

CHAPTER 3

Resilience:
Turn Liabilities Into Pluses

"Courage is grace under pressure."

—ERNEST HEMINGWAY

Many people become overwhelmed by adversity. They are thrown off their game by small obstacles; bigger problems stop them dead in their tracks. Leaders cannot afford this kind of reaction to difficult situations. On their way up, they must be able to deal with whatever is thrown in their path. Once they are in a position of leadership, they will have to deal with rapidly changing circumstances. They must learn to recognize challenges as opportunities, to turn liabilities to their advantage. In other words, leaders must learn to be resilient in the face of adversity.

While twenty-eight-year-old John F. Kennedy was running for his first term in the U.S. House of Representatives, James Michael Curley, the incumbent congressman whom Joe Sr. essentially bribed to step aside in order to make way for his son, was indicted for mail fraud after winning a fourth term as Boston's mayor the year before.

Unlike Curley's earlier brush with the law (he spent sixty days in jail after arranging for a substitute to take a civil service exam for a needy but dull-witted constituent), this indictment involved Curley's efforts to enrich himself by using dubious means to obtain war contracts for paying clients. The evidence was so damning that not even the Democratic Truman administration in Washington dared quash the prosecution. The seventy-two-year-old Curley was convicted and sentenced to between six and eighteen months in federal prison.

Despite his cheeky insistence on continuing to serve as mayor, Curley was miserable behind bars and lost no time pulling the numerous political strings available to him to win early release. John McCormack, the leader of the Massachusetts Democratic delegation in Congress (and a future speaker of the House of Representatives), immediately began circulating a petition among his fellow Bay Staters in the Capitol asking President Harry Truman to commute Curley's sentence. The "Purple Shamrock," as Curley was known, was a figure of such sentiment in Massachusetts politics by this time that even a few Republicans signed the petition. Joe Sr. was in favor, as was Archbishop Richard Cushing.

No doubt McCormack thought that signing up Joe Kennedy's son would be a mere formality. But when the powerful McCormack mentioned it to the freshman congressman, instead of immediately agreeing, Kennedy inquired whether the president had been consulted.

"No," the startled McCormack replied. Then, his anger rising at the impudence of the young man, McCormack sputtered, "If you don't want to sign it, don't sign it." Kennedy didn't.

Still finding his feet in Washington and in a new profession, Jack seemingly had little to gain and potentially much to lose by his defiance. Alienating McCormack over such a minor issue would appear unwise on the face of it. Besides, Curley was popular in Kennedy's district and the Boston area generally (250,000 people had signed the clemency petition in Massachusetts). For a time, young Kennedy wondered if he hadn't made a mistake. To his aide Ted Reardon, he expressed fears that he was "politically dead, finished."

But as was so often the case in Kennedy's career, where others saw only problems, he saw opportunity. To be sure, there were some close-to-home reasons for refusing to be gracious to Curley. The latter had, after all, refused Jack any help in the 1946 race while his maternal grandfather, John Francis "Honey Fitz" Fitzgerald—whose career Curley had ruthlessly snuffed out in 1914 by threatening to expose an affair Fitzgerald was having with "Toodles" Ryan—had lent every assistance. But the wider political consequences couldn't be ignored.

Larger Ambitions

If JFK was content to make his political career in Massachusetts, then supporting Curley—with or without Honey Fitz—would have been the smart thing to do. But Jack's ambitions ran to bigger things, and in the rest of America, roguish figures such as Curley were viewed with a distinctly jaundiced eye. Although perhaps tolerable enough at a distance, most Californians, Ohioans, and Coloradoans had no desire to see Curley—or his friends and supporters—with their hands on the machinery of state in Washington, D.C. By conspicuously refusing to come to Curley's aid, young Kennedy was putting some daylight between himself and the less-savory aspects of the Irish political tradition in the United States and, not incidentally, from his own father.

In setting himself apart this way, Kennedy was, in fact, turning what might have been a liability into a strength. To underscore the implications of his decision, biographer Robert Dallek speculates that Kennedy and his father staged a discussion for a reporter's benefit as a way of underlining young Jack's independence of his father. Certainly, it was to JFK's benefit to distance himself somewhat from his father's less popular views, such as prewar appeasement and a track record of anti-Semitic cracks.

The story goes that at a reception soon after taking office as a congressman, Joe Sr. turned to journalist Kay Halle in front of Jack. "I wish you would tell Jack he's going to vote the wrong way," the patriarch said. "I think Jack is making a terrible mistake."

The new representative didn't back down.

"Now, look here, Dad, you have your political views and I have mine," he said. "I'm going to vote exactly the way I feel I must vote on this. I've got great respect for you, but when it comes to voting, I'm voting my way."

Joe Sr. smiled and said to Halle, "Well, Kay, that's why I settled a million dollars on each of them, so they could spit in my eye if they wished."

Dealing with the Catholic Issue

One of the biggest obstacles Kennedy had to overcome was his religion. In 1928, Alfred Smith became the first Roman Catholic to win the presidential nomination of a major American political party. The result was one of the

ugliest campaigns in modern times, with Smith openly attacked for his religion by a revived Ku Klux Klan, among many other groups. Voter turnout,
especially in Protestant areas, was up sharply that year, leading to the Democratic candidate's landslide defeat to Herbert Hoover. To Smith's everlasting
sadness, he even lost his home state of New York, which had elected him its
governor four times.

Thus, Catholics found themselves radioactive when it came to nomina-
tions for national office. Of the persistence and power of anti-Catholic bigotry, there could be little doubt. In 1949, Paul Blanshard's *American Freedom
and Catholic Power,* an alarmist anti-Catholic tract, became a national best-
seller. Worried articles appeared in Protestant journals calling attention to the
aggressive efforts by the Roman Catholic Church to win converts. Jim Far-
ley, FDR's postmaster general and a Catholic himself, spoke for many in the
Democratic party establishment in 1956 when he declared, "America is not
ready for a Catholic yet."

Indeed, Catholics were still a distinct subgroup in American society. Led
by a celibate clergy, they worshiped in a dead language that few members of
the congregation even understood fully. On average, they had more children
than other Americans and were prohibited from seeking divorces. They also
tended to be concentrated in urban areas and thus were often associated with
big-city politics and its attendant reputation for corruption and vote rigging.

"Hanging a Lantern on Your Problem"

This was the challenge that faced John F. Kennedy as he set his sights on
national office in the 1950s. He responded as he did on other occasions: He
followed his brother Robert's advice to "hang a lantern on your problem."
He would turn his seeming liability into an advantage.

Kennedy's initial reaction to what came to be known as "the religious
issue" was irritation. Why did he, alone among the major candidates, have
to answer questions about his faith? It must have been especially galling given
the fact that Kennedy's own attitude toward active Catholicism could chari-
tably be described as feeble at best, unlike his mother Rose, brother Bobby,
and sister Eunice, who were strong and regular practitioners of their faith.

The possibility that Kennedy's religion might be a bar to his reaching
higher office was broached as early as his 1952 Senate race. But it really
began to jell in 1956. President Dwight Eisenhower suffered a heart attack
late in 1955, and for a time it was widely assumed he would not run for

reelection the next year. Suddenly, the Democratic nomination seemed worth having, after all. Adlai Stevenson, who had run unsuccessfully four years earlier, would almost certainly be the nominee. But who would be his vice presidential running mate?

Kennedy thought it just might be him, *if* he could lay to rest questions about his religion.

So the Kennedy team began gathering facts to demonstrate that, far from being a liability, a Catholic would help the Democratic ticket. Speechwriter Theodore Sorensen drafted a memo laying out this scenario. John Bailey, the near-legendary Connecticut Democratic chairman and close Kennedy friend, agreed to put his name on the document, giving it added credibility. Then it was circulated to every delegate and alternate to the party's convention, as well as other party leaders.

The size of the Catholic population of the United States had increased since 1928, the memo said. Furthermore, because Catholics were clustered in large cities in large states, their votes were crucial to achieving an electoral college majority. The Catholic vote was also reliably Democratic. The one time when it went Republican was in Eisenhower's 1952 victory. Therefore, if Democrats were to win, they needed to get those Catholic votes back. One of their coreligionists on the Democratic ticket might just do the trick.

Stevenson, however, wasn't convinced. Neither was Joe Sr. At least not on *this* ticket. Certain that Stevenson was a goner once Eisenhower ultimately decided to seek reelection, the family patriarch feared his son would be blamed for the inevitable defeat. The younger Kennedy, however, didn't share his father's pessimism and waged a spirited fight for the nomination when Stevenson unexpectedly threw the choice of a running mate to the convention itself. Nevertheless, the delegates chose Senator Estes Kefauver of Tennessee. It did Stevenson no good, and he lost convincingly in November 1956 for a second time.

Turning the Issue Around: The West Virginia Primary

Still, the religious issue would not go away as Kennedy aimed for the top spot in 1960. He tried knocking it down by calling it irrelevant. That hadn't worked. He had appealed to political facts in the Bailey memo. That hadn't worked. Now Kennedy knew the issue had to be confronted in a more forceful, emotional fashion. Instead of his religion being the issue, he would turn it around and make those who made an issue of his religion an issue themselves.

The young Massachusetts senator was, in many ways, the ideal bearer of such a message, for he fit none of the stereotypes that had dogged Catholics in the United States for so long. Instead of being poor or working class, he was rich. Instead of being part of a big-city political machine, he had run against it. Instead of having a large family, he had only one child. Instead of attending Notre Dame or Holy Cross, he had gone to the WASP bastion of Harvard. He was, as one observer noted, "What every Irish grandmother wanted her grandson to be."

Kennedy tried out the new approach in the West Virginia primary. In a state where Catholics were extremely thin on the ground and where fundamentalist Protestantism ran seemingly as deep as many of the state's coal mines, Kennedy was thought to stand little chance. Minnesota Senator Hubert H. Humphrey, a Protestant, was the clear favorite. (Humphrey even raised the issue obliquely, running a radio commercial with the tune "That Old Time Religion" playing in the background.)

The religious issue was confronted head-on. Appearing on a television program with Franklin D. Roosevelt Jr.—a shrewd choice, given FDR's iconic status in the state—Kennedy pledged that if he ever placed his religious beliefs above his constitutional oath of office, he would be committing a sin against God. He placed his hand on a Bible to emphasize the point.

The Kennedy campaign theme was relentless: The only reason anyone could possibly have for opposing Kennedy's religion was bigotry, plain and simple. This appeal was skillfully welded to the veteran issue (Humphrey had been medically excused from duty in World War II) when Kennedy and his spokesmen noted that no one had asked JFK or Joe Jr. their religion before they served in World War II.

Kennedy's smashing upset victory in West Virginia was only the beginning. When a group of Protestant ministers led by the famed Norman Vincent Peale attacked the idea of electing a Catholic as president, Robert Kennedy simply denounced Peale as a bigot and a Nixon supporter. Friendly Protestant ministers and Jewish rabbis, primed and ready, added their voices to the denunciations of Peale. (The Kennedys used the religious issue effectively in mobilizing Jewish voters as well, with Bobby telling one Jewish audience that a successful attack on one religion might mean an attack on another.)

Taking a Firm Stand

Nixon never raised the issue of Kennedy's religion, and he very much wanted blue-collar Catholic voters, among whom his scrappy, bulldog image had considerable appeal. But as Catholics showed signs of rallying to their coreligionist, Nixon fervently sought to tamp down the issue. "The best way the candidates can keep it out of the campaign is not talking about it," he said, with just a hint of desperation. "I've issued orders to all the people in my campaign not to discuss religion. . . . I would hope that Senator Kennedy would reach the same conclusion."

Kennedy, however, made one final effort to make clear that rank prejudice was the only possible reason to oppose his candidacy on account of religion. The denouement came in Houston before a meeting of the city's Protestant ministers in September 1960. "It is apparently necessary for me to state, once again, not what kind of church I believe in, for that should be of importance only to me, but what kind of America I believe in," he said. "I believe in an America where the separation of church and state is absolute, where no Catholic prelate would tell the president—should he be a Catholic—how to act. And no Protestant minister would tell his parishioners for whom to vote."

His peroration was quite simply extraordinary. Kennedy offered to resign the presidency should he ever perceive a conflict between his duty to the country and his duty to his faith. Kennedy correctly perceived that only an unreasonable person—a bigot, perhaps—could ask for more. Kennedy's opponents were too cowed to raise the issue again, while Catholics (and an even greater percentage of Jews) were all too willing to troop to the polls to show their support.

Kennedy and Organized Labor: An Uneasy Relationship

Organized labor was, and remains, a bedrock constituency of the Democratic party. As such, John F. Kennedy needed the support of most of its constituent unions to be elected president and to govern once he had been elected. But he was by no means "in the pocket" of the labor bosses. Indeed, they sometimes wondered whose side he was really on.

Kennedy was a strong supporter of labor unions. He admired the way they had raised the wages and reduced the hours of their members. Unions were also credited with preventing communist takeovers in France and Italy following World War II.

But there were problems with unions as well, ones that deeply concerned Kennedy. Organized labor had won major bargaining rights under Franklin D. Roosevelt's New Deal and did not hesitate to exercise them. There seemed to be continual strikes—so many that the bulk of Americans, who were not union members, were increasingly fed up and wanted the organizations reined in.

Worse, his father's brief and unhappy tenure on the U.S. Maritime Commission in the mid-1930s had demonstrated to Jack that union leaders could be as moneygrubbing and irresponsible as the most Scrooge-like capitalist. At the same time, Kennedy couldn't possibly stake out an openly antiunion stance and hope to survive politically.

Investigating Union Leadership

At one point, Jack Kennedy was given the opportunity to sit on the so-called McClellan Committee that was set up to investigate union abuses. He had not wanted to join what was later known as the "Rackets Committee." But his brother Robert had defied their father's advice to steer clear of investigating labor unions and took the job as its chief counsel. (Reportedly, their argument on the subject at Hyannis was described as "furious.") Joe Sr. thought the threat to Jack's presidential chances in 1960 from angering organized labor was plainly obvious. Other pro-labor senators with White House ambitions, such as Henry "Scoop" Jackson and Stuart Symington, avoided serving on the committee. Lyndon Johnson told Jack he thought serving on the committee would be a mistake.

But where others saw danger, Jack and Bobby saw opportunity. It wasn't unions per se they were opposing; it was corrupt union bosses who put their own interests ahead of the interests of their members. The brothers were helped by the fact that the late 1950s was not exactly a banner time for attractive union leaders. Crooked bosses such as David Beck and Jimmy Hoffa of the Teamsters union, for example, were sent seemingly from central casting as villains. Jack also was not unmindful of the fact that highly publicized investigations had helped launch the national reputations of such senators as President Harry Truman and Estes Kefauver, the man who beat Jack out for the 1956 vice presidential nomination. Besides, even if the committee came up empty, Jack and Bobby would have associated themselves with the cause of clean unionism, and that wouldn't hurt Jack with rank-and-file union voters, and it might help him with voters from nonunion households.

Introducing Reform Legislation

Ultimately, the Rackets Committee uncovered so much evidence of union wrongdoing and corruption—Beck went to prison almost immediately and Hoffa did eventually (before he was finally murdered)—that some sort of reform legislation seemed certain to pass. Teaming up with Republican New York Senator Irving Ives, Kennedy introduced the Kennedy-Ives bill that would prohibit the use of union dues for improper activities, forbid the extension of loans from union pension funds, and mandate the regular auditing of union accounts.

Labor leaders reacted as if poked in the eye with a sharp stick. "God save us from our friends," muttered AFL-CIO President George Meany about Kennedy's legislation. Al Hayes of the Machinists union compared Kennedy (rather implausibly) with Argentine dictator Juan Perón.

Meany's ruffled feathers were soothed when Kennedy pointed out that it was labor's refusal to play a constructive role in 1947 that resulted in the tough, antiunion Taft-Hartley legislation. Something similar might happen again unless labor got on board a train that was clearly leaving the station.

Eventually, Kennedy crafted a bill that was acceptable to Meany and company, and it passed the Senate by a vote of 88–1. However, the Eisenhower administration came out against it as being too favorable to labor, and Kennedy-Ives died in the House. It was revived in 1959 and once again passed the Senate. But this time Eisenhower threw his support behind the more restrictive Landrum-Griffin bill, which ended up passing and being signed into law. Kennedy's most sustained effort to attach his name to a piece of major legislation had failed.

In the end, the effort was not wasted. The public was mesmerized by the sight of Jack, and especially of Bobby Kennedy, grilling crooked labor leaders on television. Jack had associated himself with a good, if losing, cause and had shown he did not march unquestioningly to the tune of a major Democratic constituency—and he did it without alienating that constituency.

How to Turn Liabilities into Pluses

➧ *"Hang a lantern on your problem."* Robert Kennedy's advice to his brother still rings true today. By pulling his Catholicism out of the shadows and bringing it into the light, Kennedy faced his perceived problem head-on. Was there some shame in being a Catholic? An emphatic "No!" Would he take orders from Rome? Again, a resounding "No!" Do opponents reveal their own shortcomings by attacking a candidate for his religion? Yes, they do. Although there may have still been anti-Catholic bigotry in the country, few in the public arena would dare speak it aloud.

➧ *Treat each challenge as an opportunity.* To be a leader is to take on difficult problems, to learn from them, and to turn them to your advantage. That's leadership 101. If a business hits hard times, employees look to their boss to come up with a plan for turning things around, not to close up shop at the first sign of difficulty. Often, out of such adversity, creative business leaders take their companies in new directions, explore new markets, and expand their business horizons in ways not thought of before. In many cases, business success has been achieved on the heels of perceived failure.

➧ *Be resilient in the face of adversity.* Strong leaders don't crumble when faced with stressful circumstances. Their ability to stand up to adversity often arouses their people to do the same. Kennedy's hero Winston Churchill rallied his countrymen in their darkest hour when London was under nightly bombing attacks by the Germans, his stirring speeches urging them to never give up. Inspired by their leader's resilience, the British were able to withstand the Nazi assault and eventually emerge victorious from World War II.

➧ *When things go wrong, find out why.* Any leader worth his salt has encountered and overcome many obstacles along the way. But there will also be times when you aren't so successful. The key is to use each situation as a learning experience, a challenge to do better the next time. Thomas Edison often said there was no such thing as failure when it came to inventing. He felt that every wrong attempt was a step toward the solution.

CHAPTER 4

Charisma:
Set a Style

"Beauty is life, life, Beauty."

—JOHN KEATS

What is your style? Do you dress to the nines every day and seek to project a calm, confident, in-control image? Or do you seek to stand out by "dressing down"? Do you decorate your office with antiques, or cultivate a spare, modernistic look?

No matter what you choose, you *will* have a style. "Style" is a much-maligned word, usually juxtaposed with "substance," as if the two are locked in eternal opposition. There's no reason, though, that style and substance can't complement each other. Leadership style means simply how you present yourself to others. Do you look and sound like someone others would like to follow? The answer to this question powerfully affects the rest of your leadership.

One reason for paying attention to style is that, quite simply, the rest of society does. Stroll along the streets of a major city (and even many smaller ones) and count the number of people wearing black, piercing their eyebrows, and donning narrow, European-style glasses. By now, we all rely on style to express identity. If you are going to stand out amid all this "clutter," among all your fellow human beings, then you have no choice but to pay attention to style.

"From airport terminals decorated like Starbucks to the popularity of hair dye among teenage boys," writes Virginia Postrel in her book, *The Substance of Style,* "one thing is clear: We have entered the Age of Aesthetics. Sensory appeals are everywhere, and they are intensifying, radically changing how Americans live and work. We expect every strip mall and city block to offer designer coffee, a copy shop with do-it-yourself graphics workstations, and a nail salon for manicures on demand. Every startup, product, or public space calls for an aesthetic touch, which gives us more choices, and more responsibility."

John F. Kennedy pioneered the use of style in modern American politics; that is, he created an aesthetically appealing image of himself. On a personal level, he crafted a charismatic "image." On a public level, he imbued the presidency with a regal "look" that it never had before and retains to this day.

Learning to Be Charismatic

"Charisma" is a word so frequently associated with John F. Kennedy that it actually began to grate on his successor. "I may not have charisma," Lyndon B. Johnson growled to an aide, "but I got the bills passed."

LBJ makes a valid point. Many successful leaders have gotten by on little or no charisma. Nevertheless, charisma remains a potentially powerful leadership tool. Lee Iacocca, generally considered one of the most charismatic business leaders of recent years, made masterful use of his powerful public personality to convince a highly reluctant Congress and a skeptical public to go along with a publicly financed bailout of the ailing Chrysler.

New York Times columnist William Safire, in his *New Political Dictionary,* describes charisma (which is rooted in the Greek word *charism,* or "gift") as "political sex appeal." It is a certain magnetism and charm that draws others to you. It is, to some extent, a bit of a confidence trick played on those around you. People will not follow an individual in whom they repose little confidence. Charisma can help generate that confidence. To be described as a charismatic leader is almost always a compliment; to be described as "charisma challenged" definitely is not.

Charisma is widely believed to be a sort of innate trait; you either have it or you don't. The weight of the evidence, however, does not support this view. We have all known people who seem to be naturally charismatic, possessing an enviable kind of innate confidence in their abilities and judgment. But it is equally true that many people who did not appear charismatic early in their lives subsequently come to be seen that way.

John F. Kennedy was among the latter. A glance at one of his earliest appearances before a newsreel camera shows an awkward, self-conscious, almost impossibly young-looking man explaining his vague and inchoate plans to one day work for the government. "Charismatic" is not a word that would leap immediately to the viewer's mind.

It is advisable to note that charisma can be used for evil as well as good. Many of Adolf Hitler's comrades in the trenches of the First World War, or those who knew him as a failed artist in Vienna, were later flummoxed when this man they had recalled as an oddball loner emerged as one of the most evilly charismatic personalities of all time. Plainly, charisma is an attribute that *can* be learned and acquired.

Not everyone is best equipped to develop a charismatic leadership style. It is also true that even the most successful student is not going to convince everyone. There will always be plenty of people who won't view you as charismatic no matter what you do. Nevertheless, trying to develop a certain degree of charisma can't hurt. People who work for charismatic bosses seem almost to draw energy from them. They seek to please the boss. They feel as if they have let the boss down when they fail. Having a charismatic boss is just one more reason to get up in the morning and go to work.

Kennedy's own interest in the subject appears to date from an extended visit in 1945 to his father's old stomping grounds, Hollywood. Chuck Spalding, one of Kennedy's closest friends, recalled that the future president was fascinated by Hollywood's star-making system. Jack had dinner with Gary Cooper, one of the screen's brightest stars, and found him almost stunningly pedestrian. How could such a man be turned into the very epitome of a Hollywood hero, a person others looked up to and sought to emulate?

"How *does* he do it?" Kennedy asked Spalding repeatedly. "Do you think I could learn how to do it?"

Once Kennedy decided to go into politics, he set out to become the first movie-star politician. One of the ways Hollywood turns people into stars is by getting their names and photographs into newspapers, magazines, and today, on television. The public has a seemingly insatiable appetite for celebrity "news." (*People* magazine, which has no reason to exist other than to publish such material, is one of the world's most profitable titles.) By labeling the people who appear in such media as "stars," Hollywood can very often convince the public (by a technique psychologists call autosuggestion) to accept them as such, even if they have made only small appearances in a few films or sometimes no films at all.

These techniques were old hat in Hollywood by the late 1940s, but no one had thought of applying them to politics before the former Hollywood producer, Joseph P. Kennedy Sr.

Developing an Image

Joe Sr. was an early and avid believer in the then-new art of public relations. (He was apparently the first American ambassador ever to keep a full-time press officer on the embassy staff.) Beginning in the 1920s, he courted reporters and hired press agents to keep himself and his large, rambunctious, and photogenic family in the public eye. The "rolled-up sleeves" look that later came to be associated with Bobby Kennedy was in fact pioneered by his father on Wall Street in the 1920s.

Having grown up in such an atmosphere, John F. Kennedy was unusually well prepared to step into a public world increasingly dominated by the concept of celebrity (i.e., people who are famous for being famous). He moved almost seamlessly into using these techniques to promote himself from being merely another junior representative or senator into someone to watch.

Thus, Kennedy's PT-109 experience was chronicled in *Reader's Digest,* the largest-circulation magazine in America at the time. Newsreel cameras captured his first campaign for Congress, with the newsreels, naturally, being shown first in Massachusetts theaters. *Look* magazine profiled him in that first campaign. Kennedy's name and picture appeared regularly in print during his tenure in Congress, not only in Massachusetts, but also nationally, in spite of his rather thin legislative record.

"In all my years in public life," recalled future House Speaker Thomas P. "Tip" O'Neill, who succeeded Kennedy in Congress in 1952, "I've never seen a congressman get so much press for doing so little work."

Sometimes, the Kennedy publicity machine could go into hyperdrive. When Kennedy invited Jacqueline Bouvier to go sailing with him during their courtship, she was taken aback to discover that a *Life* magazine reporter and photographer were also invited aboard. What she thought would be a romantic sail turned into a major cover story. ("Senator Kennedy Goes A-Courting" was the headline over a photograph of the beaming couple on the sailboat.) Later, when they were engaged, Kennedy asked Jackie to hold off on making a public announcement for a few weeks. It seems *The Saturday Evening Post* was about to run a photo spread on "The Senate's Gay Young Bachelor."

Jack's good looks and natural charm, as well as his father's press connections, were a solid foundation on which to build. But assembling the superstructure of the charismatic Kennedy took years.

"Image *is* reality," was one of Joe Kennedy's favorite aphorisms, and like many of his opinions, it is overdrawn. But it would be naive not to admit there is a degree of truth in it. As the ambassador's concern with public relations demonstrates, part of developing charisma is an intense interest in how others perceive you.

How do you come across? As a gloomy Gus, or a sunbeam whose rays brighten everyone around you? How do you perceive problems? As frustrating defeats, or obstacles to be overcome? Are setbacks a reason not to try again, or a learning experience?

Projecting Optimism

An essentially optimistic outlook appears to be one of the major ingredients of charismatic leadership. Franklin D. Roosevelt's jaunty smile and confident mien, even in the midst of the Great Depression and looming world war, are recalled fondly by millions of Americans even today. New York City in 1993 was teetering on the brink of bankruptcy, under siege from crime and reeling from failed political leadership. ("Do Something, Dave!" was the *New York Post*'s desperate front-page plea to the seemingly clueless Mayor David Dinkins after yet another wave of shootings.) Rudy Giuliani took a city that was flat on its back and turned it, almost by sheer force of will that it *could* be done, into one that he could describe, utterly without irony, as "the capital of the world." The charisma he generated paid huge dividends on September 11, 2001, when Giuliani was a major calming figure during the terrorist attacks.

It's not hard to see why this should be so. There's never any shortage of naysayers or critics. By contrast, it takes some effort and will to see the positive in even the most adverse circumstances.

Kennedy's optimism, especially in the face of all the physical pain he was suffering much of the time, is one of the most remarkable things about him. Someone in his position, wealthy and privileged, could easily have given in to feeling sorry for himself because of his endless physical ailments, much less set a course for high political office. Instead, Kennedy just smiled through the pain.

During his first campaign, for example, he had to climb endless flights of stairs to shake hands in the tenements of Charlestown, home of the Boston Navy Yard, which was murder on his back. Confronting yet another flight of stairs, the increasingly pale and haggard-looking candidate was finally approached by an aide. "You don't look so good," the aide averred. "I *feel* great!" Kennedy replied through a clenched smile, and kept climbing.

The symbols of Kennedy's optimism were his electric smile, his enthusiasm, and his relaxed, almost casual yet still serious, demeanor. He was well aware of the importance of his smile, so much so that when *Time* magazine named him its Man of the Year in 1961, Kennedy was actually dissatisfied because the specially commissioned cover portrait did not show him smiling. ("But he didn't smile!" protested the artist, who had spent several days in Kennedy's office preparing the portrait.)

Showing Enthusiasm

Real enthusiasm for your job can also infect those around you. "He loved being president," recalled aide Arthur Schlesinger Jr. "And at times he could hardly remember that he had ever been anything else. He never complained about the 'terrible loneliness' of the office or its 'awesome burdens.'" Aide Dave Powers echoed that view, saying, "He loved being where the action was. He was always at his best under pressure. He became more determined after each disappointment."

Dressing the Part

Kennedy also learned to dress his part. For most of his life, Jack was famously casual about clothes. He wore a Churchill-like blue pinstripe suit for nearly a decade, until the seat of the pants was literally falling out. Even as a congressman, he would appear on the floor of the House of Representatives in a sport coat with his shirttail flapping in the breeze. Still, he was not entirely without a fashion sense. When it came time to replace the blue pinstripe, he selected a gray suit, which was not common then and which served to set him somewhat apart from his blue-suited colleagues.

Once more, it was Hollywood to the rescue, this time in the shape of his actor brother-in-law, Peter Lawford. Drawing on his screen image as a debonair Englishman, Lawford succeeded in convincing Jack that a U.S. senator with aspirations to the presidency simply could not afford to dress like a Harvard undergraduate. Under Lawford's direction, Kennedy bought a wardrobe of finely tailored suits with narrow lapels; custom-made shirts with monogrammed cuffs; and narrow, conservative ties. (Kennedy also popularized two-button suits; most American men at the time wore three-button jackets.) Lawford also taught Jack how to tie a tie properly, something he had done only half-wittedly since his teens, and also convinced the senator to stop wearing button-down shirts. "Looks juvenile," Lawford said.

But he didn't go in for ostentation. Until Jackie gave him an expensive wristwatch for their fourth anniversary, he had made do with inexpensive models. He never wore a diamond stickpin or even rings. His only adornment was the PT-109 tie clip.

Lawford also got Kennedy to deal finally with the fact that his left leg was half an inch shorter than his right. A dozen pairs of custom-made shoes came equipped with a slightly thicker sole and heel on the left shoe. This finally evened out Kennedy's walk and made him appear much more graceful and light on his feet.

Although Kennedy is often given credit (if that is the proper word) for moving American life toward more casual styles of dress in the early 1960s—his wearing of sports shirts and dark sunglasses is an example—he confined such attire to casual locales, such as Hyannis, Newport, or Palm Beach. In a business setting, he liked to stay more formal. Unlike his brother Robert, who made a habit of doffing his suit coat and loosening his tie whenever possible, there are relatively few photographs of JFK in his shirtsleeves. Even indoors, he tended to keep his suit coat on and buttoned. Also, unlike many politicians who address people informally, Kennedy did not use phrases such as "fellow," "son," "old boy," or similar terms. The wives of his associates were always "Mrs.," and most officeholders were addressed by their titles or as "Mr."

Kennedy also developed the habit of changing clothes from the skin out four times a day, so he would always appear fresh to everyone he met. (He may have picked this up from Frank Sinatra, who had a similar habit.) He was surprised when a friend, Newsweek Washington bureau chief Ben Bradlee, told him that many men wore the same shirt two days in a row.

Looking Good

Attention to personal grooming didn't stop with clothes. At a time when many, if not most, American men slicked their hair back with "greasy kid's stuff," Kennedy was one of the first politicians to try the "dry" look. He employed a hair stylist who would appear regularly at Kennedy's Senate office with a hair dryer, thus creating the signature JFK bouffant hairstyle. Kennedy also had his fingernails regularly buffed and manicured, and he had heat lamp treatments to give him a tanned look even in the depths of winter.

A lean, fit-looking body was also high on Kennedy's list of concerns. Though he was thin to the point of cadaverousness at times, Kennedy viewed with horror any possibility that he might be putting on too much weight. The cortisone injections he began taking in the late 1950s to control his Addison's disease had the effect of puffing out his face, thus unintentionally creating the "JFK look" that became so familiar during the 1960 campaign. Initially, however, Kennedy did not like the effect at all.

Photographs were something approaching an obsession for him. He spent hours in the photographer's studio, trying out different poses and lighting. Early in his congressional career, he noticed that Boston newspapers often ran photographs of his colleagues that were years and sometimes decades out of date. Kennedy made certain that news outlets always had up-to-date (and flattering) shots available.

Richard Nixon's unfortunate tendency to be caught in embarrassing, candid photographs was not lost on Kennedy. He took care to avoid such episodes whenever possible. One reason Kennedy disliked wearing hats was because he wanted to avoid the politician's bane of having to don funny headgear. Knowing that drinking and eating photographs were rarely flattering, he would hand proffered drinks off to nearby aides and crouch down in the seat of his car, out of camera range, while wolfing down a quick meal on the campaign trail.

A charismatic leader also knows when and how to cultivate a certain distance, even from those he knows best. Kennedy kept his life tightly "compartmented." He rarely socialized with members of his staff, for example. (He could take this habit to ridiculous extremes; not once during his administration, for example, did he invite his brother Attorney General Robert Kennedy to a private meal in the White House family quarters.) By thus "rationing" himself, he made the private moments all the more valuable to those around him.

Cultivating Candor

A charismatic leader also cultivates a certain candor, with subordinates and with the public. It is an ability to be candid without being offensive. Kennedy could often be disarmingly candid, both in public and in private, about his reasons for certain actions. Asked why he was running for president, he didn't reach for the easy soliloquy about wanting to accomplish great things for America. Instead, he frankly cited his own ambition.

"I look around me at the others in the race, and I say to myself, well, if they think they can do it, why not me?" he said. "That's the answer. And I think it's enough."

Maintaining Composure

Kennedy didn't like to hurry and disliked being hurried, even by his own staff. ("How long has Mr. McCormick been here?" Representative Kennedy asked as he leisurely ate breakfast while an aide was urging him to get to a meeting called by House Majority Leader John McCormick. "Twenty-six years," the baffled aide replied. "Well," said Kennedy, "do you think he can wait another ten minutes?") His self-assurance and easy manner came to epitomize the new ideal of "cool" (one of Kennedy's favorite words) and went down well with the public during one of the most terrifying periods in American history.

Tips from Kennedy on How to Be More Charismatic

Why not you, too? Try taking a few steps toward a more charismatic you:

➡ *Publicize yourself.* You don't need a PR agency to place glossy articles about you in major magazines to publicize yourself and your achievements. If you garner professional recognition, let people know. E-mail is wonderful for this purpose. Write for professional journals and accept speaking invitations. Before you know it, folks will begin looking to you as an authority.

➡ *Be optimistic.* Try to see the opportunities in apparent setbacks. People are naturally drawn to those who maintain a positive outlook, and they tend to shy away from negativity. True leaders recognize this fact and always try to project confidence and hope.

➻ *Remember, appearances count!* Stop fantasizing about losing weight and do it. If you've been wearing the same horn-rimmed glasses since high school, trade them in for something with a more contemporary look, or ditch them altogether in favor of contact lenses. Give a new hairstyle a try. Invest in stylish clothes and learn to wear them with confidence.

➻ *Be candid.* If you have a better idea, don't be afraid to speak up. Wall-flowers don't get promoted. If subordinates aren't measuring up to the required standard, let them know, and then work to help them develop the skills needed. You can be candid without being unpleasant.

Creating the "Look" of the Modern Presidency

From the earliest days of the American republic, the issue of how the president ought to present himself to the American people, and the world, was a critical issue. John Adams thought the president should be styled "His Majesty." George Washington settled for "Mr. President." For most of American history, the tension between the nation's small "r" republican ideals and the reality of an increasingly industrial, prosperous, and self-confident country was never really resolved—until John F. Kennedy. He came down firmly on the side of a presidency that was "imperial" in look as well as fact. And the American people loved it.

The changes began on Kennedy's first day in office. Dismayed at the reproduction antique furniture they found throughout the White House, John and Jacqueline Kennedy began an effort to remake the executive mansion as a showpiece that would impress all visitors with its stylishness and flair. Genuine antique furniture and paintings were brought out of storage or donated by the public, and new draperies were hung. The First Lady's televised tour of the redecorated White House became one of the most highly rated television programs of all time until then.

Under Harry Truman and Dwight Eisenhower, White House state dinners were fairly sedate affairs, with the men attired in business suits and a lightly spiked punch the only alcohol in evidence. Prohibition was still only two decades in the past, and considerable areas of the country remained "dry." Kennedy state dinners, however, became "events" in a way they had never been before. Trumpets heralded the arrival of the First Couple, and "Hail to the Chief" was played when they entered the East Room. White tie and tails were the order of the day. Wine was on the tables and hard liquor available at the bar for all who wanted it.

Reflecting the president's interest in the world of ideas, the guest list was expanded from the usual politicos and business leaders to include Nobel Prize recipients, artists, authors, and playwrights. Famous musicians were invited to the White House, notably cellist Pablo Casals. Controversial figures, such as scientists Linus Pauling and J. Robert Oppenheimer, also received invitations.

The Kennedys also changed the way guests were received at the White House. Before the aviation age, state visitors generally arrived by train and were greeted by the president or an official delegation at Washington D.C.'s Union Station. Presidents Truman and Eisenhower usually journeyed to Andrews Air Force Base outside of Washington to greet foreign guests. So did Kennedy in the early months of his presidency.

But after a visit to London following the Vienna summit with Nikita Khrushchev in June 1961, Kennedy discovered how the British royal family received its guests. Instead of the queen going to the airport, the visitor came from the airport to the queen at Buckingham Palace, there to be formally welcomed. When Kennedy returned to Washington, he sketched out his ideas for an event to be held on the White House lawn, featuring military bands, march-pasts by soldiers attired in colonial dress, and speeches by the president and his guest. Since that time, what has become known as the State Arrival Ceremony is a standard feature of Washington life.

The most obvious change, though, was in the way the president traveled. Before Kennedy, presidents tended to be low-key travelers, partly for reasons of security, partly for fear of appearing too regal or detached from the nation's business. Instead, Kennedy turned travel into a leadership tool.

The Boeing 707 jet that Kennedy inherited from Eisenhower was nothing much to look at. Painted in an orange, black, and white scheme, the functional, boxy aircraft had the prosaic words "Military Air Transport Service" stenciled on the fuselage.

For JFK, this simply wouldn't do. Previous presidents viewed their planes as a utilitarian item, a machine for getting them from here to there. With his longtime interest in aviation, Kennedy knew it could be much, much more. It could be a symbol of the presidency itself and the awesome power at the command of the office's holder.

For years, the Air Force had identified the plane carrying the president by the call sign Air Force One. The code was kept secret for security reasons. Kennedy, however, thought the phrase had tremendous resonance and authorized his aides to start using it publicly. Presidential arrivals became media events, with the plane descending majestically from the sky and coming to a stop right before the assembled cameras of the waiting press. Kennedy would then emerge from the interior almost as a god descending from Mt. Olympus to dwell among the mortals. The technique has been used by every president since.

When Kennedy received a newer, more powerful 707 in October 1962, he enlisted famed industrial designer Raymond Loewy—who designed the Ritz Crackers logo and the Lucky Strike cigarette package—to come up with a new color scheme. Loewy produced the pale blue and white design that became world famous and is retained on the presidential jet today. This was the aircraft that carried Kennedy to Dallas in November 1963 and brought his body back to Washington. So identified had JFK become with this plane that it flew over the president's grave at Arlington on the day of his funeral. "This aircraft told everyone we were a world power—we were here, and we were here to stay," says Jeffrey S. Underwood, historian of the U.S. Air Force Museum at Wright-Patterson Air Force Base. "We were containing communism, and we wanted to be the symbol for the Free World to look toward. And this was as good a symbol as any, because this symbol was not in New York Harbor, the Statue of Liberty, this symbol could go around the world."

How to Set Your Own Style

John F. Kennedy's style suited him well. He came from a privileged background and definitely liked the finer things in life; thus, he wasn't about to make pretenses at being a plebian. You have to decide what style suits you best if you want to have maximum impact as a leader.

Although your leadership style will reflect in how people perceive you, it is not just a personal thing. Kennedy didn't just work on his personal style, he worked to change how the presidency and the entire country was perceived. You need to also consider how your company, brand, and products are perceived. Just as Kennedy's choices affected how the United States was perceived, so too do your choices as a leader reflect on how your company is perceived both internally and by the public.

Here are some tips on setting your own style:

➡ You will have a leadership style whether you like it or not; choose one that suits your personality and that best represents the company. Likewise, choose an image that works best for your company and products. Sometimes changing the presentation of your products or your mission can change the way it is received. Consider, for example, Starbucks and its vision of a coffee shop. It's more like a café, with music, murals on the wall, and the coffee individually prepared for the customer. By changing the environment in which consumers use their products, Starbucks was able to change the way people perceive coffee as well as their relationship to the coffee provider.

➡ Charisma is not a gift. Its basic elements can be learned. JFK's transformation from awkward young man to smooth, confident, "cool" young leader certainly shows this. If necessary, get professional help with both your personal image and that of your brand and product.

➡ Pay attention to how others perceive you. Get an honest review of yourself—including your outward appearance and your style of presentation and communication. Then work on the individual elements, strengthening your weak points and making sure that they all add up to a style that supports your vision. Also, take the time to research how your products and company are perceived by your intended audience. If your brand or product needs a face-lift, take this seriously. If changes are needed, make them.

➡ Don't lose sight of how style can help you set yourself apart as a leader. You don't need to have your own jet, but you can keep up with the latest fashions and trends. Don't be afraid to try new hairstyles or new clothing styles. They can help you stand out and get people to pay attention to what you have to say.

CHAPTER 5

Communication:
Present Your Ideas Effectively

"Words with me are instruments."

—THEODORE ROOSEVELT

"He couldn't communicate."

—HOUSE SPEAKER "TIP" O'NEILL,
ON WHY JIMMY CARTER FAILED AS PRESIDENT

Communication is at the heart of leadership. You must be able to communicate in all directions—to your subordinates, to your bosses, to your peers both inside and outside your organization, to your customers, and to the public at large. Someone who aspires to leadership and is unable or unwilling to cultivate the ability to communicate is in the wrong line of work.

There is a tendency among some of us to dismiss people who are strong communicators, especially on television or in the news media, as somehow superficial and not substantive. The particular people involved might indeed be superficial, but the general proposition is nonsense. We live in a world dominated by media as never before.

Kennedy's Ability to Communicate

The image of John F. Kennedy flickering on a television screen represents for many Americans their most enduring impression of him: smiling and joking with reporters at a news conference, looking grave and serious in a nationally televised address on an international crisis, or relaxing in an informal family setting at Hyannis or Newport.

This was not an accident. For Kennedy, says scholar James L. Golden, communication "became the central element of his leadership." Kennedy believed that the fundamental problem of a democracy was its tendency toward drift and contentment. The public had to be roused to action. Kennedy's instrument for this task was compelling rhetoric and persuasive argument—leavened with some good humor. Therefore, he devoted a great deal of time and effort toward perfecting his communication skills.

John F. Kennedy had certain advantages when it came to developing as a communicator. He grew up in the public eye. His heroics in the South Pacific were widely reported and turned him into a national figure in his own right. Physically handsome and naturally quick-witted, he also had a facility with words and seriously considered becoming a journalist or a teacher before settling on a political career.

It is therefore tempting to describe Kennedy as a "natural" communicator or public speaker. He was not. Joseph De Guglielmo, one of Kennedy's earliest political staffers, said that Kennedy's efforts on the stump in 1946 lacked "oratorical polish. He would fumble for words. . . . He would be hesitant." He also tended to speak too fast, and his voice was somewhat tense and high pitched. Surprisingly, for a man known for the later forcefulness of his style, some Kennedy aides thought he was too tentative in those early days. Even as late as 1958, aide Fred Dutton characterized Kennedy as "a terribly inadequate orator. . . . He raced through his script, no dramatic emphasis or anything like that. . . . [H]e disappointed just about everybody in terms of his speech." His inauspicious beginnings show that any leader can learn this fundamental skill.

Communication Lessons from JFK

Because he worked so hard on honing his own skills in this area, Kennedy offers us many lessons in developing as a communicator.

Believe in Your Message

The United States, John F. Kennedy believed, was in a "long, twilight struggle" for its very survival against a ruthless and opportunistic foe. The

America of the early 1960s, however, seemed more interested in what was going to happen on *Father Knows Best* than the country's strategic situation.

This was a potentially dangerous circumstance, as Kennedy well knew. In answering the question of *Why England Slept,* he concluded that few people prominent in public life (Churchill being the major exception) had sought to rouse the public from its mundane, day-to-day concerns and confront the Nazi threat. On page four of that book, Kennedy italicizes this sentence: *"For the Englishman had to be taught the need for armaments;* his natural instincts were strongly against them."

The same could be said for many Americans in 1960, not a few of them in Kennedy's own party, who were strongly opposed to what they called the "arms race." That situation had to change, Kennedy believed, not because America wanted war, but because America did *not* want war. Weakness and irresolution tempted dictators to aggression. If there is a central, unchanging polar star in Kennedy's worldview, this is it. His domestic emphasis on service to country and the alleviation of poverty and suffering served this worldview. By making things better at home, America set an example to those nations tempted to choose communism over freedom and democracy. He transparently believed in this message, and that belief communicated itself to his audiences.

Know Your Audience

Whereas many people close to Kennedy were not impressed with his earliest efforts at public speaking, at least one person in a position to know thought differently. In 1945, Joe Kane, a Kennedy cousin and Boston political professional, watched an after-dinner speech delivered by the young veteran and was impressed. Afterward, Kane told Joe Sr. that his son might have a future in elective politics.

"[H]e spoke with perfect ease and fluency but quietly, deliberately and with complete self-control, always on the happiest terms with his audience," Kane recalled later.

"On the happiest terms with his audience." Whether Kane realized it or not, he had hit upon the secret that was to make John F. Kennedy so effective as a communicator. Once he became fluid at it, JFK always kept in mind that he was speaking *to* people, not *at* them, *over* them, or *around* them.

At first glance, this lesson seems obvious. Yet it is rarely as well understood as it ought to be. It is a simple matter to get a text in one's hands and go out and read it before a group of people without regard for context, audience reaction, or press interpretation. That's speechmaking, not communication. The worst thing a leader can do is view a major speech as a one-off, a commitment that must be fulfilled and then forgotten. The best communicators know they are engaging in a *conversation* with the audience, not ordering a Happy Meal at McDonald's.

Kennedy learned early on to connect with those who came to hear him speak. His loose, deceptively casual style on the platform contrasted well with the more formal presentations of the other candidates, making him look like an "unpolitical" politician. His habits of jabbing the air with his forefinger or chopping the air with the flat of his hand to emphasize a point were unique. And therefore memorable.

Pronounced regional accents are sometimes seen by political consultants as off-putting, but they can make a speaker seem more authentic. Kennedy never made an effort to soften or mute his heavy New England accent, even in parts of the country where it might not go over well (such as the South). Occasionally, he was heckled when he "ahsked" voters for their support. But it eventually became his trademark. "I recall we were all fascinated by Kennedy's New England accent" was the observation of one attendee at an early Kennedy appearance in Pennsylvania in 1947.

The best way to establish a personal bond with an audience, though, is to demonstrate shared values and experiences. A large percentage of Kennedy's listeners in 1946 were war veterans, or the parents, wives, or siblings of veterans. So he spoke directly to them and their concerns about the lack of housing and jobs in the postwar economy with the authority of someone who had been in combat himself. To Italian audiences in the North End of Boston, Kennedy reminded them that his grandfather, Boston Mayor John "Honey Fitz" Fitzgerald, had appointed the first Italians to city office.

This technique can work just as well, and sometimes better, in more intimate settings. In the wake of the Bay of Pigs disaster, Kennedy met in the Oval Office with the leaders of the Cuban exile community, some of whom had sons who were captured with the exile brigade that had landed in Cuba. The situation was potentially explosive. Kennedy disarmed it with a rare reference to his own wartime experiences, pointing out that he had lost two men in combat in the South Pacific, as well as a brother and a brother-in-law in World War II. Thus, he made clear that he knew what it was like to lose people who were close to him in war.

Many leaders, in business especially, are reluctant to discuss personal details in a public forum. But a pertinent personal reference can do wonders to "humanize" you before an audience. The CEO who, say, opens a new child care center at headquarters by mentioning that the idea came from his daughter makes a much stronger impression than someone who simply cuts the ribbon and walks away.

Learn to Address Multiple Audiences

Every time you stand up to speak, you are facing more than one audience. There is the one in the room with you. There are those not in the room who will hear of what you have said after the fact. In the case of a public figure, there may be another audience watching on television. The speaker has to make a choice about which one of these audiences will receive his primary attention. That depends on who is in the audience, how large the group is, and how influential its members are as opinion leaders. But generally, the speaker aims to reach the broadest audience possible. If there is both a live audience and one watching at home, the speaker is usually advised to focus on the home viewers rather than on the studio audience.

John Kennedy accomplished this technique masterfully in his famous first debate with Richard Nixon, which took place before the largest audience ever assembled up until that time. "Kennedy took the thing much more seriously than Nixon," recalled Don Hewitt, who produced the debate for CBS and later went on to create *60 Minutes*.

Hewitt remembers how Kennedy insisted on meeting with him a week before the encounter, asking such questions as "Where do I stand?" and pressing for other details that might give him an edge with those watching at home. For example, Kennedy chose to dress in a dark blue suit that contrasted well with the light background of the set, whereas Nixon's gray suit tended to get lost in the picture.

During the actual debate, Kennedy focused almost exclusively on the television audience, ignoring not only his opponent, but the questions from the panel of journalists. The subject of the debate was supposed to be domestic policy, but in his opening statement, Kennedy deftly shifted the ground beneath Nixon's feet, insisting that domestic policy was inseparable from foreign policy. Nixon, caught flat-footed, could only agree with Kennedy in his own opening statement. Instead of concentrating on the audience at home, Nixon, who had been a champion debater in college, focused instead on answering Kennedy's points, thus allowing the Democrat to set the agenda.

The polls after the debate showed Kennedy had reached the audience more effectively than Nixon, giving the Massachusetts senator his first clear lead in the campaign. Kennedy credited his performance with eventually winning him the election.

A more sophisticated variation of this technique is addressing multiple audiences at the same time. Rarely do speakers encounter a roomful of people who will agree wholeheartedly with everything they say. People have different backgrounds, ages, experiences, and interests. To get your message across to them in a single talk, you have to address these people separately yet at the same time.

Kennedy accomplished this in his famed inaugural address. In the third paragraph, for example, he invoked the people who had brought him this far: the World War II veterans and the ideals they fought to preserve:

> Let the word go forth from this time and place, to friend and foe alike, that the torch has been passed to a new generation of Americans born in this century, tempered by war, disciplined by a hard and bitter peace, proud of our ancient heritage—and unwilling to witness or permit the slow undoing of those human rights to which this Nation has always been committed, and to which we are committed today at home and around the world.

In the very next paragraph, he issued a warning directly to the Soviet Union and anyone else who might be tempted to test American resolve:

> Let every nation know, whether it wishes us well or ill, that we shall pay any price, bear any burden, meet any hardship, support any friend, oppose any foe, in order to assure the survival and the success of liberty.

In Latin America, Fidel Castro was beginning his third year in power. To the Latin American republics nervous about Castro's influence, Kennedy offered friendship and assistance, while at the same time issuing a stern warning to Castro and his patrons in Moscow:

> To our sister republics south of our border, we offer a special pledge—to convert our good words into good deeds—in a new alliance for progress—to assist free men and free governments in casting off the chains of poverty. But this peaceful revolution of hope cannot become the prey of hostile powers. Let all our neighbors know that we shall join with them to oppose aggression or subversion anywhere in the Americas. And let every other power know that this Hemisphere intends to remain the master of its own house.

This speech has been characterized as bellicose or warlike. But people who make such criticisms are not listening carefully. There is a dual thread running through the speech, and Kennedy makes it clear in several passages that it is peace, not war, that he seeks:

> Finally, to those nations who would make themselves our adversary, we offer not a pledge but a request: that both sides begin anew the quest for peace, before the dark powers of destruction unleashed by science engulf all humanity in planned or accidental self-destruction. . . .
>
> We dare not tempt them with weakness. For only when our arms are sufficient beyond doubt can we be certain beyond doubt that they will never be employed. . . .
>
> But neither can two great and powerful groups of nations take comfort from our present course—both sides overburdened by the cost of modern weapons, both rightly alarmed by the steady spread of the deadly atom, yet both racing to alter that uncertain balance of terror that stays the hand of mankind's final war. . . .
>
> So let us begin anew—remembering on both sides that civility is not a sign of weakness, and sincerity is always subject to proof. Let us never negotiate out of fear. But let us never fear to negotiate.

Kennedy was thus signaling that although he would be strong in any international confrontation, he was not looking for an opportunity to start World War III.

He then turned his attention to the youth of America. Unlike Kennedy and his peers, who went off to fight World War II, this new generation of baby boomers had no obvious challenge before them. Kennedy thus offered them one:

> In your hands, my fellow citizens, more than in mine, will rest the final success or failure of our course. Since this country was founded, each generation of Americans has been summoned to give testimony to its national loyalty. The graves of young Americans who answered the call to service surround the globe.
>
> Now the trumpet summons us again—not as a call to bear arms, though arms we need; not as a call to battle, though embattled we are—but a call to bear the burden of a long twilight struggle, year in and year out, "rejoicing in hope, patient in tribulation"—a struggle against the common enemies of man: tyranny, poverty, disease, and war itself.
>
> And so, my fellow Americans: Ask not what your country can do for you; ask what you can do for your country.
>
> My fellow citizens of the world: Ask not what America will do for you, but what together we can do for the freedom of man.

Stand Ready to Debate

Whether in business, politics, or even religion, leaders find themselves in the middle of controversial issues. It is critical that you understand the other side's arguments as well as your own. One of the best ways to familiarize yourself with them is by meeting with an advocate from the opposition to debate the issue. A debate, if done publicly, can be a high-risk occasion, of course, but the potential rewards can also be substantial.

When John F. Kennedy entered politics, the political debate was something close to a lost art form, and he played no small role in reviving it. While the debates with Nixon during the 1960 campaign are widely recalled, JFK in fact engaged in several high-stakes debate performances from the beginning of his career.

In 1947, for example, he and Nixon had their first debate—over the Taft-Hartley Labor Act—jousting before a mostly pro-labor crowd in McKees-port, Pennsylvania. Both men had been in Congress barely four months, and neither was from Pennsylvania. But both thought it would be good practice for the future. Christopher Matthews, who wrote a book on the Kennedy/Nixon rivalry, described this first clash as "grit versus charm," and it was widely believed that Nixon had won on points, though Kennedy was clearly the crowd favorite. Even then, Kennedy knew the importance of playing to the wider audience rather than sticking to the formal rules.

Kennedy also later debated Norman Thomas, leader of the Socialist party in the United States, and had a televised encounter with Senator Henry Cabot Lodge during their 1952 Senate campaign. These encounters gave Kennedy credibility with voters. Simply by being there, he appeared as an equal with his rivals and got credit from those watching the debates for being willing to climb into the arena and defend his views.

With the possible exception of a "perp walk," there is no less flattering image of the modern business executive than the sight of him fleeing a camera crew that's asking questions about the company's business practices, or declaring "No comment" when confronted by hostile questioning. The opportunities to debate are now almost endless, with entire cable news channels being devoted to little more than debates between representatives of different points of view. To set yourself apart, you must be ready to defend yourself and your organization in a public forum. Likewise, you must be ready to defend your decisions internally to your people to gain their support to make initiatives successful.

Learn to Cope with the Press

Many, perhaps most, business executives dislike and fear the news media. Virtually all large enterprises, and many medium-size and even some small ones, employ "media relations" experts—usually former reporters—whose primary job is to shield their superiors from having to actually meet with the reporters who cover them and their industry. Some managers adopt a similar practice with staff. They close their doors to most employees and have the next manager in line deal with questions on policies.

Dealing with your people—or if you're in a higher position, the media—does indeed have potential pitfalls, but ignoring it is not going to make it go away or protect you from criticism. Avoiding representatives of the media, or treating them as the enemy, is not only unlikely to protect you from criticism, it represents a major missed opportunity for getting your message out.

If you are the top leader at a substantial organization, the vast bulk of people inside or outside of it will never get to meet you personally, much less deal with you on intimate terms. Most will only get to know you through the news media. How you present yourself to the media will make a difference for your organization and for yourself personally. Likewise, most employees don't get daily personal interactions with their managers. You will be judged by the e-mails, memos, and telephone broadcasts you send out, as well as how you present yourself in meetings.

One reason John F. Kennedy worked well with reporters was that he had been one himself briefly. He covered the founding conference of the United Nations in San Francisco in 1945 for the Hearst newspapers, as well as the British general election that year. Joseph P. Berry Jr., in his book *John F. Kennedy and the Media: The First Television President,* thinks it was Kennedy's experience as a reporter that early clued him in on how reporters worked— and how he could work with them.

Another reason Kennedy concentrated on the shoe-leather reporters was because he believed the press to be fundamentally Republican, at least at the level of editors and publishers. He also liked television because it enabled him to "go over the heads" of reporters and get his message directly to the public. One way to do this as a manager or leader in your organization is to "manage by walking around." The more you walk around and talk to your people, the more you get to personally reinforce your message. Likewise, the more you are in front of your people by actively participating in meetings, the more they get a sense of what you're trying to do. This technique allows you to deliver your message directly to the people without relying on your middle managers to get the message out there.

As friendly as he could be with members of the press, Kennedy never lost sight of the fact that he was fundamentally in a different business. He never hesitated to let reporters know if he thought he had been wronged, for example. In fact, he could be so obsessive about anything negative written about him that a few stories appeared accusing the president of whining. Nevertheless, the knowledge that Kennedy was paying attention, and would remember, undoubtedly served as a brake on some reporters, dissuading them from publishing some items.

Kennedy had several techniques for increasing the odds that he would get favorable news coverage.

Increased Access. Although reporters had been allowed to set up shop in the White House since William McKinley's administration, they generally had to operate under an onerous set of rules. For decades, the president could not be quoted directly, unless he specifically said otherwise. (He rarely did.) Under the Eisenhower administration, reporters had to deal exclusively with Press Secretary James Haggerty. Press conferences were shown on television but were taped beforehand. Eisenhower's own diction and syntax often seemed impenetrable. (The fact that this was later shown to be deliberate on Eisenhower's part didn't keep him from being labeled as inarticulate at the time by cranky reporters.)

Kennedy's White House loosened things up considerably. Reporters were free to contact the president's aides and cabinet secretaries directly, though as Kennedy's popularity grew, few of them bothered anymore as they focused more and more on Kennedy himself. Press Secretary Pierre Salinger briefed the press twice a day. Out-of-town reporters and editors, who were more easily starstruck than the White House press corps, found themselves being invited to the White House for intimate lunches. For the resident reporters, invitations to state dinners and other glamorous events were employed as instruments of ingratiation. For the overwhelmingly male press corps, the desire of their wives to be invited to such functions and get the chance to rub shoulders with "Jackie" was a strong incentive not to be too hard on Kennedy.

"Backgrounder" meetings, where reporters were invited to interview the president or his top aides but could not quote them directly (information was usually attributed to a "high White House source"), were another Kennedy press innovation. In his memoirs, aide Theodore Sorensen described how these backgrounders worked:

> During his Christmas holidays in Palm Beach, both in 1961 and in 1962, he invited the two dozen or so regular White House correspondents accompanying him to a freewheeling three- to

four-hour "backgrounder," . . . dividing each session into domestic and foreign affairs discussions. Year-end "think pieces" (which would have been written anyway, he reasoned) were in this way better informed of views attributable to "the highest authority" or "sources close to the administration." Although these phrases deceived no one in the know, it made for a freer and fuller exchange than would have been true of a regular press conference or a larger background group in Washington.

Open Communication. Kennedy also always seemed prepared with a quote or quip that diverted a difficult or embarrassing question or situation. Although Kennedy was unquestionably light on his feet in interpersonal situations, only a few insiders knew that these seemingly spontaneous comments were often prepared and rehearsed in advance. He could also be startlingly candid (if not necessarily honest) about his motivations for certain actions. This bred a sense of intimacy with reporters that helped when he sought to squelch or tone down unfavorable stories.

The new openness with print reporters, however, didn't compare with the special treatment in store for television reporters. Kennedy agreed to the first-ever "informal" televised presidential interview when he met three network reporters in the Oval Office for an hour and a half. Kennedy also sanctioned a number of television specials, including Jacqueline Kennedy's famous tour of the redecorated White House. Before the confrontation with Alabama Governor George Wallace over the admission of black students to the University of Alabama in 1963, Kennedy even allowed a documentary film crew to tape him and his brother, the attorney general, as they actually dealt with the crisis.

Support for Those Who Help the Cause. Rowland Evans Jr. once told a story about how, during a breakfast meeting in 1959, he was asked by then-senator Kennedy to accompany him—that day—on a campaign trip to Wisconsin. Evans protested that he had nothing with him, not even a shaving kit or a change of clothes.

"Don't worry about it," Kennedy said, and Evans agreed to go.

That night, as Evans was preparing to turn in for the night in the hotel room the Kennedy campaign had secured for him, a knock came on his door. Mystified, Evans opened the door and found a smiling Salinger standing in the hallway, holding out to him a fresh shirt, a change of underwear, a razor, and shaving cream.

It was an example of what Kennedy's friend Florida Senator George Smathers later described as a Kennedy rule: "If they were for Kennedy, Kennedy was for them."

As the anecdote about Rowland Evans demonstrates, Kennedy saw to reporters' comfort. He brought banks of telephones to national politics, as well as stenographers who could provide transcripts of speeches and press conferences in time for deadline.

Up Close and Personal. Another way Kennedy ingratiated himself with the working press was by using his genuine curiosity about people and their lives. He would flatter reporters by talking to them about *their* lives and *their* jobs, not his own. He regularly inquired after wives and children, then would feed the reporters bits of gossip and give them leads for stories they could follow up on. Kennedy knew that it was not good to let a reporter walk away empty-handed. He tried to give them something they could use, especially if it would divert attention from something else Kennedy preferred to play down.

Jack Welch, the legendary CEO of General Electric, adopted a similar approach with select reporters, inviting them into his operation and letting them get to know top GE executives. He knew there were risks, but he also knew that such solicitude could pay large dividends. Given the overwhelmingly positive press he received, Welch was right.

Get the Help You Need to Master All Mediums

There is an art to delivering a speech effectively. One of the most tempting pitfalls is to speak too quickly. Eager to "get it over with," the speaker may simply go too fast for his audience. Other nervous tics can include smiling at inappropriate moments, using awkward hand gestures, or absent-mindedly fiddling with one's speech notes or text.

Kennedy had plenty of these tics. He was constantly fussing with his hair, drumming his fingers on a table, or moving his right hand nervously. (That last mannerism is one reason he so frequently jammed his hand into his suit coat pocket.) He learned to control these habits while speaking by turning them into rhetorical trademarks—his jabbing the air with his forefinger to drive home a point, for example. You have to generate within yourself the self-confidence to realize you are doing these things and set about fixing them.

One of the most frequent criticisms of Kennedy's speeches as a congressman and as a senator was that he spoke too fast, sometimes at a rate of 200 words per minute. (Speech at 150 to 180 words per minute is considered optimal.) In a speech to a union audience, Kennedy couldn't understand why union members weren't reacting to his pro-labor positions. Both Mrs. Kennedy and Stephen Smith, his brother-in-law and campaign aide, told him that he was speaking too fast for the audience to absorb what he was saying.

Instead of becoming resentful of this criticism, Kennedy set about fixing the problem. He took four or five of his basic stump speeches and memorized them, consciously working to slow down his rate of delivery. He also threw in more humor and learned to pause for audience reaction. These efforts made him much more effective as a speaker as the 1960 presidential campaign began.

But another problem soon manifested itself. The heavy speaking load of the campaign took an unexpected toll on Kennedy's voice. Several times, he developed laryngitis and had to stop campaigning. John Saltonstall, a friend from Boston, recommended a Boston University voice professor named David Blair McCloskey.

McCloskey clued Kennedy in on techniques for relaxing his throat muscles and breathing more fully when speaking. (One of his techniques was getting Kennedy to bark like a seal, which he often did while relaxing in the bathtub.) McCloskey taught Kennedy to speak from the diaphragm rather than the larynx. For a time, McCloskey accompanied Kennedy on speaking tours, signaling him from the audience whenever he thought the candidate was in danger of falling back into his old habits.

Making the best impression on television is also not usually an accident. Television can show you off to best advantage or destroy you in an instant. It is both a mass medium and an interpersonal one. While television allows you to reach the largest number of people, the individual viewer has a personal experience. That is why so many television watchers come to believe they "know" people they have only ever seen on television. It is a medium that requires special handling.

Kennedy and television grew to maturity together. Initially, he was slow to pick up on its importance, but he learned fast. In the summer of 1952, he enrolled in a course that the CBS television network offered on how to be effective on television. It was the opinion of the course's director that Kennedy's "natural approach" was exceptionally well suited to the medium. Kennedy understood the value of being natural. In a 1959 article in *TV Guide,* Kennedy observed that the "slick or bombastic orator, pounding the table, is not as welcome in the family living room as he was in the town square." An audience's impression of a candidate on television—often telegraphed by how the candidate looked, the quality of his voice, and his non-verbal body language, as much as by what he actually said—was "likely to be uncannily correct."

Thus, Kennedy paid extraordinary attention to his television appearance, especially lighting. Hollywood director Franklin Schaffner (who would later direct the film *Patton*) was brought in by the Kennedy White House to review the lighting and acoustics in the State Department auditorium, where Kennedy held his press conferences. When television technicians insisted that the air-conditioning in the Oval Office be turned off, so as not to affect the sound quality during a Kennedy speech on the Berlin crisis in 1961, JFK perspired profusely under the lights during the address. Determined not to let it happen again, Kennedy banished nonessential guests from the Oval Office during future addresses and had fans installed at his feet.

But all the stagecraft in the world won't save the speaker who has nothing substantive to say. What made Kennedy so tremendously effective on television was not only that he had first-class stagecraft, a natural wit, and telegenic good looks, but that he had important things to say. In the next chapter, we will examine the importance of becoming your own best speechwriter.

Use Other Media to Get the Message Out

Speeches, whether before a live audience, televised, or both, aren't the only forums for communicating your message to a wider audience. Newspaper and magazine articles, and, for the truly ambitious, full-fledged books, are among the others.

Articles published under your own name accomplish several communications objectives. First, you can reach an audience of people with facts and arguments larger than a mere "sound bite" on television or radio. Second, depending on the publication, you can reach a discrete audience of potential opinion leaders on a particular subject. Third, a substantive article or book under your own name gives you weight as an opinion leader in your own right.

For four of the fourteen years he served in Congress, John F. Kennedy was a member of the minority party. For much of the rest of that time, he was a very junior member of first the House of Representatives and later the U.S. Senate. His prospects for impacting major legislation were close to zero. One way he could become better known nationally, however, was by writing articles for important magazines. As his presidential campaign gathered momentum in the late 1950s, the articles he penned became more frequent and more substantive.

Kennedy's byline became a common sight in the 1950s, in such different periodicals as *Foreign Affairs* ("A Democrat Looks at Foreign Policy"), *Living for Young Homemakers* ("Young Men in Politics"), *Life* ("Where the Democrats Should Go from Here"), and *Progressive* ("If India Falls"). Kennedy articles also appeared in *Reader's Digest, TV Guide,* and even *America,* the journal of the Jesuit order in the United States. The articles were produced in the same collaborative manner as Kennedy's speeches and by the same team.

More controversial is the subject of Kennedy's books, particularly *Profiles in Courage,* an account of U.S. senators such as John Quincy Adams, Daniel Webster, and Robert A. Taft, who had placed principle above party and personal interest. Initially conceived as a magazine article, it grew into a book following Kennedy's long convalescence after his spinal fusion surgery in late 1954. Bored and restless, Kennedy began assembling the material and sketching out notes for the book. He met frequently with Sorensen, to whom the book undoubtedly owes its flow and literary flair.

The book was published on January 1, 1956, and became a best-seller. It was widely and favorably reviewed, and Kennedy appeared on numerous talk shows and gave many interviews about the book. Written at a high school level, it was widely assigned in history courses and became exceptionally popular with young people. Suddenly, Kennedy wasn't just another freshman senator.

Kennedy acknowledged the help he received from Sorensen in the book's preface, and had things simply been left there, it's likely that would have been the end of the matter. But in early 1957, the book unexpectedly won the Pulitzer Prize for biography, greatly magnifying the issue of the book's authorship. It has been widely rumored that Joe Sr. pulled strings with his *New York Times* friend Arthur Krock, who sat on the Pulitzer board, to get his son the prestigious award. The rumors persist, though no one has been able to prove that undue influence was used.

While biographers such as Herbert Parmet have concluded that Kennedy did little or no work on *Profiles in Courage,* new research, especially by author Thurston Clarke, has revealed otherwise. Uncomfortable with solitude and unable to write in longhand for long periods because of his bad back, Kennedy did much of his "writing" via dictation to his secretaries, Evelyn Lincoln, Mary Davis, and Gloria Sitrin. (This was also how Churchill did much of his writing.) Sitrin always maintained that although Theodore Sorensen did most of the research, much of *Profiles in Courage* was based on Kennedy's dictation to her.

Today, of course, no one really expects busy people such as U.S. senators to actually sit down and write from scratch the words that appear under their names. (The late Daniel Patrick Moynihan was a notable exception.) Even Churchill, who won the Nobel Prize for Literature, employed ghostwriters and researchers on several of his books, especially near the end of his life.

If you're not a skilled writer—and even if you are—don't take chances. Get second opinions from people whose business it is to write polished prose for a living.

How to Improve Your Own Communication Skills

➡ *Know your audience.* The audience is your customer. Be "on the happiest terms" with them. Before you speak or try to communicate, take the time out to discover what's on audience members' minds. If you don't address their immediate concerns, they will be less open to your message. If you can relate to people on a personal level, it will increase their receptiveness to your ideas. Always remember that you are talking to people, not at them. That connection *to* people is so often missed by leaders when they get in front of a podium.

➡ *Stay focused on your audience.* Don't be mesmerized by what is going on immediately in front of you; keep the broader audience in mind. When you are addressing multiple audiences, such as a live group of listeners and a larger public one, remember you have the choice of which one to emphasize. Ideally you should find a way to reach all audiences in your communications, but if you have to choose, it is more important to address the larger audience.

➡ *Respond to your audience.* Don't be so "locked in" to your talk that you lose the ability to be spontaneous; read your audience's reaction and gauge your responses accordingly. Part of the trick is making eye contact and pausing for effect. If you see that you are losing the audience, it might be better to acknowledge that than to just plow on.

➡ *Get the help you need.* Very few people are "natural" communicators; don't be afraid to get coaching in the necessary skills. You can get professional help from speechwriters and voice coaches, for example. You can even take courses on presentation skills. When you know the audience you are trying to reach, many issues—such as subject matter, how long to speak, what to emphasize—become readily apparent. Get some input from your advisers on these issues as well.

➡ *Work with the media.* The media is a fact of life. It cannot be controlled. It can, however, be managed. Rather than ignore reporters, prepare to deal with them directly. It will help with damage control. When seven people died from ingesting poisoned Tylenol capsules in 1982, a huge nationwide panic set in. Johnson & Johnson had to move quickly to save both the integrity of its product and the company as a whole. The company immediately alerted consumers across the nation, through the media, not to consume any type of Tylenol product, and it recalled all Tylenol capsules from the market. Johnson & Johnson's handling of this crisis and use of the media to get the word out quickly were universally praised. A product many people thought could never be sold again under its old name is still one of the top-selling over-the-counter drugs on the market.

➠ *Be authentic.* Not all strong communicators become great leaders, but nearly all great leaders are strong communicators. It helps to have enthusiasm and to believe in your message. Authenticity emphasizes your message and helps inspire people. Mary Kay Ash set out with the intention of helping women achieve personal and financial success, a goal she believed in deeply. She took her $5,000 in life savings and launched Mary Kay Cosmetics in 1963. A dynamic speaker and motivator, Mary Kay would hold increasingly larger national conventions for her people, which would turn into huge pep rallies as her contagious enthusiasm spread through the assembled crowd of "independent beauty consultants." Mary Kay Inc. has grown from a small, direct sales company to the largest direct seller of skin care products in the United States.

CHAPTER 6

Speechwriting:
Master the Art of Delivering Your Message

"He prepared his speeches with the utmost care, but seldom wrote them out in a prepared text. It has been said that he could think out a speech sentence by sentence, correct the sentences in his mind without the use of a pencil, and then deliver it exactly as he thought it out."

—JOHN F. KENNEDY, *PROFILES IN COURAGE,* ON DANIEL WEBSTER'S SPEECHMAKING ABILITIES

"Words can do more than convey policy. They can also convey and create a mood, an attitude, an atmosphere—or an awakening."

—JOHN F. KENNEDY

Public speaking can be an extremely intimidating experience. Polls frequently show that more people fear being asked to speak in front of an audience than fear dying. It's not hard to see why this is so. The prospect of making a fool of oneself before a large group of people is the stuff of nightmares. But mastering, or at least becoming comfortable with, the art of oratory is indispensable to effective leadership.

Indeed, Winston Churchill thought oratory probably the most important skill a leader could cultivate. "Abandoned by party, betrayed by his friends, stripped of his offices, whoever can command this power is still formidable," he noted. Churchill's career, which was declared to be over on several occasions, is not the only example. Abraham Lincoln was thought to be a political has-been in 1854 when he delivered a powerful speech at the Illinois State Fair attacking Stephen A. Douglas's proslavery Kansas-Nebraska Act. Almost overnight, Lincoln found he was in demand as a speaker and political candidate.

Kennedy himself had a not dissimilar experience. Asked to deliver the nominating address for Adlai Stevenson at the 1956 Democratic convention, Kennedy rejected the speech draft that was handed to him by the Stevenson campaign and worked all night with Ted Sorensen to prepare a completely new speech. They finished at 6 A.M.; Kennedy got some sleep and then, that afternoon, went before the convention to deliver a rouser that came within an ace of making him Stevenson's vice presidential candidate. Most political prognosticators recognized that this speech automatically put Kennedy on the short list of candidates for the 1960 nomination.

The public rhetoric of John F. Kennedy, delivered in his distinctive Boston twang, echoes down the decades to us, serving for many Americans as the single most memorable facet of his public career. The great words and phrases are familiar even to those too young to have heard them at the time: "We choose to go to the moon in this decade and do the other things, not because they are easy, but because they are *haaard*. . . ." "The weapons of war must be abolished before they abolish us." "Liberty without learning is always in peril. Learning without liberty is always in vain." And there are many more.

This is remarkable given that Kennedy, by his own admission, had no formal training in public speaking or elocution. For many years, he betrayed no likelihood of leaving a rich rhetorical legacy. How he developed as a compelling public speaker holds many lessons for today's executive.

Being Your Own Best Speechwriter

Critics have tended to give speechwriters the entire credit for John F. Kennedy's public eloquence, as if he were an audioanimatronic mannequin at Disney World, mouthing platitudes programmed by someone else.

If that were the case, no one would likely have remembered much of what John F. Kennedy had to say. Merely repeating words someone else has written robs the speaker of the ability to put his whole effort behind what he is saying. One thing great public speakers have in common is that they largely write their own speeches. Kennedy placed a high priority on public speeches, and one reason he is so well remembered today is because he was intimately involved in their preparation and writing. He was, in short, his own best speechwriter.

When you begin to view speechmaking as an integral part of your leadership, as opposed to simply seeing it as something you do "in addition" to your job, new vistas will open up to you. Actually putting your words down on paper can help you discipline your thoughts and flesh out ideas. In *The Strategy of Peace,* a collection of Kennedy's foreign policy speeches published during the 1960 campaign, he noted that "the statements in this volume represent my own attempt to make plain to myself and to others my thoughts on the leading questions of foreign policy that have borne down so hard on all of us."

The key in becoming your own best speechwriter is that you must put effort into it and make time for it. Note interesting facts or ideas that you come across in the routine of daily business. Clip and save articles you find interesting, and don't neglect your reading. Above all, come up with a system for your public communications and make time in your schedule for it.

Kennedy's Speechwriting System

Time is at a premium for any executive, especially a president, so rarely can they actually sit down and compose a speech in its entirety. Many people believe that Kennedy was among the first presidents to employ a speechwriter. This is not true. While Woodrow Wilson appears to have been the last president who wrote major speeches entirely on his own, American chief executives have employed amanuenses from the beginning.

Alexander Hamilton, for example, largely drafted George Washington's famous farewell address. (This fact was actually kept secret for decades after it was discovered, for fear it would damage Washington's reputation.) Theodore Roosevelt, undoubtedly an accomplished writer, had help from aides and friends. Even Abraham Lincoln, widely considered the most eloquent of American presidents, got help on occasion. The famous "better angels of our nature" line from the close of Lincoln's first inaugural address, for example, was supplied by Secretary of State William Seward.

Kennedy did much of his own writing. Steven R. Goldzwig and George N. Dionisopoulos, writing in their book, *"In a Perilous Hour": The Public Address of John F. Kennedy,* note that when time permitted and the occasion inspired him, Kennedy could write an excellent speech on his own, selecting the topic and emphasis, gathering much of the supporting material, and writing it out in longhand on a legal pad. As his career gathered momentum, however, Kennedy realized that this approach was inadequate and that he needed to develop a systematized approach to preparing speeches.

Central to Kennedy's system was his "brain trust." He liked input and feedback, not only from those on his staff, but from an outside coterie of informal advisers. Naturally enough for a senator from Massachusetts, these advisers included professors from Harvard and MIT, but also journalists, ambassadors, and experts in various fields. Meyer Feldman, who later worked in the White House as a speechwriter, described how "an issue is studied beyond what is known, and an answer is arrived at by slow growth."

A Kindred Spirit to Help Hone the Message

Kennedy's most important hire in terms of his speechmaking career would take place shortly after his election to the Senate in 1952 when, on the basis of two five-minute interviews, he brought aboard Theodore C. Sorensen.

Like many great partnerships, Sorensen and Kennedy's was a marriage of apparent opposites. In complete contrast with the casual, fun-loving, Irish-American Brahman Democrat that was Kennedy, Sorensen was a serious, studious, half-Jewish Nebraskan from a Republican family. Together, they created some of the most memorable rhetorical moments of the twentieth century.

Like most speechwriters, Sorensen did not set out to ply that trade. A lawyer by training with little experience in writing or speaking, he was initially supposed to develop policy positions for Kennedy, in which capacity he crafted a number of speeches for Kennedy to deliver in 1953. As Sorensen recalled it, his life changed on March 17, 1954, when Kennedy delivered a speech in Boston written by Sorensen for St. Patrick's Day (an occasion,

Sorensen admitted, that was quite alien to his own background). Kennedy liked the speech so much that he began giving his aide more and more speechwriting assignments.

Although they were oddly matched in some superficial respects, Kennedy and Sorensen were alike in ways that counted. Like his boss, Sorensen was well-read and articulate. He also wrote in a straightforward style that suited Kennedy and others found difficult to emulate. (When historian Arthur Schlesinger Jr. tried his hand at writing for Kennedy, for example, he often found his drafts rejected as too wordy and high-flown.)

Sorensen's main value to Kennedy was not only as a speechwriter but, in Kennedy's words, as "my intellectual blood bank." He was continually calling Kennedy's attention to obscure items in the news or odd facts and bits of information that could buttress a case Kennedy wanted to make. Principals who use their speechwriters as a kind of in-house think tank get far more than good speeches: They get food for thought and facts to chew on that can help them do their jobs more effectively.

Before a major presidential speech, Kennedy would sit down with Sorensen to sketch out his own thoughts. Beyond outlining the main topics he wished to discuss, he would often put forth ideas for a compelling introduction, appropriate quotes, as well as the required length (rarely more than twenty minutes; thirty minutes at the outside).

Sorensen would then call a meeting of relevant aides and writers to help with research for the speech. Depending on the speech's importance, as many as twenty people might be in the room, and the meeting could go for three or four hours. All attendees would be expected to be familiar with Kennedy's previous statements on the topic in order to guide their thinking. All angles would be discussed. Sorensen would then undertake a first draft, which he would pass around to the other writers for their input before sending it on to Kennedy. The president would then spend considerable time going over the address line by line, crossing out words and phrases and writing in substitutions, making notes in the margins, and occasionally rejecting the entire product and demanding that his team start over.

Kennedy eventually recruited other writers, of course, such as Meyer Feldman and Richard Goodwin, who were usually detailed to write on specific areas, such as agriculture, civil rights, or the Peace Corps. All were intellectually accomplished in their own right. Goodwin, for example, was first in his class at Harvard Law School, had helped unravel the TV quiz show scandals in the late 1950s, and spoke Spanish. Sorensen always insisted, however, that the final product of any speech was Kennedy's. "[T]he more time he had to edit and rewrite, the better the speech would be," he recalled later.

But probably the single most important reason that Kennedy's system worked was the time he devoted to it. Sorensen wasn't just "the speech-writer," although many called him that. He was probably Kennedy's closest aide other than the president's brother Robert, and he saw Kennedy more often than any other member of the president's official family. Thus, Sorensen became intimately familiar with Kennedy's style of speaking, presenting himself, and way of thinking. He became JFK's alter ego, giving him advantages most other speechwriters can only dream about.

It isn't necessary for you to be as close to your main speechwriter as Kennedy was to his, but it is necessary to make time for this professional and the speechwriting process. Ronald Reagan met with his speechwriters at least once a week and brought them along whenever he was scheduled to deliver an address. Like most of life's worthwhile objectives, your public communication will be only as good as the time and effort you invest in it.

Developing a Distinctive Style

At the time Kennedy entered public life, political speechmaking in Irish-American Massachusetts was a set-piece occasion for forensic fireworks. Political orators such as James Michael Curley gave speeches that were long, flowery, and heavy on emotion. It would be hard to imagine a style less suited to the cool, analytical Kennedy.

In his short stint as a reporter, when he was covering the 1945 British general election, Kennedy observed a different sort of political speechmaking. In Britain, candidates on the stump tended to deliver short talks, leaving time for questions from the voters. It allowed the speaker to "get closer" to his audience. It was this general style—which was new in Massachusetts at that time—that Kennedy adopted in his first campaign and maintained, with modifications, thereafter.

Keeping the Message Focused on the Audience

Kennedy's speaking style was *audience centered*. That is, he and Sorensen always sought to write for the *ear* as opposed to the *eye*. When assembling a

Kennedy speech, Sorensen said, the "chief criterion was always audience comprehension and comfort." To achieve that effect, they relied on:

➡ Short speeches, short clauses, and short words wherever possible

➡ A series of points or propositions in numbered or logical sequence, wherever appropriate

➡ The construction of sentences, phrases, and paragraphs intended to simplify, clarify, and emphasize

Creating a Style That Works for You

Rhetorically, Sorensen's greatest contribution to Kennedy's speechmaking style was his fondness for the *contrapuntal phrase*. A method of rhetorical antithesis, it uses a repeated rhythm with an inversion or substitution of words for emphasis—for example, "While we shall negotiate freely, we shall not negotiate freedom," or "Mankind must put an end to war, before war puts an end to mankind." Although other presidents had used this device before, Sorensen helped Kennedy bring it to a high pitch of perfection, and it became his rhetorical trademark, adorning almost all his major addresses.

Another favored Kennedy rhetorical device was use of the *antithetical construction*—repeating a parallel syntactic structure with contrasting terms or a reversal of words. He would use it to lay out two extreme positions on an issue, and then present his own view, which he hoped the audience would perceive as the more moderate and reasonable alternative.

Kennedy used antithetical construction in the inaugural address, of course. Another good example is his speech on world peace at American University. Kennedy sought to distance himself both from those who believed that some sort of peaceful coexistence with the Soviet Union was impossible and those who sought "peace at any price" when he said:

> Let us examine our attitude toward peace itself. Too many of us think it is impossible. Too many think it is unreal. But that is a dangerous, defeatist belief. It leads to the conclusion that war is inevitable—that mankind is doomed, that we are gripped by forces we cannot control.
>
> We need not accept that view. Our problems are man-made;

therefore, they can be solved by man. And man can be as big as he wants. No problem of human destiny is beyond human beings. Man's reason and spirit have often solved the seemingly unsolvable and we believe they can do it again.

I am not referring to the absolute, infinite concept of universal peace and goodwill of which some fantasies and fanatics dream. I do not deny the value of hopes and dreams but we merely invite discouragement and incredulity by making that our only and immediate goal.

Let us focus instead on a more practical, more attainable peace—based not on a sudden revolution in human nature but on a gradual evolution in human institutions, on a series of concrete actions and effective agreements which are in the interest of all concerned.

Alliteration—the repetition of the same consonant or sound in consecutive words or sentences—was another characteristic of Kennedy's speechmaking. Some examples:

"Let us go forth to lead the land we love. . . ."

"[R]ace has no place in American life or law. . . ."

"Peace need not be impractical and war need not be inevitable. . . ."

"For we prefer world law, in the age of self-determination, to world war in the age of mass extermination. . . ."

These and other aspects of Kennedy's speechmaking were not simply cute rhetorical tricks intended to show off the speaker's erudition. Rather, they functioned as mnemonic devices designed to aid the audience in recalling what they had just heard. A speech has no impact if the people who have heard it can't recall what was said five minutes after it was delivered. Although you might not deliver words that will live decades after your death, as Kennedy did, a distinctive style will, it is hoped, cause your words to ring in your audience's ears long after you have left the podium.

Finding the Right Words

The purpose of communication is not merely to entertain the members of your audience but to enlighten and inform them and, hopefully, stimulate them to action. A leader incapable of this kind of message will have a hard time reaching his full potential. One reason that the late Washington Senator Henry "Scoop" Jackson failed to achieve the presidency, many believe, was his ponderous speaking style. "If he gave a fireside chat," one wag commented, "the fire would go out."

Kennedy understood the value and power of his words. Sorensen says that words for Kennedy were "regarded as tools of precision, to be chosen and applied with a craftsman's care to whatever the situation required." Thus, Kennedy and Sorensen understood Mark Twain's injunction that choosing the right word or words can be the difference between a "lightning bug and lightning."

An instance of Kennedy's care with words, even in a fairly mundane case, was an introduction for Lyndon B. Johnson that Arthur Schlesinger drafted for Kennedy to deliver at a political dinner in 1959. Schlesinger's draft hailed Johnson as a leader "without peer or precedent" and said that Kennedy would always "cherish" the Texan's friendship. Kennedy changed this to praise Johnson as the best parliamentary leader since Henry Clay and said he would merely "value," as opposed to "cherish," Johnson's friendship.

A much grander instance of finding exactly the right words to fit the audience and the occasion was Kennedy's June 26, 1963, speech in West Berlin:

> Two thousand years ago the proudest boast was "civis Romanus sum." Today, in the world of freedom, the proudest boast is "Ich bin ein Berliner."
>
> There are many people in the world who really don't understand, or say they don't, what is the great issue between the free world and the communist world. Let them come to Berlin.
>
> There are some who say that communism is the wave of the future. Let them come to Berlin.
>
> And there are some who say in Europe and elsewhere we can work with the communists. Let them come to Berlin.
>
> And there are even a few who say that it is true that commu-

nism is an evil system, but it permits us to make economic progress. *Lass' sie nach Berlin kommen*. Let them come to Berlin.

The "Ich bin ein Berliner" oration is classified by the John F. Kennedy Library as "remarks," rather than a speech or an address. The reason is that Kennedy delivered them extemporaneously. He had planned to use the German phrases in a prepared text that he carried with him to West Berlin. (They were Robert Kennedy's idea, and JFK added them, with McGeorge Bundy's help, while flying on *Air Force One*.) But as he drove through the city streets packed with West Berliners chanting his name over and over, Kennedy realized that the occasion demanded something much more than what he had prepared. Thus, what became probably his second most famous public address was delivered largely off-the-cuff. The result was a smash, with the words meshing perfectly with the mood of the occasion.

Kennedy had gotten much better at extemporaneous speaking as time went on and he became a more experienced public orator. It even got to the point where he could edit a speech as he delivered it. This technique, however, is definitely not for beginners or inexperienced speakers. It's best to come as prepared as you can possibly be.

Making the Message Clear

Disliking verbosity and pomposity in others, Kennedy avoided them like the plague in his own addresses. He wanted both his message and his language to be plain in both meaning and delivery, and to avoid sounding patronizing or condescending. In making policy recommendations, he preferred citing definitive courses of action, avoiding terms such as "suggest," "perhaps," and "possible alternatives for consideration." Sorensen said he sought to avoid slang, dialect, legalistic-sounding phrases, contractions, elaborate metaphors, and ornate figures of speech. He considered certain words to be hackneyed or overused, such as "glorious," "dynamic," and "humble." Generally, he tended toward understatement rather than overstatement.

Using Imagery and Symbols Where Appropriate

Kennedy honed distinctive phrases and images to make his points or create a mood or atmosphere. As examples:

"Khrushchev reminds me of the tiger hunter who has picked a place on the wall to hang the tiger's skin long before he has caught the tiger. This tiger has other ideas."

"We cannot negotiate with those who say, 'What's mine is mine and what's yours is negotiable.'"

"Those who make peaceful revolution impossible will make violent revolution inevitable."

"Too often we enjoy the comfort of opinion without the discomfort of thought."

"Victory has a thousand fathers, but defeat is an orphan."

"We have the power to make this the best generation of mankind in the history of the world or to make it the last."

"If we are strong, our strength will speak for itself. If we are weak, words will be of no help."

Making Your Arguments with Reason, Logic, and Facts

Many amateur speakers think the way to an audience's heart is to use emotion. Emotional arguments, however, are rarely persuasive to large numbers of people over the long term. It is much better to use facts and argument to persuade them of the rightness of your case. Emotion can supplement facts, but not substitute for them.

John F. Kennedy wasn't much of a political storyteller, and his speeches are notable for the lack of overt emotional appeals. Some observers thought this a mistake. One of Hubert Humphrey's 1960 supporters commented, "When you see him [Kennedy] on TV reading statistics about how poorly the farmers and workers are doing, you'd think he was a professor up on Mars. Just statistics. When Humphrey does the same thing your heart bleeds."

Of course, Kennedy's speeches were more than just statistics, and the overall effect often packed an emotional wallop. But he did indeed like using statistics. In his justly famous 1963 speech calling for equal rights for blacks, Kennedy rejected any idea of appealing to emotion as a primary reason for assuring equal rights for all Americans. Instead, he cited facts:

The Negro baby born in America today, regardless of the section of the state in which he is born, has about one-half as much chance of completing a high school as a white baby born in the same place on the same day, one-third as much chance of completing college, one-third as much chance of becoming a professional man, twice as much chance of becoming unemployed, about one-seventh as much chance of earning $10,000 a year, a life expectancy which is seven years shorter, and the prospects of earning only half as much.

While making it clear that equal rights for all was the right thing to do, Kennedy did not simply leave it at that. He made it clear that equal rights for America's blacks were in the interest of white Americans as well, saying that the price of delay would be to weaken the nation in the worldwide struggle against the Soviet bloc, while breeding fear and insecurity at home:

We preach freedom around the world, and we mean it, and we cherish our freedom here at home, but are we to say to the world, and much more importantly, to each other that this is the land of the free except for the Negroes; that we have no second-class citizens except Negroes; that we have no class or caste system, no ghettos, no master race except with respect to Negroes?

Now the time has come for this nation to fulfill its promise. . . . The fires of frustration and discord are burning in every city, North and South, where legal remedies are not at hand. Redress is sought in the streets, in demonstrations, parades, and protests which create tensions and threaten violence and threaten lives.

Other speeches, notably the ones on foreign policy, are quite fact-heavy. (Kennedy's staff was known as one of the heaviest borrowers of materials from the Library of Congress.) His July 2, 1957, speech calling on France to seek a negotiated solution to her war in Algeria, for example, was organized in the classic Kennedy problem-solution order. He devoted 90 percent of the address to discussing the problems of French rule in that North African country. He attacked France's claims that Algeria was an integral part of France and, therefore, none of the world's business by pointing out that few

Arab Algerians were in fact French citizens and therefore entitled to vote. Unlike mainland France, where education was free and compulsory, schooling was not universally available to non-French Algerians, and so on. He appealed to French rationality by arguing that France's constant warfare since 1939, as well as her brutal attempts to suppress the Algerian independence movement, were only harming France itself.

Even though Kennedy's recommendation for a U.S.-brokered solution was ultimately rejected by the Eisenhower administration as well as by France, the fact that Kennedy had clearly done his homework gave the speech weight. It was the first speech that drew Kennedy international attention.

Kennedy liked to call himself "an idealist without illusions," and appeals to rationality and the quest for pragmatic solutions to national and international problems are a *leitmotif* of his oratory. As examples:

"Our most basic common link is that we all inhabit this planet. We all breathe the same air. We all cherish our children's future. And we are all mortal."

"Let us not seek the Republican answer or the Democratic answer, but the right answer. Let us not seek to fix the blame for the past. Let us accept our own responsibility for the future."

"Let us not emphasize all on which we differ, but all we have in common. Let us not consider what we fear separately, but what we share together."

As Kennedy demonstrated in the civil rights speech, facts need not be presented in a dull or dry manner. In his famous speech in Houston, Texas, on the subject of his Roman Catholicism, he challenged Texas pride by citing some facts about a place he had visited earlier that same day, the Alamo:

For side by side with Bowie and Crockett died McCafferty and Bailey and Carey—but no one knows whether they were Catholic or not. For there was no religious test at the Alamo.

Kennedy sometimes softened his use of complex arguments with the rhetorical device of a short, declarative sentence to sum up his argument. In a speech on the Middle East, for example, he followed a long section on the sources of conflict in the region by declaring, "The true enemy of the Arab world is poverty and want." Transitioning to a discussion of South Asia, he said, "India is a somewhat different story." This simple device served to both make his point and "wake up" the audience.

Being Prepared

As Richard Nixon's dismal performance in the first 1960 debate demonstrates, rehearsal and preparation are essential before any important public appearance. Some people prefer to rehearse alone; others use a selected audience. Some recite the speech before going to sleep, when all is quiet and it is easier to listen for how it will sound. Regardless of *how* you do it, do rehearse.

At the same time, there is such a thing as being overprepared. Rehearse too much and you risk appearing tense and uneasy when the actual moment comes. Kennedy ceased formal preparation the day of the famous first debate with Nixon and sought to be as relaxed as he could be in the hours beforehand.

Another part of preparation is dealing with an inevitable part of public speaking on controversial issues: hecklers. There is an art to putting down a heckler without seeming rude yourself. Kennedy often dealt with them by noting, "If you're booing you're not listening. If you're not listening you're not learning. So maybe, right now, you should be listening."

Using Humor

In the same way that everyone wants to go to heaven but no one looks forward to dying, most speakers want to use humor but few are confident it won't bomb. The speaker has to decide when and where humor is appropriate, and if he is comfortable using it. But humorous observations, usually at the beginning of one's remarks, are a time-tested means of establishing audience rapport. Choosing to forgo humor is to throw away one of a communicator's great tools.

Even people who are not known for humor can use it effectively, especially if it is self-deprecating. A pharmaceutical executive who was known for his droning, uninteresting speeches began a talk by noting that it was the anniversary of the first use of sleeping gas in a surgical procedure. Looking up at the audience, he then deadpanned, "I have sometimes been accused of having the same effect on people." The audience howled.

Despite his natural wit, early Kennedy speeches contained little humor, and he stuck closely to his prepared text. Certainly, the major foreign policy and "crisis" speeches of his presidency were humor free. But Kennedy came to see humor as crucial to his public persona and speaking style. Sorensen says that Kennedy "would work diligently for the right opening witticism, or take as much pride the next day in some spontaneous barb he had flung, as he would on the most substantive paragraphs in his text."

Some of Kennedy's barbs were indeed spontaneous, but a great many were not. Humor was serious business to John F. Kennedy and his speech-writing staff. The humor could not be bitter or acerbic; rather, it had to be topical, tasteful, and relevant. It could also be pointed, irreverent, subtle, and self-deprecating. In other words, one reason Kennedy's wit worked so well was because it reflected his own style and personality.

Sorensen kept a "humor file" in his office where he secreted jokes that people had passed on to him or that he had heard on television or read in the newspaper and would then adapt for Kennedy's use. When the president would be traveling, advance men would scout the local newspapers and talk to local politicos in search of locally oriented humor that would immediately allow Kennedy to bond with the audience. Finally, there was Kennedy himself, who was often the richest vein in the humor mine. William "Fishbait" Miller, who served for years as the House of Representatives doorkeeper and who was not a particular fan of Kennedy's, nevertheless said he was among the best people he ever knew for "witty lines and snap comebacks."

Entire books have been written detailing Kennedy witticisms. Here, again, are some examples:

➡ Asked if he had as much time to read the papers as he did before becoming president, Kennedy responded, "I am reading it more and enjoying it less."

➡ Asked if he recommended running for president, he said, "No, I don't recommend it to anyone right now."

➡ When he was criticized by some Catholic leaders for his opposition to using government funds for Catholic schools, he said, "[S]ome circles invented the myth that after Al Smith's defeat in 1928 he sent a one-word telegram to the Pope: 'unpack.' After my press conference on the school bill, I received a one-word wire from the Pope: 'pack.'"

➡ Inspecting the newly replanted White House gardens, Kennedy said, "This may go down as the real achievement of this administration."

➡ Commenting during the 1960 campaign on the fact that the first astronaut dogs were called Belka and Strelka rather than Rover and Fido, Kennedy recalled the name of his opponent's dog, saying, "It was not named Checkers, either."

➡ Surprised at receiving the endorsement of the *New York Times* in 1960, Kennedy keyed off the newspaper's then-popular advertising slogan: "In part, at least, I am one person who can truthfully say, 'I got my job through *The New York Times*.'"

Not that Kennedy never bombed. Early in his Senate career, he opened a speech by noting that he arrived in a taxicab and was going to give the driver a healthy tip and urge him to vote Democratic. "Then I remembered the advice of Senator Theodore Green [D-RI] and gave him no tip and told him to vote Republican." A reporter wrote up the comment as if Kennedy had told it straight, and the Senate was deluged with angry letters, many of them from Republicans and cab drivers. Kennedy resolved to be more careful about his use of humor in the future.

What Ghostwriters *Can't* Do for You

This is as good a place as any to point out that not even the best speechwriters or ghostwriters can make a person into something he is not. As president, Jimmy Carter had in his employ some of the sharpest writing talent available. His speechwriters included Michael Kinsley, James Fallows, and Hendrik Hertzberg, all of whom went on to distinguished careers in journalism in the years after Carter left Washington. Yet not even his most fervent admirers would likely claim Carter was an eloquent or memorable speaker. (Fallows actually wrote an unflattering memoir of his White House experience for *Atlantic Monthly* titled "The Passionless Presidency.") Carter's vice president, Walter Mondale, used as his speechwriter Charles Krauthammer, who became a syndicated columnist and went on to win the Pulitzer Prize for distinguished commentary. Yet Mondale could never escape being tagged as a dull public speaker.

In short, if you want to be an effective communicator, it involves much more than simply finding a strong writer. Sorensen helped Kennedy write *his* speech, not Sorensen's speech. Your speechwriter must do the same for you, but only if you do your part as well.

How to Master the Art of the Speech

→ *Live your speech.* Public speaking is an integral part of your leadership, not an add-on responsibility. Become skilled at it and be your own chief speechwriter. Adopt a style that feels natural to you, use words you would normally use, and work on appearing at ease (even if you are not) when addressing others. One reason Kennedy's inaugural address worked, author Thurston Clarke believes, is because Kennedy didn't merely believe in the speech, he *lived* it. The speech summed up and distilled virtually all of Kennedy's life that had gone before it: his war service, his period in London preceding it, his experience watching his father make mistake after mistake as the European crisis gathered momentum, his early identification of Churchill as the man of the hour. Another person delivering the same speech could not have achieved the same impact.

→ *Get input from your staff.* Tell them the message you'd like to get across and brainstorm with them about the best way to convey that message. Come up with key phrases that will encapsulate what you are trying to say. Using others to help craft your speech, as Kennedy did with Sorensen, can be a great benefit, especially as the writer gets a feel for your message and your way of delivering it. However, the final speech must be your own, one you feel comfortable delivering.

→ *Be brief.* Your speech should be short, no more than twenty minutes ideally. Your words should also be short and your style straightforward yet memorable. Ideally, you should use language and stories that the audience will be able to relate to. Avoid language that will lose your audience; that means avoiding legalese, lots of acronyms, and flowery sentences. Make the message as clear as possible and as directed to your intended audience as you can make it.

➡ *Use examples, statistics, and facts to make your points.* People seem to be able to remember numbers and facts longer than they can remember other information. Punctuating your message with facts and figures makes it more memorable. However, don't overwhelm your listeners with a flurry of numbers and facts. Zero in on the specific examples or statistics that will make your case.

➡ *Be* very *sparing with the use of PowerPoint slides.* No more than two or three at the most. If the audience is busy reading slides, it is *not* paying attention to you.

➡ *Tell a story when appropriate.* Storytelling is an incredible leadership skill that has recently become popular. If you can find a story that makes your message personal for the audience, you can make the issue resonate for them. Ronald Reagan, one of the greatest presidential storytellers, initiated the practice of inviting citizens who had distinguished themselves in some field to be his personal guests at the State of the Union Address. He would tell the story of their achievement to underscore some major element of his message and then introduce them in the gallery. Every president since Reagan has used this same technique.

➡ *Remember that your speech reflects you.* Even if you get help from a professional writer, never forget who has the final say. Blaming your speechwriter if you misspeak is a good way to scare off speechwriters; it also makes you look silly. It's *your* message; make sure it reflects who you are.

CHAPTER 7

Commitment to Learning:
Challenge Your Assumptions

"There's no school for presidents either. We'll learn together."
—JOHN F. KENNEDY TO ROBERT MCNAMARA, WHO SAID HE
DIDN'T FEEL QUALIFIED TO BE DEFENSE SECRETARY

Although you should avoid getting bogged down in minutiae, as a general rule, you can never learn too much about your line of work, or someone else's. But information and skills are only as good as the uses to which you put them. Kennedy was not afraid of using new information to change his mind about an issue or of learning new skills to help him do his job better. Being able to learn new facts and step back to see if your assumptions are correct is essential to good leadership. Too often leaders won't change their position even when they are wrong because they are afraid of looking weak or indecisive.

"We all learn," Kennedy observed in 1960, "from the time you are born until the time you die. Events change, conditions change, and you would be extremely unwise to pursue policies that are unsuccessful."

Getting the Country Moving Again

"Now tell me again," Kennedy said to his chief economic adviser, Walter Heller, "how do I distinguish between monetary and fiscal policy?"

Kennedy freely admitted that he knew little about economics (even though it had been his major at Harvard) or business or the corporate world. But as president, he knew he couldn't afford to remain ignorant for long. He had pledged to "get the country moving again" in 1960 and that's what he intended to do. Besides, Western Europe's economies seemed to be growing faster than the U.S. economy during the 1950s and, more worrisomely, the Soviet Union was reporting huge feats of economic strength (both of which proved illusory, of course). The United States could not afford to be perceived as an economic weak sister and continue to lead the Western alliance.

Heller, whose previous position had been as an economics professor at the University of Minnesota, had experience teaching beginners and spoke in terms the president could understand.

"Well," Heller answered, "Monetary is M, like Martin [William McChesney Martin, the chairman of the U.S. Federal Reserve]. So remember Martin and think of the federal reserve board."

Such mnemonic tricks may seem juvenile, but they are a wonderful way to learn and keep concepts straight in your mind. These conversations were the beginning of John F. Kennedy's economic education—an education that would result in one of the most inspired pieces of economic policy making of the twentieth century: the Kennedy tax rate cut. Ironically, the Kennedy policy would, twenty years hence, be given a catchy name—"supply-side economics"—and become a cornerstone not of Democratic economic policy, but of the Republican party.

At the time Kennedy became president, there had been three recessions in seven years. The one in 1958 had been exceptionally deep, briefly rekindling fears that another Great Depression might be in the offing. Through it all, President Dwight D. Eisenhower and his economic team adopted a steady-as-you-go policy, endeavoring to keep budget deficits to a minimum by keeping income tax rates relatively high. The rate of economic growth during the Eisenhower years thus averaged a steady, but hardly spectacular, 2 to 3 percent.

That wouldn't be good enough for Kennedy. The question was: how to get from here to there?

Exercising Caution

The economists who surrounded Kennedy in the early 1960s had all been steeped in what was known as the Keynesian school of economics. Named for British economist John Maynard Keynes, author of the highly influential 1936 treatise *The General Theory of Employment, Interest, and Money*, the Keynesians generally advised deficit financing and cutting taxes as a way of stimulating demand in a slack economy.

Large deficits, however, were anathema to Treasury Secretary C. Douglas Dillon and to House Ways and Means Committee Chairman Wilbur Mills, as well as the Republican–Southern Democrat coalition that dominated Congress. Liberals were willing to go along with a temporary tax cut to stimulate demand, but Dillon, Mills, and company wouldn't buy that, either. The fear of large deficits thus caused Kennedy to steer clear of large tax cuts early in his administration or the kind of public works projects that Franklin Roosevelt had used in the 1930s. JFK feared being seen as a reckless spender, and he was determined to show his sense of fiscal responsibility by pledging he would balance the budget.

He made his first cautious stab at stimulating economic growth in the spring of 1961 by proposing an 8 percent investment tax credit aimed at business. (Businesses could deduct 8 percent of any new investment from their tax bills.) To appeal to liberals, Kennedy coupled the proposal with such familiar "tax reform" devices as tightening up on perceived loopholes. Liberals, however, objected that the plan was too generous and conservatives fretted that it was not generous enough. The tax credit idea went nowhere.

It was Commerce Secretary Luther Hodges, the token "graybeard" in the Kennedy cabinet (he was sixty-three years old in 1961), who seems to have first pushed the idea of steep and permanent cuts in both personal and corporate tax rates. Hodges was the odd man out in the Kennedy cabinet in several respects other than his age. Neither an academic nor a career politician, he had made a fortune in the textile business and turned to politics only late in life. As governor of North Carolina, he had successfully lured businesses to the state by advertising its low tax rates. Unfortunately for Hodges, general economic policy was not seen as part of his portfolio and he had a hard time making his voice heard in the administration's economic councils.

Despite the lack of action, Wall Street in general seemed to like the noises that were coming out of the Kennedy White House on economic policy. The Dow Jones Industrial Average, which was at around 600 points when Kennedy was elected, reached a high of 741 by November 1961. But as the internal economic debate dragged on in the administration with no sign of a resolution, the stock market began drifting downward to about 700 by April 1962.

Provoking "the Kennedy Crash"

Then Kennedy made his biggest economic mistake. United States Steel Corporation, the nation's largest steelmaker, announced a series of price increases after Kennedy had persuaded the steelworker's union to moderate its demands for wage increases in the name of fighting inflation. The president felt double-crossed by U.S. Steel Chairman Roger Blough. "My father always told me that all businessmen were sons of bitches," Kennedy was quoted as saying. "But I never believed it until now."

When the remark leaked to *Newsweek,* a White House spokesman lamely claimed Kennedy was referring only to steel industry executives. The damage, however, was done. Memories of the business-bashing rhetoric and policies of the Roosevelt and Truman administrations were still fresh, and many business executives and owners feared the campaign against steel signaled that it was making a comeback under Kennedy. The situation wasn't helped by the often-overzealous attorney general. Robert Kennedy convened a grand jury to investigate the steel industry, and FBI agents appeared at the doors of steel executives and even journalists covering the industry at odd hours. (Some have said that J. Edgar Hoover was responsible for the latter ploy, seeking to deliberately embarrass the Kennedys.)

As Jude Wanniski points out in his account of the Kennedy tax cut in *The Way the World Works,* Wall Street began skidding almost immediately, falling to 655 at the end of April. A national economic conference held in Washington, D.C., during the third week in May only seemed to aggravate the situation. United Auto Workers President Walter Reuther called for national economic planning, à la the Soviet Union. AFL-CIO President George Meany said he would begin a campaign for a thirty-five-hour workweek to free up more jobs. Kennedy's failure to offer an effective alternative made Wall Street fear the worst. The market fell 22 points in one week, to 611, the biggest weekly drop since 1930. On May 28, the market plummeted a then-eye-popping 35 points in one day, settling below its pre-Kennedy level. The newspapers quickly dubbed it "the Kennedy Crash" and comparisons with Herbert Hoover were in the air.

Turning Things Around

The Kennedy economic team convened at 10 A.M. on May 29, Kennedy's forty-fifth birthday. The market continued falling throughout the two-hour conference. To underline the gravity of the situation, Treasury Secretary Dillon and, crucially, Commerce Secretary Hodges both emerged at noon to brief reporters. While Dillon held to his cautious line on tax cuts, Hodges declared his belief that a major tax reduction package was in the offing. It was Hodges's statement that got picked up by the newswires. Almost immediately, the market turned around, rallying to close the day 50 points higher.

That was all Kennedy needed to see. (It helped that Robert Lovett, a New York–based Democratic party "wise man" who had declined an invitation to serve in Kennedy's cabinet, urged him to cut taxes come what may.) In little over a week after the May 29 crisis, the president—who had dismissed tax cuts early in his administration—sent proposals to Capitol Hill for a net tax reduction, though the idea was still freighted down with the "loophole closing" bric-a-brac so beloved by Democratic liberals. He demonstrated his newfound faith by not waiting for Congress to act, instead issuing executive orders in the summer of 1962 that created more generous depreciation schedules for machinery and equipment, a break worth $1.5 billion to business in the first year alone.

A Lesson Learned

The fallout from the steel and stock market crises convinced Kennedy that he hadn't paid sufficient attention to the concerns of business. The entire administration thus embarked on a "charm offensive" designed to banish any thought that the Kennedy White House might be antibusiness. Kennedy hosted a series of black-tie dinners to which top corporate executives were invited. He even managed to patch things up somewhat with Roger Blough.

None of this escaped the notice of many old-line Democrats. Supreme Court Justice Felix Frankfurter, one of the last New Dealers still active in government in the early 1960s, gave Kennedy a finger-wagging lecture about being too close to "moneyed interests." The president, however, was unpersuaded. He had promised the American people jobs; he couldn't afford to be beastly to those who created them.

The entire effort climaxed with a speech given by Kennedy to the Economic Club of New York in December 1962. As always, he put national security first:

> If the economy of today were operating close to capacity levels
> with little unemployment, or if a sudden change in our military

requirements should cause a scramble for men and resources, then I would oppose tax reductions as irresponsible and inflationary; and I would not hesitate to recommend a tax increase if that were necessary. . . .

But then he cut to the heart of the matter:

It is increasingly clear that no matter what party is in power, so long as our national security needs keep rising, an economy hampered by restrictive tax rates will never produce enough jobs or enough profits.

The final and best means of strengthening demand among consumers and business is to reduce the burden on private income and the deterrents to private initiative which are imposed by our present tax system; and this administration pledged itself last summer to an across-the-board, top-to-bottom cut in personal and corporate income taxes to be enacted and become effective in 1963.

John Kenneth Galbraith, the liberal Harvard economist and Kennedy adviser, privately derided the address as "the most Republican since McKinley." (Galbraith was still upset that Kennedy had chosen to "exile" him to India as ambassador rather than offer him a major economic post in Washington.) A journalist marveled that the speech made Kennedy sound more like the president of the National Association of Manufacturers than a Democratic president of the United States. Kennedy had not only learned from his crash course on economics, he had turned around and used those lessons to rethink his position and boost the economy.

Taking a Bold New Step

The final piece of the puzzle came together as 1963 dawned. Kennedy wasn't much inclined to listen to the liberals anymore, at least on economic policy. They carped frequently and delivered little. Organized labor was so anxious to grow the economic pie and create more jobs that it had little interest in the liberals' determination to eliminate the three-martini business lunch and similar corporate tax breaks they often targeted for elimination.

With labor safely on board, Kennedy felt free to ditch any attempt at "tax reform" and move toward a general tax reduction on both individuals and businesses. He had become convinced that the budget deficits that would result in the short run would later be made up by higher tax revenues resulting from a higher level of economic growth. Although this belief has been labeled Keynesian by many historians, it is, in fact, the precursor of supply-side economics.

Kennedy's tax bill would not pass until the year after his death. The punitive tax rates that had been put in place to finance World War II and had largely remained untouched since then were slashed. (The top rate of 91 percent was brought down to 70 percent, for example.) By the time Lyndon Johnson signed the bill in February 1964, the Dow Jones was cresting 800. The recession ended; unemployment and inflation both fell. In the next two years, per capita income rose $320 in inflation-adjusted terms, versus $112 in the entire eight years of the Eisenhower administration.

By his own admission, Kennedy had shown little interest in economic policy. He felt the true mission of the president centered on foreign affairs. However, he learned that economic decisions could have far-reaching effects, touching the lives of most Americans and strengthening or weakening the country as a whole.

As he delved into the economy, Kennedy challenged some of his own long-standing assumptions. Confronting his fear of running up deficits and being labeled a reckless spender, he did an about-face on tax cuts. When his general distrust of businessmen began to be perceived as an antibusiness bias, he adopted a new business-friendly attitude to the chagrin of his liberal friends.

Strong leaders are not afraid to reverse course when confronted with new information challenging their old assumptions. In fact, part of true leadership is to keep learning and adapting all the time.

Rethinking America's Response to the Threat of Nuclear War

John F. Kennedy knew that, as president, he was the only individual who could authorize the use of nuclear weapons. But once he had given the word, what happened then? He found out on a September afternoon in 1961.

Events in the first months of his presidency—the Bay of Pigs, the Vienna summit with Nikita Khrushchev, among them—caused Kennedy to delay until this comparatively late date a detailed briefing by the Joint Chiefs of Staff on his nuclear options. Or, more accurately described, his *option*.

Armed with easels and flip charts, the Joint Chiefs of Staff presented the president with the nation's doomsday war plan. More than 3,700 targets in the Soviet Union and communist China were identified. Upon presidential authorization, these targets would be blasted by more than 3,000 U.S. nuclear weapons. At any given time, Kennedy was told, more than 1,500 missiles and bombers were on fifteen-minute alert, with 50 percent of the fleet of B-52 long-range bombers kept airborne at all times and in all weather conditions. Another 1,700 delivery vehicles could be brought to readiness within six hours.

Asked if it were possible to execute only a portion of the plan, the chairman of the Joint Chiefs of Staff, General Lyman Lemnitzer, responded that such a course would involve "grave risks. . . . There is no effective mechanism for rapid rework of the plan, after order for its execution, for a different set of conditions than for which it was prepared."

Those who knew Kennedy, as Richard Reeves recounts in *President Kennedy: Profile of Power,* recognized as a bad sign the way he was tapping the front of his teeth with the nail of his thumb as he listened. Finally, the chief executive spoke.

"Why do we hit all those targets in China, general?" Kennedy asked. China was thought to be working on nuclear weapons but had not yet exploded one or deployed a missile that could deliver one.

For a president who liked flexibility and options, Lemnitzer gave the wrong answer. "It's in the plan, Mr. President."

Kennedy was shaken by what he had just heard. After the generals and admirals had left, he muttered, "And we call ourselves the human race."

Facing a New Reality

Kennedy had just come face-to-face with "massive retaliation," the official doctrine of the U.S. government for more than a decade. In the event of a Soviet attack on the United States or its closest allies, Uncle Sam would hit back with everything in his toolbox. In theory, the Soviet Union and communist China would all but cease to exist. American casualties would be far fewer, given the vastly less capable nuclear arsenal of its foe and the likely damage it would suffer in the American attack. But if even only a couple of Soviet bombs managed to detonate on U.S. soil, millions of Americans would likely be killed. And none of this was to mention the enormous damage the planet itself would suffer, with unpredictable consequences for the survivors.

For all the easy manner with which he carried his presidential authority, John F. Kennedy was discovering there was a big difference between ruminating about nuclear warfare in the Senate cloakroom and actually having to give the "go" code under unimaginable circumstances. He was reminded of this grim reality on a daily basis whenever he happened to catch sight of the lone military officer clutching the so-called football (an oversize valise containing the nation's nuclear codes) who trailed him wherever he went.

And Kennedy had seen, up close, just what kind of damage all-out war could wreak on a major metropolis. Just a week before Adolf Hitler attacked Poland on September 1, 1939, the event that ignited World War II, the young Kennedy had been visiting Berlin. Despite six years of Nazism, the German capital was still a bustling, cosmopolitan city of four million people with world-class hotels, theaters, shops, and restaurants. Its sweeping boulevards, plazas, and monumental architecture combined to proclaim Berlin one of the world's great cities.

Almost exactly six years later, Kennedy returned, having hitched a plane ride with Navy Secretary James V. Forrestal. The great buildings had been blasted into heaps of ruins, basic utilities were spotty, and the streets were filled with hollow-eyed refugees begging for food and fuel. The kind of destruction that Kennedy saw had taken years; nuclear destruction would be worse—and much, much faster.

Stoking Nuclear Fears

The nuclear issue was central to American politics and even culture in the early 1960s. Major cities continued to conduct air raid drills on a regular basis. Schoolchildren still did duck-and-cover exercises in their classrooms, diving under their desks at the first sign of a nuclear flash. Hollywood tapped into the popular unease by churning out a succession of "nuclear nightmare" films, including *On the Beach* and *The World, the Flesh, and the Devil* (both in 1959), as well as 1962's *Panic in the Year Zero,* among others.

Hollywood wasn't alone in stoking public fears. Kennedy did his part, too. Determined never to be portrayed as "soft on communism," Kennedy moved to Richard Nixon's political right on foreign policy in the 1960 campaign. One of the ways he did this was by insisting there was a "missile gap" between the United States and the Soviet Union that favored the Soviets.

The missile-gap theory had had its origin in a report issued by a panel of academics chaired by H. Rowan Gaither Jr., president of the Ford Foundation, and appointed by President Eisenhower in the spring of 1957. Originally tasked with examining the feasibility of civil defense, it broadened its scope to the overall vulnerability of U.S. nuclear forces in the wake of the Soviet launch of Sputnik in 1957. Using CIA and U.S. Air Force data, the committee painted a frightening picture of hundreds of Soviet missiles pointed at America within five years.

The reason this was important was because, at the time, the United States relied almost exclusively for nuclear deterrence on a fleet of long-range B-52 bombers. These aircraft, however, were concentrated at comparatively few bases. A Soviet missile would have a flight time of only thirty minutes, and the U.S. Strategic Air Command was simply not organized for such a short reaction time.

If the Soviets built a massive intercontinental ballistic missile (ICBM) force before the U.S. equivalent was ready, the Russians would be in a position to destroy most of the U.S. nuclear forces on the ground. Accordingly, the ability of the United States to deter the Soviets from making such an attack in the first place was in doubt.

Unfortunately, there was simply no way of knowing how many ICBMs the Soviet Union had. American intelligence had almost no agents on the ground in the tightly controlled Soviet Union. Virtually all that could be done was to electronically observe the test firings of Soviet missiles and extrapolate from the results. When the U-2 spy plane, which began flying in 1956, surprised everyone by photographing no Soviet missiles at all, many in the intelligence community insisted that was possible only because the Soviets were camouflaging them.

At Eisenhower's direction, General Earle Wheeler of the Joint Chiefs of Staff at the Pentagon briefed Kennedy that there appeared to be no missile gap, but he was reluctant to reveal how the United States knew that. Fearful of leaks about the U-2, Eisenhower preferred to remain vague. Kennedy, however, was hearing differently from air force sources. The situation was aggravated by Khrushchev's table-thumping insistence that the Soviet Union was cranking out missiles "like sausages." For a man like Kennedy, who was steeped in Winston Churchill's lonely fight to prove the reality of the Nazi air threat against a seemingly complacent government in the late 1930s, Eisenhower's "trust me" stance must have had an eerily familiar ring.

Thus, the supposed missile gap became a staple of Kennedy's 1960 campaign rhetoric. "We are facing a gap on which we are gambling our survival" was a standard line.

Once in office, however, Kennedy found himself blindsided by his own rhetoric. Spy satellites, which became operational in Kennedy's first year in office, definitively confirmed that the Soviet Union had only four operational ICBMs. Faced with the reality of overwhelming U.S. military superiority, the Kennedy White House began ordering "studies" and generally talking around the missile–gap issue. Even Kennedy himself seemed confused on the history of the controversy, asking National Security Adviser Mc-George Bundy to research it. Unexpectedly, however, the public seemed not to care. The fact of American superiority, it appeared, trumped any questions over who knew what when.

Nevertheless, Kennedy was determined to further strengthen U.S. defenses, conventional as well as nuclear. Draft calls were bumped up; reservists slated for demobilization were kept on active duty. JFK doubled the building rate of the new Polaris missile-carrying nuclear submarines. He ordered 1,000 American ICBMs (though the air force wanted 3,000) and increased the number of B-52 bombers on airborne alert.

Kennedy's aim, however, was not a mindless military buildup. Rather, he sought to secure a strong position from which to negotiate some kind of new understanding with the Kremlin. A collection of his foreign policy speeches from the 1950s was titled "The Strategy of Peace." Once again, the words of Churchill were his guide: "You arm to parley."

Recognizing the Dangers of Nuclear Diplomacy

For all of the awesome military strength at his command, Kennedy was smart enough to know that it couldn't last. The Soviet nuclear arsenal was certain to grow in size and sophistication as time went on. China was developing an arsenal of her own. A policy of "massive retaliation" would simply have no credibility in a world of near-equal nuclear capabilities. In its place, Kennedy substituted "flexible response," a new nuclear war plan that would give him and his successors a range of options to fit different scenarios, options designed to hold any possible nuclear exchange to the most minimal level possible.

We know now that Khrushchev and the rest of the Kremlin leadership found Kennedy's moves alarming at the time. Insecure at the best of times, Khrushchev almost seemed to use his overblown rhetoric and frequently crude personal behavior as a weapon to compensate for his actual lack of hardware. His occasional noises about improved understanding and cooperation between the superpowers tended to be vitiated by other antics, such as his banging his shoe on the table at the United Nations and his verbal pummeling of JFK at their Vienna summit in June 1961.

The Soviet leader's answer to Kennedy's moves came on August 31, 1961, just ten days after the Berlin Wall went up, when Khrushchev announced that he was unilaterally ending the informal three-year ban on nuclear testing being observed by the United States, the Soviet Union, and Great Britain. (France had tested her first nuclear weapon in 1960 and was not observing the ban.) Two months later, Khrushchev detonated what remains the largest nuclear blast in human history, a 58-megaton monster. Kennedy felt he had no choice but to respond by resuming U.S. nuclear testing.

But it was the Cuban missile crisis (discussed in detail in Chapter 10) that brought home to Kennedy the dangers and limits of nuclear diplomacy. Says Vito N. Silvestri in his study *Becoming JFK: A Profile in Communication,* "There is a linear progression between the Cuban missile crisis, Kennedy's commencement address at American University in June 1963, and the Limited Nuclear Test Ban Treaty in July 1963."

While the public strongly supported his tough stance in Cuba, Kennedy knew better than anyone how close the call had been, and it was too close for comfort. Kennedy also knew that the pictures of mushroom clouds blossoming over the Nevada desert on a regular basis were a cause of public unease about radioactive fallout. (Kennedy himself became notably pensive when it was pointed out to him that the rain falling outside the Oval Office windows might well contain fallout.) Polls showed that Americans believed stopping the spread of communism should be a major national priority; yet, the same polls also showed they thought avoiding World War III was almost as important. Furthermore, Kennedy didn't want the United States to be perceived overseas as warlike. It was time to start "cashing in" some of the credibility he had bought with his handling of the missile crisis and the military buildup he had initiated.

Talks on a limited test ban had foundered for years on the issue of verification of compliance. The United States was demanding an on-site inspection regime as the price of a treaty; the Soviet Union always rejected such plans for fear the Americans and the British would use it as an opportunity for espionage. Kennedy decided to approach Khrushchev again, this time downplaying the on-site verification issue (more advanced seismographs and spy satellites were making that less important anyway). Kennedy proposed talks at a higher level than the ones that had been taking place in Geneva up until that time.

Launching a New Initiative

The approach was laid out publicly in a speech Kennedy delivered at the commencement ceremonies of American University on June 10, 1963. According to Ted Sorensen, it was the first time an American president had specifically addressed the issue of world peace since 1945:

> I have . . . chosen this time and this place to discuss a topic on which ignorance too often abounds and the truth is too rarely perceived—yet it is the most important topic on earth: world peace.
>
> What kind of peace do I mean? What kind of peace do we seek? Not a Pax Americana enforced on the world by American weapons of war. Not the peace of the grave or the security of the slave. I am talking about genuine peace, the kind of peace that makes life on earth worth living, the kind that enables men and nations to grow and to hope and to build a better life for their children—not merely peace for Americans but peace for all men and women—not merely peace in our time but peace for all time.
>
> I speak of peace because of the new face of war. Total war makes no sense in an age when great powers can maintain large

and relatively invulnerable nuclear forces and refuse to surrender without resort to those forces.

Perhaps Kennedy even foresaw the end of the Cold War, which few could have seen or expected then, when he stated:

> World peace, like community peace, does not require that each man love his neighbor—it requires only that they live together in mutual tolerance, submitting their disputes to a just and peaceful settlement. And history teaches us that enmities between nations, as between individuals, do not last forever. However fixed our likes and dislikes may seem, the tide of time and events will often bring surprising changes in the relations between nations and neighbors.

The American University speech was delivered the day before his great civil rights speech, and so it tended to be overshadowed in public notice. In Moscow, however, the speech was minutely studied and actually printed in full in both *Pravda* and *Izvestia*. Only a month later, Ambassador Averell Harriman was in Moscow working out the details of a test ban, which was concluded about two weeks later. Kennedy was an active long-distance participant, urging Harriman to keep his eye on the ball and not allow himself to be sidetracked by minor issues.

The treaty Harriman brought home banned nuclear weapons testing above ground, underwater, and in outer space. Underground testing would still be legal, until such time as a comprehensive test ban treaty could be negotiated. Kennedy, and probably Khrushchev as well, were motivated at least in part by the threat of nuclear proliferation. If the major powers were seen as placing some modest restraints on their own arsenals, in preparation for further restraints down the road, perhaps some nations would be deterred from developing their own nuclear arsenals. (In the case of China, it failed. Contemptuously dismissing the treaty, Beijing exploded its own nuclear weapon above ground in 1964 and continued to do so for another twelve years. Thus, the treaty did have the unexpected benefit of worsening Sino-Soviet relations.)

The Limited Nuclear Test Ban Treaty was ratified by the U.S. Senate.

Kennedy called it "a shaft of light in the darkness." Although he made clear that he had no intention of relaxing America's guard vis-à-vis the Soviet Union, he made it known that few acts of his presidency had given him more pleasure than the test ban treaty.

Sometimes leaders discover new information or see old information in a new way after taking over in their new position. There probably was no more critical issue facing the world during Kennedy's presidency than the proliferation of nuclear weapons. After railing against the "missile gap" during his campaign, Kennedy soon got a crash course in reality: The United States actually had the superior firepower. The more he learned, however, the more he became uneasy with the heavy burden of nuclear weaponry being at the heart of our stalemate with the Russians. A macho mistake here or an idle threat there could truly result in Armageddon. In fact, the face-off with Khrushchev over the missiles in Cuba was a brief glimpse into the abyss. Kennedy learned on the job, as all great leaders do, and he launched an initiative resulting in the first nuclear test ban agreement.

How to Challenge Your Assumptions

➡ *Never stop learning.* Being a one-trick pony is a quick route to career obsolescence in today's fast-changing economy. A few years ago, most cellular phone companies assumed their competition was restricted to a few other phone companies. Today, other small electronic devices are being developed that may compete. For example, new BlackBerry e-mail devices from Research in Motion also have the capacity to make phone calls. Similarly, cell phones not only make calls, they play games, take pictures, and let you send and receive e-mail. If you are not continually changing your assumptions, you can miss new threats and opportunities.

➡ *Be prepared to change your mind.* Don't allow your initial assumptions to govern your actions. When presented with new facts and realities, be prepared to change your mind. In fact, before making any kind of changes, you should have done sufficient research to determine whether they are correct. For example, many companies have decided to refocus their attention on the older generation. That's fine, but by directly appealing to seniors or the "aging population" and such, many of these companies have missed their mark, because no one wants to buy products that make them feel old. A more successful approach is to meet consumer needs without labeling them as products for older people. For example, Kohler now makes toilets with a higher seat and bathtubs that are more accessible, which better meet the needs of many people, but it doesn't identify them as products for "elderly" or "handicapped."

➠ *Beware the "If I were king . . ." syndrome.* Overblown rhetoric can come back to haunt you when you do finally find yourself in a position of responsibility. Many politicians have learned this lesson the hard way. Get all the pertinent information you can before making any kind of major announcement. The higher you get in an organization, the more public your speeches and comments will be. Aspire to give strong and powerful speeches, but beware of saying things you can't back up or might regret later on.

CHAPTER 8

Team Building:
Find Your "Bobby"

"[M]en of ability who can do things. Men of good judgment."
—JOHN F. KENNEDY, DESCRIBING THE QUALITIES HE
LOOKED FOR IN SUBORDINATES

*"This is the one part of the job I had hoped would be fun. But
these are the decisions that could make or break us all."*
—JOHN F. KENNEDY ON SELECTING PERSONNEL

The team you put together to surround and advise you says a lot about your leadership. So, too, does the way you go about building that team. You can't only choose friends and acquaintances, although having a few of them close to you will help get you through some rough times. You must spread a wide net so that all the people around you are not cut from the same cloth. You want a range of opinions, not just one point of view or one kind of background. You need to be sure you will receive honest advice from experts in their fields, not simply watered-down recommendations your people think you want to hear. And, finally, you want a team that is as loyal to you as you will be to it.

When *Air Force One* arrived at Andrews Air Force Base on the evening of that shocking day in November 1963, the presidential staff aboard the airplane was informed that a military honor guard was standing by outside to carry the late president's coffin. As Kennedy aide Kenneth O'Donnell recounted later in his memoir, *Johnny, We Hardly Knew Ye,* he turned to the other staff members, the ones who had been with JFK for so long, and took a silent poll. He turned back to the person who brought the news.

"We'll carry him off ourselves!" O'Donnell said.

And they did. O'Donnell, Dave Powers, along with Jacqueline Kennedy, resting her hand on the coffin lid, bore the bronze temporary casket that had carried the president's body back from Dallas. It was a fitting way for Kennedy's staff to pay final tribute to their slain chief. Although the Kennedy administration was retrospectively described as "Camelot," Kennedy himself had years earlier likened their relationship—perhaps with some exaggeration—to that of Shakespeare's Henry V and his knights:

> But we in it shall be remembered—
> We few, we happy few, we band of brothers. . . .
> And gentlemen . . . now abed,
> Shall think themselves accursed they were not here. . . .
>
> *Henry V*

JFK inspired tremendous affection and loyalty from the members of his team, emotions that, far from dissipating, seemed to grow actually stronger with the passage of time. (It is remarkable that no member of the administration or of Kennedy's inner circle ever wrote a "debunking" or even remotely hostile memoir.)

This intense devotion is all the more remarkable given that Kennedy's treatment of those around him was not always cordial or considerate. Despite his personal wealth, for example, Kennedy rarely carried money with him and was continually "borrowing" cash from friends or staff members for restaurant bills, cab fares, and even church collections and "forgetting" to pay it back. But he could be remarkably considerate as well. When he and his best friend Lem Billings set out to tour Europe together in 1937, Kennedy insisted on staying in the kind of cheap lodgings that his far less well-heeled friend could afford.

No one gets to the top of an organization, be it a company or a government, all by himself. Even a prizefighter, alone in the ring, has a retinue of coaches, managers, and trainers backing him up. A team can help bring you all the way, or it can potentially trip you up. Assembling a team is not only essential, it is one of the most important tasks you will ever undertake as a leader.

Let's look at Kennedy's team and how he assembled it.

Robert F. Kennedy: The Strong Right Arm

"With Bobby, I don't have to think about organization," Kennedy said. "I just show up."

Robert Francis "Bobby" Kennedy was a man of contradictions. To the end of his days, he veered sharply between political views that were liberal—some charged leftist—and conservative, sometimes bordering on the reactionary.

He started out unenthusiastic about civil rights, even authorizing the wiretapping of Martin Luther King Jr. because he feared the civil rights leader was consorting with communists, and later became a crusader for civil rights. A militant anticommunist, Bobby Kennedy turned against a war meant to halt its spread. As a Senate investigator and later as attorney general, he pursued a single-minded crusade against organized crime, yet he seemed unconcerned about using mobsters to assassinate Fidel Castro. There are many other examples.

Someone Who Can Be Trusted Above All Else

But there were no contradictions when it came to his most important role: as his brother's confidante and most trusted all-around adviser. He acted as JFK's "office wife," providing candid information and opinions about issues, people, and events, a role that Kennedy's actual wife was disinclined to play herself.

It was not a role that many expected for him, least of all, probably, himself. Bobby was eight years younger than his brother Jack and nine years younger than Joe Jr. Because both of his older siblings had gone off to boarding school by the time he was born, neither of them had an exceptionally close relationship with Bobby in childhood. The bucktoothed Bobby was the "runt" of the litter and self-conscious about it. Eager to prove his worth, he played football in spite of a frame that was spare to the point of being scrawny. He unsuccessfully sought to become a naval aviator, like his late elder brother, Joe Jr. His father, Joe Sr., however, refused to pull strings to aid him in this ambition, so Bobby had to serve his hitch aboard the USS *Joseph P. Kennedy*.

But he found ways to carve out his own persona. While his brothers were fun loving and delighted in skirt chasing and ribaldry, Bobby was an intensely conservative, almost puritanical Catholic. Of all the male Kennedys, Bobby is the only one it is possible to imagine becoming a priest. Instead, he became the first to marry, when he was twenty-four, beating his older brother to the altar by three years. Eventually, he and his wife Ethel would produce eleven children. He also cut rather a different figure at Harvard, where he roomed with football players and his friends and associates were more blue-collar than from the Social Register.

Jack first seemed to really notice Bobby during an overseas trip to the Middle East and Far East. His sharp observations and organizational skills impressed his older brother. When Mark Dalton (who had managed Kennedy's successful 1946 U.S. House of Representatives race) proved unable to work with Joe Sr. in the opening phases of Jack's 1952 Senate race and resigned, Jack had no doubt about who should get the call.

"I'll just screw it up," Bobby protested. Fresh out of law school, he was still learning his way around the Department of Justice in Washington and had certainly never managed a political campaign before, much less one against a formidable incumbent such as Henry Cabot Lodge Jr. Nevertheless, he couldn't refuse and headed straight to Boston.

Bobby never did anything halfway, and the campaign was no exception. He plunged into a routine of eighteen-hour days so punishing that he managed to lose twelve pounds that he could scarcely afford to lose. He viewed anyone who did not work as hard as he did as a slacker, and he let him know it. He had no truck with the professional politicians who hung around the campaign office, doing no work but expecting favors later. He threw them out. "You can't get any work out of a politician," he said.

Bobby proved adept at the hard, tedious, but necessary jobs that any organization demands. Jack detested personal confrontation; to Bobby, it was oxygen. He did not preface bad news with gentle niceties. He came brutally to the point and showed no mercy. He inherited his father's almost maniacal sense of precision. The result, as two Massachusetts journalists wrote later, "was the most methodical, the most scientific, the most thoroughly detailed, the most intricate, the most disciplined and smoothly working statewide campaign in Massachusetts history—and possibly anywhere else." Bobby's watchwords were "organization, organization, and more organization."

A Candid Critic and Sounding Board

When Jack won his Senate seat in 1952, in spite of the nationwide landslide for Republican Dwight D. Eisenhower, Bobby had earned his stripes. For the rest of JFK's life, he would serve as his brother's strong right arm. Their unique relationship enabled Bobby to candidly challenge his brother when he thought he was wrong. JFK used him as a sounding board for ideas as well as general adviser.

But RFK also had an identity independent of his brother. As a Senate staffer and against his father's advice, Bobby undertook a massive investigation of organized criminal infiltration of the U.S. labor movement. This effort became something of a war and ultimately focused on "getting" James R. "Jimmy" Hoffa, the president of the International Brotherhood of Teamsters. After initial indifference, Bobby ultimately became the administration's voice and conscience on civil rights matters (though he continued the eavesdropping on Martin Luther King Jr.).

Bringing Your Most Trusted Confidantes with You

So indispensable had Bobby made himself by the time the Kennedys moved into the White House there was no question that he would join the administration. While JFK later tried to claim that Joe Sr. had insisted on the controversial decision to secure the attorney general's post for the younger Kennedy, a more dispassionate reading of the record makes it clear that this was the plan from the start. RFK had to be in the cabinet so he could report directly to his brother, and none of the other major cabinet departments was a plausible fit for him.

For all his obvious closeness to his brother, however, JFK never hesitated to reject his advice, and he did not include Bobby in all major decisions. He also had to throw cold water on some of Bobby's wilder ideas. When a political crisis in the Dominican Republic briefly threatened to install a pro-Castro government there, Bobby urged U.S. military intervention as the only acceptable course of action. (He even toyed with the idea of setting off a bomb in the U.S. embassy to provide the necessary pretext for invasion.)

When Undersecretary of State Chester Bowles objected to this buccaneering stance, Bobby called him a "gutless coward." Bowles took the dispute to the president. "Who is in charge here?" Bowles demanded. "You are," JFK replied. To which Bowles said, "Then will you please tell that to your brother?"

RFK's influence was felt throughout the government. Almost any bureaucrat anywhere could sometimes pick up his phone and hear the attorney general barking at the other end. "Little brother is watching you" became something of an administration in-joke.

The occasional blowup notwithstanding, RFK never lost his place in his brother's affections. Bobby was even able to confront his brother—albeit unsuccessfully—about the back treatments he was receiving from New York physician Max Jacobson, who was sometimes referred to as a Dr. Feelgood. "I don't care if it's horse-piss," JFK famously told his brother. "It works."

Bobby Kennedy gave his brother something indispensable to a leader—a close and loyal ally who will give you unfettered advice with no eye toward gaining your favor. It doesn't have to be your brother, but if you have a close and loyal associate available to you, consider yourself lucky. Successful business leaders often have a "Bobby" of their own who moves with them up the company ladder or even along with them to a position with a new company.

Lyndon B. Johnson: The Fifth Wheel

To the Kennedy White House, Vice President Lyndon B. Johnson was not unlike the ornery but wealthy bachelor uncle who presents himself at your doorstep unexpectedly and announces he has arrived for an extended stay. Despite your almost desperate efforts to make him feel welcome, the uncle's quirky habits and general contrariness grate on everyone's nerves, but he has something you want badly, so you don't dare ask him to leave.

The bluff, plain-spoken Texan was a poor fit with the smooth-faced "cool" of the New Frontier. Johnson was chosen as vice president to deliver Texas to the Kennedy ticket in 1960 and, once that was accomplished, his role became largely superfluous. It sometimes taxed all of Kennedy's ingenuity to keep a man of such ego, talent, and ambition suitably occupied in a job that fundamentally required him merely to sit and wait for the unmentionable.

The former Senate majority leader had taken the post of vice president in the belief that he could make what was traditionally a powerless post into a power center. He was swiftly disabused of that notion at the first meeting he attended of the Senate Democratic caucus in his new position. Johnson tried to take over and chair the meeting but was forced to yield to Montana Senator Mike Mansfield, his successor as majority leader. The Senate Democrats had suffered under Johnson's authoritarian style of leadership and were well glad to be rid of him. The rebuff stung Johnson deeply; he never attended another caucus meeting and seemed uninterested in using his experience to move Kennedy's program on Capitol Hill.

Trying to Make the Outsider Feel Welcome

Kennedy worked hard to keep Johnson "on board," repeatedly shooting down rumors that LBJ would be dumped from the ticket in 1964. Whereas previous vice presidents had their offices on Capitol Hill (Richard Nixon's was across the hall from Kennedy's own), LBJ became the first vice president to be given a White House office, a privilege since accorded all of his successors. Kennedy also ensured that Johnson remained in charge of federal patronage in Texas, an arrangement that caused considerable friction with Texas Democratic Senator Ralph Yarborough. Kennedy's fateful November 1963 visit to Dallas was made, in part, to smooth over this controversy before the 1964 election.

Johnson chaired Kennedy's Committee on Equal Employment Opportunity, as well as the Space Council. He also represented Kennedy at numerous functions at home and around the world. He journeyed to South Vietnam early in the administration, to West Berlin after the wall went up, and to Pope John XXIII's funeral.

But all of that was poor compensation for the power and prestige Johnson had left behind on Capitol Hill. Worse was the often-condescending attitude of Kennedy White House staffers toward Johnson, who not infrequently addressed him as "Lyndon" rather than "Mr. Vice President." Johnson often discovered after the fact that he had not been invited to meetings on subjects in which he had an interest, such as civil rights. He once attended a meeting only to discover that aides had failed to take account of his presence and make enough copies of the necessary documents. Johnson had to read them over an aide's shoulder.

This was minor league, however, compared to the fire-and-water relationship Johnson had with Bobby Kennedy. Bobby made no secret of his opposition to Johnson's selection in 1960, and he never seemed to have warmed to him. For his part, LBJ returned the bile. "I don't like that little son-of-a-bitch and I never will," Johnson said after an encounter with the president's brother. He was as good as his word. Their relationship was essentially antagonistic until RFK's assassination in 1968.

JFK's efforts at placating Johnson, however, did not go far enough. He never truly took Johnson into his confidence, excluding him from some of the most dramatic moments of the Kennedy administration, including the Bay of Pigs and the desegregation crisis at the University of Mississippi. When Johnson's advice *was* sought on a major decision, notably on the coup to overthrow Ngo Dinh Diem, the South Vietnamese president, it was often rejected.

Part of the problem was simply the nature of the office he held. The president/vice president relationship is almost inherently a difficult one: Vice presidents cannot be fired, as can cabinet members and other aides, and they frequently hail from a section of the party or country that is at odds with the president (although subsequent presidents have demonstrated that the relationship can be effective, notably George W. Bush and Richard "Dick" Cheney). Failing to truly integrate Johnson into his team was one of Kennedy's conspicuous management failures.

There are times when you will have to work with somebody not of your own choosing or not even to your liking. You have to make the best of such situations. Assuming the other person is competent, give her important tasks to handle and ask for her advice when appropriate. Try to defuse explosive or unpleasant relationships between these people and your closer advisers.

The "Irish Mafia": Extraordinary Loyalty

"You see Kenny there?" John F. Kennedy said, motioning to the sleeping figure of Kenneth P. O'Donnell aboard *Caroline,* the 1960 campaign plane.

"If I woke him up and asked him to jump out of this plane for me, he'd do it. You don't find that kind of loyalty easily."

Of his personal secretary, Evelyn Lincoln, Kennedy once commented that if he told her that he had just cut off Jacqueline's head and would like to dispose of it, Lincoln would appear immediately with a hatbox of the appropriate size.

Kennedy was indeed a man who inspired tremendous loyalty from those he gathered around himself. On the surface, this seems a little hard to understand. The Kennedys were not known for paying particularly well. Expressions of gratitude for a job well done were, as Theodore Sorensen admitted, "rather rare." In addition to their normal political and administrative duties, staff members also were expected to perform numerous "extras" the Kennedys insisted upon, most notoriously, facilitating the president's extramarital affairs.

But loyalty there was, and it proved extraordinarily durable.

Partly, the loyalty was tribal. Kennedy was the first president not to have a drop of English or Dutch blood in his veins. From the beginning of his political career in 1946, he had gathered around him aides bound to him by ties of blood and ethnic kinship, tempered by service in war. The closest of these were the so-called Irish Mafia: Kenneth O'Donnell, David Powers, and Lawrence O'Brien.

The Stern Gatekeeper

A veteran of the World War II U.S. Army Air Corps, O'Donnell started off as a Harvard friend of Robert Kennedy. They met while trying out for the football team together. It was the beginning of a relationship that would endure until Bobby's death in 1968. O'Donnell left Boston College Law School to work in Jack's first Senate campaign and carved out a role for himself as the keeper of Jack's schedule.

In the White House, his office was right next to the president's and he served as a stern gatekeeper, keeping away from Kennedy all those without a real need to see the president. (When even cabinet members complained that they had trouble getting past O'Donnell, Kennedy instituted a "safety valve" by directing them to enter through Evelyn Lincoln's office, thus bypassing the aide.)

O'Donnell's acerbic attitude sometimes caused trouble, especially his ill-concealed dislike for Vice President Lyndon B. Johnson. This grew so serious at one point that Kennedy felt the need to personally confront his aide on the matter.

"I just want you to know one thing," the president told O'Donnell. "Lyndon Johnson was majority leader of the United States Senate, he was elected to office several times by the people. He was the number-one Democrat in the United States, elected by us to be our leader. I'm president of the United States. He doesn't like that. He thinks he's ten times more important than I am; he happens to be that kind of fellow. But he thinks you're nothing but a clerk. Just keep that right in your mind. . . .

"Elected officers have a code," Kennedy continued, "and no matter whether they like each other or hate each other. . . . You have never been elected to anything by anybody, and you are dealing with a very insecure, sensitive man with a huge ego. I want you literally to kiss his ass from one end of Washington to the other. . . ."

But O'Donnell's tough-guy reputation (the Secret Service was alarmed to discover that he carried a gun) also came in handy. He could pick up a telephone and threaten a politician or a contributor with a loss of patronage or access if he did not fall into line. Kennedy himself could then call and smooth any ruffled feathers. Thus, the president and the aide functioned as an effective "good cop, bad cop" team.

The Day-to-Day "Pal"

Dave Powers was a milder sort. With Kennedy from 1946, he served essentially as Kennedy's general factotum, coat holder, and "body watcher." During campaigns, Powers would rise before dawn and make his way to the candidate's hotel room. He came up with an effective patter to get the groggy candidate out of bed for another endless day of events and appearances.

"I wonder where Dick Nixon is today?" Powers would say aloud as he opened the blinds to admit sunlight into the dark room. "I wonder how many factory gates he's been to already, how many hands he's shaken. . . ." Kennedy sometimes responded to this routine with what Powers delicately described as Navy language, but it got Kennedy's gears oiled up and spinning.

In the White House, Powers functioned as Camelot's court jester, keeping

JFK laughing with a steady stream of jokes, baseball trivia, and malapropisms (e.g., "He's our kind of Shah," and "Is this the real Mikoyan?"). If a guest showed signs of wearing out his welcome in the president's presence, Powers could always be relied on to escort the visitor from the Oval Office without his even realizing that he was being given "the hook."

Powers's devotion to his boss was limitless. After the assassination, he would visit the house Jacqueline Kennedy and her family occupied in Georgetown to read to John Jr. To the end of his life in 1998, he spent almost every day at the John F. Kennedy Library in Boston, speaking to the hordes of tourists and answering questions from visiting scholars.

The Political Pro

Lawrence O'Brien was a political technician. It was he who devised the system, employed in Jack's 1952 Senate campaign, of creating a Kennedy statewide organization completely separate from and independent of the state Democratic party. In the White House, he served as liaison to Congress, centralizing that function in the White House for the first time. Before O'Brien, cabinet departments and federal agencies were largely responsible for their own relations with Capitol Hill. O'Brien ended that practice, instituting weekly meetings with congressional liaison officials from the rest of the government to ensure that the entire administration was putting forth the same view.

The "Irish Mafia," as the newspaper came to call these aides—not always kindly—were Kennedy's Sancho Panzas, people with seemingly small but crucial roles to play in helping an executive get where he wants to be. Never let charges of cronyism or the like deter you from having people around that you know well and implicitly trust. It is essential that you have such people around you for your own peace of mind.

The White House Staff: Kennedy's Eyes, Ears, and Hands

John F. Kennedy largely created the modern White House staff. Although the concept of White House aides acting as a power center separate and distinct from the cabinet dated back to at least Franklin D. Roosevelt, it was

Kennedy who finally dismantled the idea of "cabinet government." After Kennedy, White House aides routinely became important figures in their own right.

It's not that Kennedy's White House staff was larger than previous ones; indeed, in many respects, it was smaller. Unlike Dwight Eisenhower and his powerful chief of staff, Sherman Adams, Kennedy had no real chief of staff. In contrast to Eisenhower's military-style "chain of command" government, Kennedy preferred to describe his White House as a wheel, with him at the center and the spokes radiating outward. He disliked bureaucracy intensely and wanted a small, more fluid organization that could respond to his needs quickly and without a lot of fanfare.

The reasons for the increased profile of the White House staff were rooted in how large the government had grown since the 1920s. It was humanly impossible for cabinet secretaries, let alone the president, to know all that was going on within their huge departments. The cabinet members could make recommendations on major issues, but they could not see how those recommendations might impact the government as a whole. Also, cabinet departments would inevitably disagree with one another on the best course of action to take. (This was especially true of the Department of State and the Defense Department.) It was the president who would have to decide. To make those decisions, he would need the independent judgment of aides who, in Sorensen's words, "represented his personal ways, means, and purposes."

When a Leader Can't Be Everywhere at Once

Thus, the two dozen or so aides who represented the core White House staff in the Kennedy years acted as JFK's eyes, ears, and hands. As Sorensen described it: "They could talk with legislators, bureaucrats, newsmen, experts, cabinet members, and politicians—serve on interdepartmental task forces—review papers and draft speeches, letters, and other documents—spot problems before they were crises and possibilities before they were proposals—screen requests for legislation, executive orders, jobs, appointments with the president, patronage, and presidential speeches—and bear his messages, look out for his interests, carry out his orders, and make certain his decisions were executed."

In turn, they scrutinized what was coming out of the cabinet departments, ensuring that Kennedy's personal stamp was placed on policies likely to be popular while distancing him from those that would not. Harvard presidential historian Richard Neustadt, who functioned as an unofficial adviser to the Kennedy White House, summarized the role of the White House aides this way: They were to get "information to his mind and key decisions to his hands reliably enough and soon enough to give him room for maneuver."

Kennedy's staff members were young, most still in their thirties. (The cabinet members were young too, but mostly in their mid-forties.) Although most had portfolios concerning specific issues, they could find themselves being tasked to work on anything if they happened to be around when Kennedy wanted something looked into.

Kennedy's "Intellectual Blood Bank"

Theodore C. Sorensen was probably Kennedy's closest aide outside of his family and the old Irish Mafia circle. Sorensen was looking for a new challenge. Raised in the prairie populist tradition of Nebraska independent Senator George Norris, Sorensen was at first concerned that the new Massachusetts senator was too conservative for his taste. But shortly after the 1952 election, Sorensen agreed to sign on for a one-year trial period. The "trial" lasted until November 22, 1963. Over that decade Sorensen drove himself so relentlessly on Kennedy's behalf that his marriage collapsed and his health was put at risk. (See Chapter 6 for more on Sorensen and speechwriting.)

Sorensen oversaw the workings of Lee White (handling natural resources, housing, education, and civil rights), Meyer "Mike" Feldman (writing on most other domestic issues, such as agriculture, as well as drafting executive orders), and Richard Goodwin (who left the speechwriting staff in 1961 to become assistant secretary of state for Inter-American Affairs). He also oversaw the work of Harris Wofford, the liaison to the civil rights movement until he moved over to help run the Peace Corps.

According to Sorensen, the primary role of the speechwriting staff was to be skeptical and critical, not merely another layer of bureaucracy. They were too deferential to the supposed "experts" during the Bay of Pigs and learned their lesson afterward.

A Wide Range of Staffers

Another prominent senior staffer was Harvard historian Arthur Schlesinger Jr., who interrupted his massive, multivolume history of Franklin D. Roosevelt's presidency (never to resume it, as it turned out) to serve as the administration's in-house historian and point of contact for all-too-frequently disgruntled liberals.

Press Secretary Pierre Salinger had worked as a journalist before joining Robert Kennedy as an investigator in the Senate in 1957. Salinger's rotund physique caused him to stand out among the generally slim New Frontiersmen and made him the butt of jokes, but his good-natured bonhomie kept Kennedy laughing. "Dammit, Salinger, you've fouled us up again!" would be Kennedy's mock rebuke to his press secretary at the end of a difficult day. He was handicapped in his job by not really being a member of Kennedy's inner circle. (In addition to being his own chief of staff, Kennedy often effectively functioned as his own press secretary, calling journalists himself when he had major news.) Salinger's major contribution was his brainstorm of having Kennedy give live televised press conferences, which proved immensely popular.

The national security adviser's position had existed for a decade and half before the Kennedy administration, but it was mostly an administrative post, designed to filter reports from the departments of state and defense, as well as the CIA, for the president's consideration. Under Kennedy's National Security Adviser (NSA), McGeorge Bundy, a Republican and former dean of Harvard College, it became a powerful policy-making post for the first time and remains so today.

Bundy's power grew because of JFK's disenchantment with the U.S. State Department. "Dammit, Bundy and I get more done in one day than they do in six months at the State Department," Kennedy groused at one point. After the Bay of Pigs disaster, Kennedy brought Bundy "across the street" from the Old Executive Office Building to the West Wing. A special center was established with sophisticated communications equipment that brought reports from embassies and military bases from all over the world directly into the White House. Eventually, this center would be dubbed the Situation Room and would be portrayed in innumerable spy novels and action films as the nerve center of the U.S. government in world crises.

With such independent access to diplomatic, intelligence, and military information, the national security adviser thus had the wherewithal to be a power in his own right. This happened despite the fact that Bundy was not a foreign policy expert and seemed more comfortable in the role of a skilled adjudicator than a strong advocate. He was a strong anticommunist, but tolerated and even encouraged dissent from the conventional wisdom, as long as the argument could be made succinctly and intelligently on paper.

Unlike previous holders of his post, Bundy saw Kennedy frequently, usually several times a day and without an appointment. He largely displaced the quiet, unassuming Secretary of State Dean Rusk as Kennedy's principal foreign policy adviser. "No president kept a tighter rein on foreign policy," says James N. Giglio in *The Presidency of John F. Kennedy,* "yet few presidents learned to listen to as many divergent viewpoints."

A Loyal Boss

"I can't afford to confine myself to one set of advisers," Kennedy said to Richard Neustadt during the transition between the Kennedy and Eisenhower administrations. "If I did that, I would be on *their* leading strings."

But Kennedy was loyal to those who were loyal to him, which is a crucial element of leadership. When Sorensen was attacked for some comments he made on a trip to his home state of Nebraska, Kennedy characteristically defused the controversy with a quip: "That's what happens when you permit a speechwriter to write his own speech!" In private, when Sorensen apologized for any embarrassment he might have caused his boss, Kennedy flashed his famous grin and said, "I don't mind. They can criticize *you* all they like!"

Kennedy's advice on advisers holds true for any kind of leadership position. You need a wide range of trusted advisers who will give you their honest opinions. They can and should come from everywhere—outsiders as well as insiders—and they should have no fear of speaking their minds.

The Kennedy Cabinet and Administration: Picking from Here and There

Choosing the White House staff was a relatively simple affair. The vast majority of them were people Kennedy had known and worked with for years.

Putting together a cabinet and an administration to actually run the government was not nearly as straightforward.

"Jesus Christ, this one wants that, that one wants this," the president-elect
grumbled as he shuffled papers in the backseat of his car on the way to play
golf with his father in Palm Beach after the election. "Goddamn it, you can't
satisfy any of these people. I don't know what I am going to do about it all."

Turning around from the front seat, Joe Sr. said, "Jack, if you don't want
the job, you don't have to take it. They're still counting votes up in Cook
County [outside Chicago]."

Putting the Right People in Place

Kennedy believed that people *are* policy. You put the right man in the
right place and let him do the job. If he failed, you put in someone else. His
first decision in this regard came in August 1960, when he named his personal lawyer, Clark Clifford, a veteran of the Truman White House, to guide
the potential transition to a Kennedy administration.

"I don't want to wake up on November 9 and have to ask myself: 'What
in the world do I do now?'" he said to Clifford.

Clifford prepared the ground well, with stacks of memos and reports from
himself, as well as college professors, national security experts, and management consultants. Still, no amount of preparation can adequately account for
the chaos that inevitably confronts someone about to embark on the world's
most challenging job. Simply finding the best man for a particular position is
only part of the process. Considerations of patronage, potential conflicts of
interest, and political calculation went into the mix as well.

(And without exception, they were *men*; Kennedy became the first president since Herbert Hoover not to feature a woman in his cabinet or, indeed,
in any prominent role. There never really has been any adequate explanation
for this oversight, other than a general sense that the "locker room" atmosphere of the Kennedy administration simply wasn't conducive to female
members. This wasn't the only example of a curious myopia in this regard
on Kennedy's part. He had planned to name housing expert Robert C.
Weaver as the first black cabinet member but was thwarted when Congress
refused to create a cabinet-level housing department. He briefly considered
naming Weaver as the secretary of the U.S. Department of Health, Education, and Welfare after Abraham Ribicoff resigned but worried it might ap-

pear "racism in reverse." Kennedy had asked Representative William Dawson, a black congressman from Chicago, to become postmaster general, but only after first ascertaining that Dawson was not interested. Otherwise, Kennedy made little effort in this area.)

Putting a Personal Stamp on the Key Choices

No president, or top executive, can possibly identify all the people he will need. But for the top fifty or so positions in the government, Kennedy wanted his personal stamp on the process. Following the election, Kennedy simply sat down and began interviewing people, often for hours at a stretch. For a man as fundamentally restless by nature as Kennedy, this was often a considerable strain. During one interview with an applicant to be agriculture secretary, the president-elect fell asleep.

Kennedy supplemented the interviews with a steady stream of phone calls. "What do you know about this man?" he would ask. "How well do you know him—is he just a lot of talk?" The press was full of speculation about various names, some of them no doubt leaked by Kennedy in an effort to gauge public reaction, some of them certainly placed by the subjects themselves, in order to raise their own profiles. Occasionally, Kennedy used the press to prod recalcitrant candidates. He leaked word that he had appointed Adlai Stevenson U.S. ambassador to the United Nations, for example, in order to make it that much harder for the disappointed Stevenson—who yearned to be secretary of state—to refuse.

Recognizing Good People Wherever They Are

As with so much of Kennedy's modus operandi, serendipity played its part in his selection of his larger team. Reading an article in *Time* magazine about Robert S. McNamara, who had just become the first nonfamily member to be named president of the Ford Motor Company, Kennedy was immediately intrigued. The fact that McNamara was a Republican didn't bother him at all. He liked that McNamara was one of the "whiz kids" who had turned Ford around in the years following World War II, when he and nine other U.S. Army Air Corps veterans uniquely offered themselves to industry as a "package." They were financial disciplinarians who brought quantitative analysis, the science of modern management, to Ford. Another interesting tidbit was McNamara's refusal to live in the automotive "ghettoes" of Grosse

Pointe or Bloomfield Hills, making his home instead in the university town of Ann Arbor.

This was the kind of fresh leadership Kennedy was looking for at the Pentagon, the world's largest office building containing the world's largest bureaucracy, and the problem child of the federal government. From its creation in 1947, the Department of Defense had proved seemingly impervious to real management. Its first secretary, James V. Forrestal, suffered a nervous breakdown and committed suicide after less than two years of relentless effort to get his arms around the department. George C. Marshall, a brilliant career soldier who proved one of the nation's greatest secretaries of state, walked away from the Pentagon in befuddlement after barely a year in 1951.

The initial interview did not go well. The first question McNamara asked Kennedy was the equivalent of waving a red flag in front of a bull: He asked the president-elect whether he indeed wrote *Profiles in Courage* himself. It is a tribute to Kennedy's determination to have McNamara join his government that he ignored this question and then offered him his pick of the Treasury Department or the Defense Department.

Taken somewhat aback, McNamara protested that he didn't know anything about government. "I don't know how to be president, either," Kennedy responded. "We'll learn together." McNamara asked for time to consider the matter. After studying everything he could get his hands on, he returned a week later and said he preferred the Defense Department, provided he had right of final approval for all department appointments. Kennedy accepted immediately.

Author David Frum has described McNamara as the sort of figure who would have fascinated the tragedians of ancient Greece. His subsequent career was all but consumed by the Vietnam War, for which he rightly bears considerable responsibility. His "systems analysis" approach simply didn't take account of Ho Chi Minh's determination to extend communism from North to South Vietnam. The United States was riven by the effort to stop Ho, and nearly 60,000 Americans died as a result. This failure disturbed McNamara deeply. In his final appearance as secretary of defense in 1968—it has never been clearly established whether he resigned or was fired—he all but suffered a public breakdown.

These facts should not completely obscure McNamara's very real achievements at the Defense Department, however. In almost every respect, he fulfilled Kennedy's expectations. Aside from Attorney General Robert Kennedy, he was the New Frontier's dominant cabinet personality. His energy and intensity radiated throughout the Pentagon and no one doubted he was in charge.

McNamara presided over the buildup of U.S. conventional forces to deter Soviet aggression. In the nuclear realm, he helped create the "flexible response doctrine" that, in Kennedy's words, gave him choices between "inglorious retreat or unlimited retaliation." He built up the U.S. Army and Navy Special Forces, in the teeth of opposition from the top brass, to carry out "unconventional warfare" in distant corners of the world. (Their record in Vietnam was one of the few unalloyed successes of that conflict, and they have performed at the cutting edge in the current War on Terror.) He also made the helicopter an integral part of the army's arsenal, where it remains today. He was also a force in creating the National Reconnaissance Office, which operates the nation's network of spy satellites.

One Department Where Kennedy Wanted Control

Identifying a secretary of state was more difficult, in part because this was an area where Kennedy did *not* want strong leadership. Unlike the Defense Department, the U.S. Department of State had had a series of powerful secretaries from both parties since the end of World War II, including Democrat Dean Acheson and Republican John Foster Dulles. Kennedy didn't want a figure of such stature because he intended to function largely as his own secretary of state.

"Aren't you going to choose Stevenson?" exclaimed Dean Rusk when Kennedy sounded him out about the secretary's post. (Rusk, who was president of the Rockefeller Foundation, was referring to 1952 and 1956 Democratic presidential nominee Adlai Stevenson.) "No," Kennedy replied. "Adlai might forget who's the president and who's the secretary of state."

The one major personality Kennedy considered for the post was Senate Foreign Relations Committee Chairman J. William Fulbright of Arkansas, who badly wanted the job. "It would be nice to have someone in the cabinet I actually knew," Kennedy mused aloud. But Robert Kennedy cautioned that Fulbright's prosegregationist stand would send a bad signal to the newly independent countries of Africa. Fulbright's name was crossed off the list.

The quiet, unassuming Rusk, a veteran of the State Department during the Truman administration, seemed to be almost everyone's second choice and was thus offered the job almost by process of elimination. This caught him by surprise in more ways than one. Federal government salaries were absurdly low in those days (Sorensen discovered that the superintendent of schools in a small Missouri town made more than a cabinet member). He protested that he could not afford to give up his $60,000 annual salary at the Rockefeller Foundation to become a $25,000-a-year cabinet member.

"All right," the startled president-elect responded. "I'm going down to Palm Beach tomorrow. You come down." By the time Rusk got to Florida, Kennedy had spoken to the Rockefellers and secured for him a financial severance package that would more than make up for the lost salary. Rusk was on board.

Rusk, however, turned out to be something of a disappointment to Kennedy. If anything, he was *too* deferential. Quiet, courtly, cautious, and noncommittal in his public statements, he was virtually the only member of Kennedy's circle who insisted that Kennedy call him "Mr. Secretary" and not by his first name. So discreet was the secretary that Kennedy joked that when he and Rusk were alone, Rusk would still whisper there were one too many people present.

Nevertheless, Kennedy never warmed to the State Department. It seemed to take forever to answer his questions and it rarely seemed the source of creative or even interesting ideas. Rusk was frequently mentioned as a likely casualty in any Kennedy cabinet shake-up. But the shake-up never came, and Rusk stayed on until the last day of the Johnson administration in January 1969. The one enduring contribution Kennedy made to the State Department was to seek out ambassadors with specific knowledge of the language, culture, and politics of the country to which he was accredited. (Edwin O. Reischauer, the ambassador to Japan, for example, was Tokyo born and a scholar of Japan.)

Filling Out the Roster

No one had to tell John F. Kennedy that business and financial types were wary of Democrats in the White House. Kennedy's own father was virtually the only business leader of any stature to support Franklin D. Roosevelt in 1932. That meant JFK had to tread warily when it came to choosing a treasury secretary. Ultimately, he tapped Eisenhower's undersecretary of state, C. Douglas Dillon—yet another Republican—to take the job.

"How can you do this?" protested Tennessee Senator Albert Gore Sr., Kennedy's former seatmate in the Senate, when he heard about the offer to Dillon. "If you want someone rich from Wall Street, pick Averell Harriman."

"Too old," Kennedy averred. He wanted the New Frontier to project a youthful image. (Bobby had earlier expressed his belief that men much over forty "lose their zeal.") He also told others that he needed someone "who could call those Wall Street people by their first names." Gore thought Dillon too easygoing to sell dramatic economic policies. Ironically, Dillon would push hard for the dramatic Kennedy tax cuts, which Gore himself would oppose. Nevertheless, to "balance" Dillon, Kennedy chose liberal economist Walter Heller of the University of Minnesota as his chairman of the Council of Economic Advisers.

Kennedy had little interest in the lesser cabinet posts, filling them largely with proven elected officials. The secretary position at the U.S. Department of Health, Education, and Welfare went to former Connecticut Governor Abraham Ribicoff. The Agriculture Department went to former Minnesota Governor Orville Freeman; the Commerce Department to former North Carolina Governor Luther Hodges; and the Interior Department to Stewart Udall, a former congressman. Former AFL-CIO official Arthur Goldberg was installed as secretary of the Labor Department, and insurance executive/ lawyer J. Edward Day as postmaster general.

None of this meant these men were unimportant. It has already been noted, in Chapter 7, that Hodges played a key role in moving the Kennedy economic program forward, and the energetic Arthur Goldberg made himself so valuable at the Department of Labor that Kennedy was reluctant to appoint him as an associate justice to the U.S. Supreme Court in September 1962 because he felt he was losing his "right arm."

Making It All Fit Together

The cabinet was filled out, but the job wasn't finished yet. Putting an administration together is not unlike a Rubik's Cube puzzle, with everything having to fit together just right. There were subcabinet posts, especially in the State Department and Defense Department, in which Kennedy had a particular interest. Unfortunately, that interest sometimes didn't coincide with those of the men he appointed to head the departments. This was especially true in the case of Robert McNamara.

Paul Nitze, one of the foreign policy/defense intellectuals who were making names for themselves in Washington at that time, asked to be named deputy secretary of defense. McNamara, however, had extracted from Kennedy that agreement about having final authority over all Pentagon appointments and vetoed Nitze. Shortly after that, Kennedy leaked to the *New York Times* his intention of naming Franklin D. Roosevelt Jr. to the position of secretary of the navy, in gratitude for the role FDR Jr. played in helping him win the crucial West Virginia primary.

"I guess I'll have to take care of him [FDR Jr.] some other way," Kennedy groaned when McNamara vetoed Roosevelt. John B. Connally, who would ride in the limousine with Kennedy in Dallas, ultimately got the job, and FDR Jr. had to be content with being made undersecretary of commerce.

Recruiting Brains Doesn't Hurt

Another distinctive feature of the Kennedy administration's personnel policy was its recruitment of serious scholars from the academy. Kennedy named a substantial number of academics, including fifteen Rhodes scholars, to major posts in his administration. They sometimes were sent to unexpected places. Harvard economist John Kenneth Galbraith, for example, was made ambassador to India. Yale economist James Tobin protested that he himself was "too ivory tower" to join the administration. "That's all right," Kennedy replied. "I'm something of an ivory tower president."

Handling the Military

The area of military leadership became a sore point for Kennedy early in his tenure. Admiral Arleigh Burke, the chief of naval operations nearly caused a diplomatic incident with the Soviet Union in the first days of the administration by proposing to give a bellicose-sounding speech. A Kennedy appointee in the Pentagon prevented that, but Burke was enraged. Kennedy was amazed at the admiral's reaction. "I used to admire these people," he marveled.

The endorsement of the Bay of Pigs disaster by the Joint Chiefs of Staff in the spring of 1961 caused Kennedy to lose faith in that institution, at least until he could change the personnel involved. He brought retired Army Gen. Maxwell D. Taylor into the White House as a personal military adviser. A dashing paratroop commander in World War II, Taylor had bitterly opposed Eisenhower's cuts in the army budget to fund nuclear weapons programs.

Taylor was more cerebral than most army generals of his era (he spoke several languages), and so he was much more in tune with Kennedy than with Eisenhower. As superintendent of West Point, Taylor had placed more emphasis on academics than athletics or physical training. "If Harvard graduated generals," one observer noted, "it would have graduated Maxwell Taylor." Robert Kennedy in particular grew fond of Taylor, even naming one of his own sons after the general. John F. Kennedy appointed Taylor chairman of the Joint Chiefs of Staff in 1962, a position he held for two years until President Lyndon B. Johnson appointed him ambassador to South Vietnam.

Kennedy, however, rarely allowed poor personal relationships to blind him to an individual's virtues. He could scarcely stand Air Force Gen. Curtis LeMay, but Kennedy promoted him to chief of staff of the U.S. Air Force, in part because McNamara had served under him in World War II and because Kennedy recognized LeMay's brilliance. Besides, LeMay was undoubtedly tough. As Richard Reeves pointed out in *President Kennedy: Profile of Power,* if the Cold War suddenly grew hot, it might be a good idea to have someone like LeMay around.

"Toughness," of the mental rather than physical variety, became something of a cliché around Washington as Kennedy moved to fill the lesser slots in his administration. One apocryphal story had a prospective appointee being asked if he knew anything about the job for which he was applying. "No," he replied, "but I'm tough!"

Here again, the diversity of Kennedy's choices is a valuable guide for any leader in building a team. Whereas your closest advisers may come from people you know to some degree, your key departments can be run by people you've never met. Above all, you must know what you are looking for in filling each post. For some positions, you need brains. For others, you need brawlers. In areas where you want to maintain control, you need people who will go along with you. For posts you are less interested in or know less about, you need strong leaders in their own right.

The "Ministry of Talent": An Assessment

Sorensen said Kennedy wanted a "ministry of talent" in assembling his team. Within the constraints imposed by politics, he largely achieved it, for the team John F. Kennedy assembled in Washington proved one of the best to have served the nation in peacetime. To a remarkable extent, Kennedy ignored geography, previous political allegiances, and party factions in seeking to staff his administration with "the best and the brightest" (a phrase that came to have ironic connotations following the Vietnam debacle).

Except for Robert Kennedy, no member of the cabinet was closely identified with Kennedy. The secretaries of state and defense were strangers to the president until after the 1960 election. The treasury secretary had actually contributed $26,000 to the campaign of Kennedy's 1960 opponent, Richard Nixon.

With the possible exception of Adlai Stevenson, Kennedy saw no reason to appease old rivals with high government posts. Religion also played no role. When Sorensen felt constrained to point out to Kennedy that his entire speechwriting staff was Jewish, JFK replied, "So what? They tell me this is the first cabinet with two Jews, too. All I care about is whether they can handle it."

"Superior ability" were Kennedy's watchwords in seeking out talent, and he found a great deal of it. As historian James N. Giglio has pointed out, the administration was remarkably free of conspicuous incompetence or corruption. Hardly anyone brought aboard in the early days by Kennedy later had to be dismissed. (A major exception was the so-called Thanksgiving Massacre at the State Department in 1961, in which Undersecretary of State Chester Bowles—a man of ideas sadly miscast in a basically administrative role—was forced to resign and numerous other officials were shuffled to different posts.)

Kennedy's open, gregarious, and idealistic public stance proved a tonic to the millions of young Americans born immediately following World War II who were looking for a challenge in life. These included a young Arkansan named Bill Clinton, who shook Kennedy's hand in the White House Rose Garden, and John Kerry, who used personal connections to be invited to meet Kennedy at the "Summer White House" in Newport, Rhode Island. NBC newsman Tim Russert recalled being inspired by Kennedy's inaugural address as a ten-year-old in Buffalo, New York. Countless others had similar experiences. To a very large extent, these people could be considered a part of JFK's "team" as well.

How to Build Your Own Team

No one gets anything done alone. You must build a team. The presidential cabinet is designed to get representatives from various groups in one room to give critical advice and insights to the president. There are representatives from the departments of state, treasury, defense, health, labor, commerce, justice, and many other key groups that are fundamental to making the country run. Similarly, in business, executive advisory boards usually have representatives from various departments such as finance, HR, IT, marketing, and other key divisions. Although this is fairly common, getting a group of people together who will give constructive criticism and work together well, while still representing the needs of their division, is difficult—yet it is extremely important to achieve. This is especially critical when breaking into a new market, product, or service area, or when making any strategic decisions.

➡ *Make sure everything fits together.* A leader not only creates an executive board, but encourages functional teams to do the same. This practice will help generate buy-in as well as keep all plans realistic. Consider, for example, IBM's approach to partnering. IBM not only has a team specializing in partnering with representatives from different parts of the company, it also insists that outside companies that want to partner with IBM do the same. How else will IBM be able to determine whether the potential partner will be a good fit or whether the plans will work?

➡ *Look for honesty and loyalty.* Don't fall into the trap of seeking "yes men." Find people who bring new ideas to the table and who will help you identify potential problems from the outset. Kennedy chose men for his team who were not afraid to speak their minds. At the same time, they were also loyal. This crucial combination will ensure that you get the best ideas possible, and a dedicated team to back them up.

➠ *Overlook personal quirks.* Don't let someone's personal quirks blind you to his or her virtues. It's tempting to leave certain personalities off advisory boards because they "hold things up" or because of personal disputes. Understand that a certain amount of dissention is necessary to create superior strategies. You need people to think outside of the box and to challenge assumptions that come out of homogeneous groups. If the people on your team are doing what you need done, overlook the rest. If the individual's quirks are particularly disruptive, you may need to reconsider. But if you end up removing that person, try to find a suitable replacement.

➠ *Choose qualified people.* Don't be afraid to bring in people who are personally close to you, but make sure they have the ability to do the job. Kennedy was able to bring in his brother Robert because he was more than loyal and trusted; he was qualified. If your people are qualified, no one will complain about unfair practices.

CHAPTER 9

Decision Making:
The Buck Stops with You

"To govern is to choose."

—JOHN F. KENNEDY

"A master of time."
—DR. JANET TRAVELL, KENNEDY'S PERSONAL PHYSICIAN,
DESCRIBING HOW JFK MANAGED HIS SCHEDULE

Leaders must make decisions all the time—it's what they do. Different leaders have different approaches to reaching decisions. Some leaders like to study short reports with specific recommendations by the key people involved in the area in question and then arrive at a decision on their own. Others prefer sitting in a room full of advisers, kicking ideas around until a consensus is reached. Still others have one or two highly trusted advisers present when all decisions are made. Some leaders go with their gut reaction to a problem and make decisions on the spot. Many executives delegate decisions—especially the smaller ones—to others; some executives want to be in on every decision, large and small.

As a leader, you must find a way of making decisions that works for you. You need to be comfortable with your decision-making process, and you should be confident in your final decisions. This doesn't mean that you can never be wrong, just that you should feel you have made the right decision based on the factors as you knew them at the time. You can't know in advance if a decision will be right or wrong or somewhere in between, but you want to feel that you have done all you can to arrive at the proper decision.

In Search of Bold Initiatives

Kennedy held an expansive view of the presidency. In a speech at the National Press Club in January 1960, he articulated the kind of presidency he envisioned:

> We will need in the sixties a president who is willing and able to summon his national constituency to its finest hour—to alert the people to our dangers and our opportunities—to demand of them the sacrifices that will be necessary.

Nine months later, in a speech in Seattle, Washington, Kennedy said:

> If the president does not move, if his party is opposed to progress, then the nation does not move—and there is no progress. But this country cannot afford to stand still in the 1960s—for the whole wide world is moving around us.

Kennedy yearned to be an "activist" president, in the mold of Abraham Lincoln, Woodrow Wilson, and Franklin D. Roosevelt, who had written their names large on the pages of history with bold presidential initiatives. But all of those men were presidents in time of war or great national calamity. Perilous though the world may have seemed to many people in the United States in the 1960s, the immediate difficulties did not approach those presented by war or the Great Depression.

Kennedy was hardly the first executive to face this conundrum. Just a decade earlier his idol, Winston S. Churchill, had returned to the premiership six years after being turned out at the end of World War II. He arrived back at 10 Downing Street determined to bring to the peacetime British government the same brand of urgency he had shown in wartime. But the "Action This Day" tabs that Churchill had slapped on so many wartime documents mostly remained in his desk drawer this time. Try as he might, the old sense of urgency just wasn't there.

Kennedy seemed fated to end up less like Franklin D. Roosevelt and more like Theodore Roosevelt, another president addicted to action and movement who found himself governing in relatively placid times.

Nonetheless, John F. Kennedy would leave his mark on the presidency. He moved the White House unquestionably to center stage in American life, making it the center of national executive decision making. Although every president since has promised a return to Eisenhower-style "cabinet government," none has ever really been able to make it stick. The modern presidency, with the White House staff functioning as the president's main advisers, is largely JFK's creation.

This chapter takes a closer look at Kennedy's executive style and how he made decisions.

Kennedy's Decision-Making Process

"Ike approved decisions," Richard Reeves writes of Kennedy's decision-making process. "Kennedy intended to make them."

Few decisions are as momentous as Abraham Lincoln's to issue the Emancipation Proclamation, or Harry Truman's to drop the atomic bomb or to send U.S. troops to Korea, or Gerald Ford's to pardon Richard Nixon. But the job of the president, or any executive (the root of the word is "execute," after all), is to make decisions.

"There are costs and risks to a program of action," Kennedy said. "But they are far less than the long-range risks and costs of comfortable inaction."

Of course, Dwight Eisenhower had a much more "hands-on" decision-making approach than almost anyone outside of his inner circle knew at the time. The many committees, councils, boards, and other bodies that festooned the Eisenhower administration were mostly a filtration system, ensuring that only the major decisions reached Eisenhower's desk. Kennedy had contempt for this approach, thinking that it limited the president's options, and he set out almost immediately to start dismantling Eisenhower's chain-of-command-style superstructure in favor of his own more fluid, less structured way of doing things.

Everyone has his own decision-making process or style. It is hard to "map" the "right" process. Kennedy's and Eisenhower's styles were shaped by their respective backgrounds. Raised in the army bureaucracy and presiding over the greatest war effort the world had ever seen, Eisenhower recreated what he was used to having and what had worked for him. Kennedy, for his part, had been a junior naval officer, for whom bureaucracy was an annoying impediment to getting things done. From his perspective, he didn't see what was so wondrous about the chain of command.

Decisions rarely devolve into choices of good versus bad. Rather, decision making is usually a matter of balancing competing alternatives, both of which offer benefits and disadvantages. Kennedy's efforts to achieve inflation-free economic growth while holding the budget deficit under control is an example of the kind of choices a president makes. A corporate executive might have to decide between continuing to fund a research project that shows great promise but is difficult to execute, and pulling the plug and funding other ideas.

Yet we all need parameters by which to make decisions. Biographer Geoffrey Perret cites a quotation from Lincoln as Kennedy's lodestar for decision making: "The true role in determining whether to embrace or reject anything is not whether it [may] have any evil in it, but whether it have more of evil than of good. . . . Almost everything, especially of government policy, is an inseparable compound of the two."

Let's examine the parts of Kennedy's decision-making process.

Creating a Loose Staff Structure and an Open-Door Policy

One of Kennedy's first decisions was to eschew a powerful chief of staff, such as Eisenhower's Sherman Adams or FDR's Admiral William Leahy. As we have seen, Kennedy relied on staffers such as Theodore Sorensen to keep the White House functioning and the paper flowing. (The cool, almost emotionless Sorensen might be likened to playing Mr. Spock to Kennedy's Captain Kirk.) Staff members generally did not need an appointment to see their chief. If the Oval Office door was ajar, they were free to enter after knocking.

Although members of the staff had portfolios, Kennedy didn't adhere to them rigidly. He might ask a staffer to work on something simply because he happened to be around. There never seems to have been an actual "staff meeting," in which all the members of the staff got together with their boss. Kennedy preferred to deal with people individually or in small groups.

As Perret has commented, Kennedy inspiration for this curiously nineteenth-century structure was probably British politics. Distrustful of experts, the British exalted the talented amateur and generalist. ("You can't beat brains" was one of Kennedy's favorite maxims.) What Kennedy was doing was creating his own organizational superstructure, one that operated parallel to the existing government structure, much as he had created his own campaign structure, independent of the Massachusetts and national Democratic parties. He wanted something that would be responsive to his needs and no one else's.

Encouraging Frank Communication

Kennedy had an almost insatiable curiosity and desire for more information. The problem, once he became president, was that people naturally are less likely to give their frank and honest opinion. The Oval Office is, by its nature, intimidating (like any boss's office only more so); getting people to speak freely in such an atmosphere is a challenge. Kennedy worked hard at it. "The president is a fellow who has a foot-long needle in you all the time," remarked Budget Director David Bell.

How well he succeeded is open to some debate, but there is at least one occasion where Kennedy unquestionably did get a candid opinion: from Winthrop Brown, the ambassador to Laos, in February 1961. Preventing Laos from falling to a communist insurgency was Kennedy's first important foreign policy challenge. Eisenhower had urged him to use U.S. troops. Kennedy badly wanted on-the-spot information. After a few pleasantries, he and Brown got down to business. The president began hitting the ambassador with rapid-fire questions about the situation in that landlocked Asian country about which outsiders—including Kennedy himself—knew almost nothing.

"What kind of people are these people?" Kennedy asked, reeling off a list of names of the various faction leaders.

Uncomfortable with such questions, Brown took refuge in repeating what

U.S. policy toward Laos had been under Eisenhower. JFK immediately cut him off.

"That's not what I asked you," Kennedy said. "I said, 'What do *you* think—*you,* the ambassador?'"

Brown recalled later that he took this as a license to pour out his heart to the president.

"Laos is hopeless," Brown declared, in a comment that probably was more candid than Kennedy was expecting. "It's just a series of lines on a map. Fewer than half the people speak Lao. They're charming, indolent, enchanting people, but they're just not very vigorous. . . . The king is a total zero."

They spoke for nearly an hour, longer than Kennedy normally met with anyone. Exactly what impact his conversation with Brown had on his policy toward Laos is uncertain, but it probably contributed to Kennedy's efforts to find a nonmilitary solution.

Another way Kennedy found to encourage candor was in his dealings with the Joint Chiefs of Staff. Following the Bay of Pigs disaster, Kennedy heard that some members of the Joint Chiefs had had doubts about the operation, but they were hesitant to voice them in the presence of their fellow chiefs. When Kennedy solicited their advice in later years, he usually asked each chief for his written opinion before meeting with them as a group.

Not that frankness was always valued in Kennedy's presence. If the subject matter was unwelcome, he could turn icy in an instant.

Less than a month into the administration, for instance, Kennedy was forced to endure a meeting with the top officials of the Americans for Democratic Action (ADA), the country's flagship liberal organization. Kennedy disliked the group—he had never joined it himself—because he thought its politics emotional and unrealistic. His stereotype was instantly confirmed when one member of the delegation urged Kennedy to undertake a massive public-spending program to bring down unemployment, an idea that had no hope of succeeding in Congress.

Kennedy deflected the proposal gently. But then Joseph Rauh, the general counsel of the United Auto Workers, pressed JFK to take a more aggressive stance on civil rights for black Americans. Kennedy's demeanor, which had been relaxed and open to this point, hardened almost instantly. "Absolutely not," he snapped. "It's a totally different thing. Your criticism on civil rights is wrong."

He also elicited information in writing. JFK was an inveterate writer of memos and he could dictate several dozen per day. They often took the form of questions about something he had just heard. For example, when his friend Florida Senator George Smathers urged a prohibition on the importation of Cuban agricultural goods into the United States, Kennedy sent a memo to National Security Adviser McGeorge Bundy:

> What is [Undersecretary of State] George Ball's judgment of this? Would it save us valuable dollars in the gold reserves? Would it make things more difficult for Castro? Would it be in the public interest?

The telephone, too, was an extension of Kennedy's decision-making process. He spent considerable time calling people who had the information he needed or who might be the logjam in a decision he had made or wanted to make. "I think there is a great tendency in government to have papers stay on desks too long," he explained. "The president can't administer a department, but he can be a stimulant."

Mastering Meeting Management

Nowhere was Kennedy's White House–centered decision-making approach more evident, however, than with regard to the way he used the cabinet. Under Eisenhower, the cabinet acted something like a corporate board of directors, meeting weekly and framing important decisions.

As with most formal meetings, Kennedy found them far less productive than he liked. He thought the discussions often meandered into irrelevancies and allowed the various cabinet members, especially of the lesser departments, to simply lobby for their favorite initiatives. Under Kennedy, the cabinet met much less frequently as a body, rarely more than once a month, and sometimes not even that often. He came to think of the meetings as a waste of time. "Why should the postmaster general sit there and listen to a discussion of the problems of Laos?" Kennedy asked.

To show how bare-bones such meetings became, Sorensen reproduced in his memoirs the full agenda for the December 10, 1962, cabinet meeting:

1. Review of Foreign Situation—The Secretary of State

2. Review of Economic Situation and Outlook—Honorable Walter Heller

3. Status Report on 1963 Legislative Program—Honorable T. C. Sorensen

Kennedy much preferred to meet with the cabinet members alone or in small groups. "If we have a problem involving labor management," Kennedy said, "it is much better for me to meet with Secretary [Luther] Hodges from Commerce and Secretary [Arthur] Goldberg from Labor. I think we will find the cabinet perhaps more important than it has ever been, but cabinet meetings not as important."

So, although the Kennedy cabinet certainly had strong personalities— notably, Robert McNamara, C. Douglas Dillon, and Bobby Kennedy—the cabinet as an institution went into what appears to be final eclipse with the Kennedy administration. JFK tended to reserve its meetings for matters of general concern, such as the budget, legislative strategy, or the attitude of business toward the administration. The cabinet's days as a center of decision, however, were done. The government had simply grown too large and complex for the cabinet to function as the intimate body that had advised Washington, Jefferson, and Lincoln. From the Kennedy administration on, policy would be made by a combination of White House staffers, the cabinet members directly involved, and other advisers as the president saw fit.

Needless to say, this state of affairs did not sit well with some cabinet members, especially since many of them—generally those with domestic responsibilities—were now required to report to Kennedy through the White House staff itself. Commerce Secretary Luther Hodges, Postmaster General J. Edward Day, and Agriculture Secretary Orville Freeman, for example, had to go through Meyer "Mike" Feldman of Sorensen's staff. Health, Education, and Welfare (HEW) Secretary Abraham Ribicoff reported to Sorensen himself. These staffers had the authority, in most cases, to speak for Kennedy and decide what would and wouldn't be brought to the president's attention. If a cabinet member insisted, the matter could be taken to Kennedy personally, but cabinet secretaries soon learned that the president rarely overruled his staff in favor of the "permanent government," of which the cabinet members were representatives.

Some cabinet members learned to work within this system. Secretary of the Interior Stewart Udall, for example, was philosophical about his relative lack of access. "Kennedy was not terribly interested in natural resources and didn't really know much about the problems of conservation," Udall told Lewis J. Paper, author of *The Promise and the Performance: The Leadership of John F. Kennedy.* "Interior was simply not among his major priorities. But I felt I had broad discretion to act, and he gave my efforts strong support whenever I needed it."

Others, however, could not. HEW Secretary Abraham Ribicoff, in particular, felt he was little more than a "lackey," since he would call the White House to speak to Kennedy on a matter the secretary considered important and he would be called back by Sorensen.

Ribicoff left in early 1962 to return to Connecticut and run (successfully) for the U.S. Senate. (Kennedy didn't blame him.) Commerce Secretary Hodges, also a former governor, actually went so far as to ask that Kennedy's relations with his cabinet be placed on the agenda of a cabinet meeting, a request that got nowhere.

Kennedy found that the system worked well for him and he began applying it to other government officials as well. When the head of a federal agency early in the administration had asked for and received several meetings with Kennedy about what the president considered to be parochial issues, Kennedy called in aide Fred Dutton. "Now look, from now on I don't want that guy coming into this office," he said. "If he's got a problem, he'll have to write a memo to you, and then you take care of it."

Not that Kennedy ignored the cabinet. Initially, JFK tried to meet with each member weekly, but he found this schedule took up too much time and instead asked for weekly written reports. Some members used these reports in an effort to circumvent the White House staff gatekeepers, causing the reports to grow in length. Kennedy soon insisted the reports run no more than five or six pages. These he read carefully and returned to their authors covered with marginal notations and underlinings.

Not all cabinet members were created equal, of course. Bobby Kennedy was in a class by himself, and those involved in foreign policy, notably Dean Rusk, McNamara, and Dillon, enjoyed Kennedy's attention much more frequently than the others, usually two or three times a week (sometimes that much per day during crises). McNamara and Dillon, in particular, saw their stock rise as the administration went on, and by its final year they were close to rivaling Sorensen and RFK in enjoying the president's confidence. Largely by his own choice, Rusk kept some distance between himself and his boss. He didn't mind reporting through Bundy, the national security adviser, and he rarely spoke in large meetings, reserving his advice for the times when he met with Kennedy alone.

The other members of the cabinet sometimes employed Bobby Kennedy, because of his privileged access, as a kind of messenger to convey their dissatisfaction to the president, and RFK took their concerns seriously. He even penned a memo to his brother on the subject in March 1963, urging him to consult the cabinet on issues other than those for which they were directly responsible. "I think you could get a good deal more out of what is available in the government than you are at the present time," he wrote.

Although President Kennedy would occasionally ask cabinet members for advice outside their jurisdictions if they had particular expertise—Dillon on foreign policy, as a former undersecretary of state, and McNamara, a former business executive, on the steel-price dispute, for example—Bobby's memo did little to change Kennedy's view that such consultations were a waste of time all around. He also viewed it as an implicit criticism of those who were actually responsible for the area in question.

This was an exception, though, to Kennedy's general rule of valuing fluidity. Easily bored himself, the president couldn't stand straitjacketing his operation. Titles meant little in the Kennedy regime. He once said that if everyone could have the title "special assistant to the president" the situation would be ideal. Most White House aides had this title, with a few of the higher-ranking ones being called "administrative assistant." Formal, scheduled meetings were uncommon, and rigid attendance lists even more so. Sorensen said:

> Each of us was busy with our separate responsibilities, and each of us met when necessary with whatever staff members had jurisdictions touching our own. For example, in my role of assisting the president on his program and policy, with particular emphasis on legislation, I might meet in one day but at separate times with

National Security Assistant Bundy on the foreign aid message, Budget Director Bell on its cost, Press Secretary Salinger on its publication, Legislative Liaison O'Brien on its reception by the Congress, and Appointments Secretary O'Donnell on the president's final meeting on its contents, as well as the Secretaries of State, Defense, and Treasury and the Foreign Aid Director.

Meetings of the National Security Council (NSC) were more frequent than cabinet meetings, in part because Kennedy wanted to get major officials' views on the record, so they could not complain later that they had opposed certain decisions or had not been consulted. Still, the attendance list was kept short. "We have averaged three or four meetings a week with the secretaries of defense and state, [NSC adviser] McGeorge Bundy, the head of the CIA, and the vice president," Kennedy said in 1961. "But formal meetings of the security council, which include a much wider group, are not as effective. It is more difficult to decide matters of high national security if there is a wider group present."

Kennedy rarely announced decisions in large meetings, since that might invite objection and reopen the matter. Thus, he preferred making major decisions with as small a group present as possible, preferably only the official or officials directly involved. If he did announce a decision at a large meeting, it was usually because the decision itself had actually already been made and communicated in private.

Knowing and, If Necessary, Using Back Channels

One thing John F. Kennedy certainly learned from his father was that there was more than one way of getting something done. If the front door was locked, try the side door and then the back door. This tendency manifested itself during his administration with the creation of various "back channels," particularly in the realm of foreign policy, that bypassed normal routine.

Early in the administration, for example, he set up a back channel between his brother, the attorney general, and a Soviet diplomat/intelligence agent named Georgi Bolshakov. Unlike other officers of the generally dour, tightly wound Soviet diplomatic corps, the gregarious, fun-loving Bolshakov was a hit on the Washington party circuit. He was also a close friend of Nikita

Khrushchev's son-in-law, Alexei Adzhubei, the editor-in-chief of *Izvestia*, who would function as Bolshakov's own back channel to the Soviet chieftain.

Such *sub rosa* communications had taken place between American presidents and their counterparts overseas since at least the time of Franklin D. Roosevelt. FDR himself had opened up the most controversial back channel of all time in September 1939, when he sent a short note to the newly appointed First Lord of the Admiralty Winston Churchill, asking the Briton to keep him advised of anything he might think proper. Given that Churchill was not yet the head of the British government, the discovery of this secret correspondence could have led to a serious diplomatic incident.

Kennedy opened up his back channel to Khrushchev because he very much wanted to establish a personal bond with the Soviet leader. Faced with decisions that could conceivably incinerate the planet, Kennedy knew it would be difficult to kill a man that you knew. Also, Kennedy's distrust of the State Department and its methods has already been demonstrated. He didn't want the contents of his messages and any proposals or counterproposals contained within them leaking to the press.

The back-channel method produced mixed results for Kennedy. The initial contacts with Bolshakov, in which Robert Kennedy previewed his brother's negotiating strategy at the June 1961 Vienna summit, may have been one of the things that convinced Khrushchev he could get away with his clumsy effort at bullying Kennedy at that meeting.

Later, however, the relationship became closer, with the two men exchanging messages and letters through Bolshakov and other "cutouts." Some of the letters were quite lengthy, especially on Khrushchev's end. These communications played a key role in defusing tensions over the Berlin Wall, and later the Cuban missile crisis, when Khrushchev used ABC News television correspondent John Scali to deliver crucial messages to Kennedy. Privately, Kennedy rebuked the Russian for using a journalist for such a sensitive mission. "I have some friends among newspapermen," Kennedy wrote, "but no spokesmen."

The use of back channels proved successful enough, however, that Kennedy and Khrushchev decided to institutionalize it to some extent when, following the communications difficulties in getting messages back and forth during the Cuban missile crisis, the two leaders elected to establish a "hot line" (actually, a teletype system) linking Moscow and Washington in the event of a future crisis.

Kennedy also tried the back-channel method to broker a peace agreement between Israel and her Arab neighbors. He drafted thirteen letters to be sent to each of the Arab heads of state whose nations were technically at war with Israel. Mike Feldman was intimately involved in the drafting process and recalled it later:

> [Kennedy] wanted to give the impression that he was seeking a dialogue with them, a continuing dialogue, and that they should feel free to write to him personally and not through regular State Department channels. And, he wanted to show that he was sympathetic to all their legitimate aspirations. At the same time, he did not want to give the impression he was siding with them in their conflict with Israel. So the effort was made to achieve a nice balance between the two. Variations in the text of the letter he looked at very carefully. Indeed, he discussed the variations in some of the letters with me just to make sure that they would feel that this was a personal interest, and that this would get them involved in the discussions with us.

The letters did not succeed in their stated goal of opening the way for direct negotiations between the Arab states and Israel. But they made a positive impression, and Kennedy's sincere interest seems to have blunted Arab criticism of the United States, at least for a time.

Decision Making in Action: The Space Race

Since John F. Kennedy is the president most intimately identified with the manned space program, it may be surprising to discover that he initially opposed it. As a senator, he agreed with Eisenhower that it was a waste of money and effort. Early in his tenure as president, he held to the same view. He appointed Dr. Jerome Wiesner as his science adviser. Wiesner thought that robots and computers could perform the job of space exploration as well as or better than humans—and without putting human lives at risk. Kennedy

was even preparing to cancel the Apollo manned space program as a budget-
ary measure.

All that changed after Soviet cosmonaut Yuri Gagarin's one-orbit flight in
April 1961. Despite the effort in some quarters to pooh-pooh the achievement (*Time* magazine referred to the Soviet spaceman as "Gaga"), most of
the world was agog at the idea of sending men into space. The national
security implications of a Soviet lead in space were obvious.

But Kennedy grasped the political implications more immediately. The
idea that the United States could launch computers and robots into space
while its greatest rival was launching real, live people—and that the president
would pay no political price for such a stance—doesn't bear much scrutiny.
Kennedy immediately dashed off a memo to Vice President Lyndon Johnson, who chaired the Space Council.

"Do we have a chance of beating the Soviets," the memo asked, "by
putting a laboratory in space, or by a trip around the moon, or by a rocket
to go to the moon and back with a man? Is there any other space program
which promises dramatic results in which we could win? How much addi-
tional would it cost? Are we working twenty-four hours a day on existing
programs? If not, why not?"

Johnson had always been enthusiastic about manned space flight. (The
space program wasn't based in Houston for nothing.) He responded that
ignoring the Soviet achievement would cause many of the world's peoples,
"regardless of their appreciation of our idealistic values," to regard the
United States as weak. He finished the memo with words calculated to hold
Kennedy's interest: "Dramatic accomplishments in space are increasingly
identified as a major indicator of world leadership."

Kennedy didn't just sound out opinion in his immediate vicinity. Tunisian
President Habib Bourgiba was visiting Washington for a state dinner in the
weeks after Gagarin's flight. Kennedy spotted the Tunisian conversing with
Wiesner and wandered over.

"You know, we're having a terrible argument in the White House over
whether we should put a man on the moon," Kennedy said. "Jerry here is
against it. If I told you you'd get an extra billion a year in foreign aid if I
didn't do it, what would be your advice?"

"I wish I could tell you to put it in foreign aid," Bourgiba replied, "but I
cannot."

Kennedy also called in Wernher von Braun, the former Nazi rocket scientist who was now the chief designer of U.S. space rockets.

"Can we beat the Russians?" Kennedy asked.

"We have a sporting chance," the German responded cautiously. "With an all-out crash program, I think we could accomplish this objective in 1967–1968." It wouldn't be cheap, though. The first year would cost $562 million. The total tab would run between $7 billion and $9 billion.

The cost was irrelevant now. On May 25, 1961, Kennedy delivered his message before a joint session of Congress:

> Recognizing the head start obtained by the Soviets with their large rocket engines, which gives them many months of lead time, and recognizing the likelihood that they will exploit this lead for some time to come in still more impressive successes, we nevertheless are required to make new efforts on our own. For while we cannot guarantee that we shall one day be first, we can guarantee that any failure to make this effort will make us last. We take an additional risk by making it in full view of the world, but as shown by the feat of astronaut [Alan] Shepard, this very risk enhances our stature when we are successful. But this is not merely a race. Space is open to us now; and our eagerness to share its meaning is not governed by the efforts of others. We go into space because whatever mankind must undertake, free men must fully share.
>
> I therefore ask the Congress, above and beyond the increases I have earlier requested for space activities, to provide the funds which are needed to meet the following national goals:
>
> First, I believe that this nation should commit itself to achieving the goal, before this decade is out, of landing a man on the moon and returning him safely to the earth. . . .

The scientific value of the moon landing was a subject of debate then and since. (A few lines further on in his address, Kennedy asked for $50 million for communications satellites, which unquestionably revolutionized life on Earth.) But the attraction of manned space flight continues. In spite of the loss of two space shuttles and their crews, there has been no hue and cry from the public demanding that such flights be ended. And China's decision in 2003 to send astronauts into space shows that the prestige factor associated with space flight continues.

But it is noteworthy that Kennedy did not blindly announce a decision without checking with experts to see if the idea was feasible. He expected to be president in 1967 and 1968, and the last thing he wanted was a high-profile, high-cost fizzle on his hands. He encouraged debate within the White House and, in the end, chose to disregard the advice he received from his scientific adviser and made his own decision.

The Importance of Pace and Routine

To be in the best frame of mind for making decisions, you need a personal routine. Getting to the office before dawn every day and retiring well after nightfall is a recipe for burnout in the long run. Kennedy sought to avoid seeming frazzled or overwrought and structured his time accordingly. Here's a quick look at a typical day in the life of President Kennedy.

"I'm awake" or "Good morning, George" were usually the first words John F. Kennedy spoke every day in the White House, as his valet, an African-American named George Thomas, who had worked for him since 1947, knocked on his bedroom door. Never an early riser except when on campaign, Kennedy didn't expect Thomas before 8:00 A.M. (though Kennedy would sometimes arise earlier, depending on the day's schedule).

Next stop was the bathtub, which would soothe JFK's aching back muscles. (On mornings when his back was giving him exceptional trouble, Thomas would help him get dressed.) Kennedy would shave while bathing, using a wooden board stretched across the tub to read memos and papers sent for his consideration. Staffers sometimes would get these documents back decorated with water stains and shaving cream. Reading while doing something else, not only shaving, but dressing or eating, was a Kennedy hallmark. It was one way he fit so much reading into a busy schedule.

He ate breakfast in his quarters at about 8:45 A.M. A confirmed meat-and-potatoes man (his wife described her husband's palate as "distressingly normal"), Kennedy would partake a morning repast that usually consisted of boiled eggs, bacon, toast, and coffee with generous helpings of cream and sugar. After a few minutes with his wife (who slept in a separate bedroom) and children, he would begin the journey downstairs to his office in the West Wing, arriving between 9:30 and 10 A.M.

After meeting with his national security adviser and press secretary, his round of daily appointments would begin, with few lasting longer than fifteen minutes. Kennedy would either remain at his desk or, if his back was bothering him, would move his guest to a set of sofas that faced one another in front of the Oval Office fireplace while Kennedy sat in his rocking chair. People who met with Kennedy testify he generally said little for the first ten minutes or so, listening intently to what his visitor had to say without "sounding off." He would reserve his rapid-fire questions for the final five minutes or so before gently but firmly escorting his visitor out the door.

Kennedy was no slave to his schedule, however. An article that appeared in *The New Republic* called "The Mind of JFK," which became required reading in the Washington press corps, described Kennedy as having "an ability to live with chaos":

> There is nothing he dislikes more, it is testified, than a nice, orderly day with five appointments neatly spaced. . . . [H]e keeps filling in the gaps in the appointment list until he has guaranteed himself a twelve-appointment day of continuous action . . . [s]harp, drift-free tuning which permits movement from one problem to another without overlap or confusion . . . [a]n unflagging intent of action. A zest which confers absurdity upon all the melodramatic and maudlin folklore about the loneliness, anguish, and burdens of the presidency.

Around noon, the president would disappear for physical therapy and exercises, followed by a swim in the White House pool, which was kept heated to ninety degrees to soothe his back muscles. He would then retreat to the family quarters for lunch and a two-hour nap (another habit he picked up from Winston Churchill). He would return to the Oval Office around 3:30 P.M. for more appointments and meetings. Late in the afternoon, he would often return to the pool for another swim and a massage, watch *The Huntley-Brinkley Report* (the television news show), and gather with Sorensen, Pierre Salinger, and other staffers in the Oval Office for a review of the day's happenings. If he didn't have a formal event that night, he would usually return to the family quarters around 8 P.M. for dinner and to see his children off to bed.

About twice a week, Kennedy enjoyed having friends over for dinner. These guests rarely included political figures or staffers; Kennedy wanted to relax at the end of the day and not talk "shop." On evenings when no one was coming over or he and his wife did not have a formal engagement, Kennedy would relax in the family quarters and he would catch up on his reading. Sometimes these were state papers, but he usually stuck to light reading in the family quarters.

Kennedy liked to listen to music before retiring, his tastes running to Broadway show tunes rather than the symphonies and operas his wife enjoyed. (This was the origin of the Camelot myth that took hold after his death.) He usually went to bed between 11 P.M. and midnight.

As you can see, Kennedy had a basic routine he stuck to when he was in the White House. Most successful leaders have similar routines. This gives them a feel for the consistent pace of their day and allows them to make decisions in a thoughtful, unhurried manner as part of their daily routine.

Kennedy and Decision Making: An Assessment

The adjustment to being an executive from having been a legislator was a difficult one for Kennedy, especially in the early months. He found much truth in the old saw that it's easy to criticize a leader when you are not the leader.

Kennedy's decision-making process and general managerial style had its strengths and weaknesses. Among the latter, the most obvious was his decision to eschew a chief of staff. Since Kennedy had decided to function, in effect, as his own secretary of state as well as his own press secretary, it was simply too much to take on the functions of his own chief of staff as well. This was the root of the seeming disorganization that concerned such old Washington hands as transition chief Clark Clifford and Solicitor General Archibald Cox.

After the Bay of Pigs, National Security Adviser Bundy took on a much more extensive coordination role, though it was still well short of the duties that an actual chief of staff would perform. As a result, Kennedy sometimes became bogged down in day-to-day details that would have been much better left to staff members at lower levels. In this respect, there was much to be said for Eisenhower's more structured approach to the presidency.

On the plus side, Kennedy's "loose ship" style suited his personality and leadership style; he enjoyed a moderate degree of chaos around him and thought that it served as a stimulant to creativity and new ideas. Whether he would have left this system in place during a second term, had he won one, is, of course, impossible to say.

For Kennedy, clearly his decision-making style worked. Few of his decisions were obviously wrong or incompetent, in retrospect. And at least one that fell into that category, the Bay of Pigs, came about after he had consulted widely and closely with established experts.

No one should be blind to the potential difficulties of such a relatively unstructured style, however. It is best suited to a highly confident executive who does not rattle easily and is able to attract strong talent whose abilities can take best advantage of the lack of a formal structure.

How to Develop Your Own Decision-Making System

➡ *Find your style.* Decision making is the essence of what a leader does; some kind of process is essential to carry it out. Your decision making will leave much to be desired if it is haphazard and random. Establish your style; then adapt it to circumstances. No one process is replicable for all executives at all times. Find one that suits your personal style and circumstances.

➡ *Get into a routine and learn to pace yourself.* Overwork is a recipe for inattention and mistakes. Determine when you are at your best in contemplating decisions and then try, within reason, to work on your decision making at these optimum times. If you do your best thinking in the morning, for example, you should try not to push yourself to reach a hurried decision toward the end of the workday. Remember, too, that you can mull over decisions while doing other things, such as commuting or working out.

➡ *Attend fewer meetings.* Most office environments feature too many meetings. Decide which ones are essential and keep them to a minimum. As
the leader, you may find that you should step away and allow some
meetings to take place without you. There may be many meetings that
will accomplish much more without your presence. Your people can
come up with their recommendations, then pass them on to you for
the final decision. Not only does this free up your valuable time, it
helps your people grow into their own roles as advisers and decision
makers.

➡ *"Go to the source" if you need more information.* People are generally flat-
tered when higher-ups call and ask for their specialized knowledge. A
U.S. president has many advisers in a wide range of fields to call upon
when necessary; as a business executive, you have many resources at
your command, too. Find out whom in your organization to go to for
the answers to what kinds of questions. Keep in mind that smart, talented people have many fields of expertise, often outside their main
responsibility, so take the time to find out what areas your people
know. Ted Sorensen was a lawyer with little interest in writing or
speaking who was brought in to develop policy positions for young
Senator Jack Kennedy. He came to be JFK's trusted speechwriter and
one of his closest aides.

➡ *Try to get people to speak openly and candidly.* This is frequently difficult
to do but is essential to get the information you need to make the right
decisions. Your people should never be afraid to speak their minds in
your presence or to deliver information you may not want to hear. You
may disagree with them or disregard their advice, but they should always feel free to give it. However, insist that your people be able to
back up their statements if you question them beyond their surface
recommendation.

➡ *Let some advisers go, if necessary.* Not everyone is going to be happy with
your decision-making style. Some advisers may become openly frustrated if you fail to follow their advice. Some will adapt, but others may
simply have to leave.

CHAPTER 10

Miscalculations and Misjudgments:
Make the Best of Them

"[Y]our advisers are frequently divided. If you take the wrong course, and on occasion I have, the president bears the burden of the mistake quite rightly. The advisers may move on to other advice."
—JOHN F. KENNEDY

It's often said that we learn much more from our mistakes than we ever do from our successes. All leaders make mistakes; you can't avoid them. However, you can look at your mistakes, figure out where you went wrong, and try to avoid making the same mistake in the future.

Leaders also have to be able to admit when they have made a mistake. They can't foist responsibility off on someone else. If you do this, you'll soon find resentment and a lack of respect growing among your subordinates and peers.

"Do you ever admit a mistake?" an increasingly frustrated John F. Kennedy asked Soviet chieftain Nikita Khrushchev during their contentious summit meeting in Vienna in June 1961.

"Certainly I do," the Russian replied. "In a speech before the Twentieth Party Congress, I admitted all of Stalin's mistakes."

Clearly, the bilious Russian was not without a sense of humor. Admitting we make mistakes even in the most innocuous of circumstances is difficult.

When one holds a position of great responsibility, the reluctance is magnified many times over.

Mistakes and misjudgments, by both individuals and organizations, are inevitable. John F. Kennedy and his administration made their share. True leadership involves recognizing when you have made a mistake, learning from that mistake, and trying to correct it going forward. Kennedy did seek to learn from his mistakes and misjudgments. Sometimes he learned incompletely, as in Cuba.

Cuba: From the Bay of Pigs to "Operation Mongoose"

Cuba was the most consistently frustrating foreign policy problem John F. Kennedy faced in the White House. From the first day to the last, it gnawed at him. The United States lives with the consequences of his actions to this day.

The so-called Bay of Pigs invasion of the island by Cuban exiles in April 1961 is a story that has been told often before and in greater detail elsewhere. It has been termed "the perfect failure." Here we will confine ourselves to examining the mistakes and misjudgments on Kennedy's part that made it so.

➡ *He was trapped by his own rhetoric.* In the last days of the 1960 campaign, Kennedy pounded the Eisenhower administration relentlessly on the subject of Cuba, accusing the administration of negligence in allowing a hostile regime to install itself on America's doorstep. Kennedy never said what he would have done differently, a fact that didn't bother him. "Hell," he told aides, recalling Republican attacks on Harry Truman eight years earlier for "losing" China, "they never said how *they* would have saved China." (Of course, neither had Kennedy; and he had joined in many of those same attacks early in his career.)

Thus, once in office, Kennedy found himself compelled to take a hard line on Cuba. This put him at an immediate disadvantage in assessing the pros and cons of the plan the CIA had begun developing under Dwight Eisenhower to invade the island with a force of 1,500 Cuban exiles. Kennedy wanted the plan to succeed, but as a former naval officer, he knew how many things could go wrong in military affairs. But he also feared, probably rightly, that Republican critics would assail him for appeasement if he canceled the operation. Caught between a rock and a hard place, Kennedy allowed the plan to stumble almost relentlessly forward to its tragic and bloody denouement.

➡ *His expectations were unrealistic.* Throughout the run-up to the Bay of Pigs, Kennedy was preoccupied with reducing the international "noise level" and the American "footprint" in the operation to a totally unrealistic extent. (He even told an aide that he doubted the operation would make the front page of the *New York Times*—Kennedy's definition of "news.") Kennedy meddled in the planning to achieve his aim.

Instead of landing near the populous port of Trinidad, the exiles would land at the isolated Bay of Pigs, many miles to the west. That made it even less likely that the action would spark the popular uprising that everyone conceded was necessary for the invasion to have any chance of success. Worse, the Bay of Pigs was surrounded by swamps, so it would be difficult for the exiles to move inland from the invasion beaches, or scatter in the event they were overwhelmed by Fidel Castro's forces.

The idea that the United States could "plausibly deny" any involvement in the scheme was so laughable it is hard to imagine how anyone could have taken the idea seriously. (Former President Eisenhower made exactly this point to Kennedy later, though he never said how he would have handled the problem.) The exiles had been equipped with a few old World War II B-26 bombers to provide air cover. Where would they have gotten those? What about the ships that took them to the beaches? Presumably, Kennedy thought that if the invasion succeeded, he, like a winning football coach who had taken a daring chance, would not have to answer any embarrassing questions.

Finally, Kennedy made it clear that no U.S. forces would be used under any circumstances. That last directive should have submarined the entire operation. The exiles themselves—a mishmash of former Cuban soldiers, middle-class intellectuals, and high-society party boys—couldn't understand how they were supposed to stand up to a force anticipated to be many times their own size. E. Howard Hunt, later one of the Watergate burglars but at this time a CIA agent assigned to the Cuban operation, told the exiles that they were assured of American air cover. But Kennedy would not give that assurance. Even if he had, it seems unlikely that the small exile force could have succeeded with anything less than full-scale U.S. military support, complete with marines and army troops. That was a commitment Kennedy simply wasn't prepared to make.

➡ *He brushed aside contrary advice.* CIA Director Allen Dulles and Deputy Director Richard Bissell were the prime movers in advocating the invasion. Both men had long and reasonably successful track records in covert operations (although they also had a few failures about which they were far less vocal). The Joint Chiefs of Staff, although lukewarm in their support to Kennedy's face, were privately dismissive of the agency's plan as "weak" and "sloppy." Defense Secretary Robert Mc-Namara and National Security Adviser McGeorge Bundy—neither of whom had a high-level military or intelligence background—endorsed the idea.

Wanting so badly for the plan to work, Kennedy thus did not take seriously the contrary advice that he was getting. J. William Fulbright, the chairman of the Senate Foreign Relations Committee, was firmly opposed on moral grounds, saying the invasion would violate numerous treaties and U.S. laws. Dean Acheson, the former secretary of state, objected on practical grounds, noting that you didn't have "to call in Price Waterhouse" (the accounting firm) to see that 1,500 Cubans were unlikely to defeat the 25,000-man army Castro was training. Nor did JFK consult two members of his cabinet with relevant experience: Agriculture Secretary Orville Freeman, a Marine Corps veteran of World War II landings in the Pacific, and Labor Secretary Arthur Goldberg, a former army intelligence officer.

➡ *He ignored evidence that secrecy had been compromised.* Worse, there was no shortage of evidence that the operation's security had been hopelessly compromised. Most of the brigade's members had been recruited from Miami's burgeoning Cuban exile community, which was also riddled with pro-Castro informers, so the impending invasion was common knowledge. Worse, CBS News and the *New York Times* ran stories giving the basic outline of the invasion preparations in the weeks before the operation was launched. "Castro doesn't need agents over here," Kennedy complained. "All he has to do is read our papers. It's all laid out for him."

→ *He was unwilling to call it off.* Why, then, did Kennedy not call the invasion off? At this point, it seems, the plan had advanced so far that it had taken on a life of its own. He had also been influenced by an exceedingly optimistic assessment of the exile brigade by a decorated and experienced marine colonel named Jack Hawkins, who said he had never seen a better-prepared fighting force. Furthermore, CIA Director Dulles had warned Kennedy several times of the "disposal problem"—what to do with 1,500 armed and angry Cuban exiles—they would face with regard to the brigade if the operation were called off.

In the end, though, a combination of political cowardice and overconfidence in his own abilities proved to be JFK's downfall at the Bay of Pigs. Unwilling to bite the bullet and call off the operation, he trusted the incredible string of luck he had enjoyed for most of his life to see him through. At the Bay of Pigs, however, the only luck Kennedy experienced was bad.

When Brigade 2506, as it had been designated, arrived on the beaches of the Bay of Pigs on April 17, 1961, Castro was only momentarily surprised. He was personally very familiar with the area and used his knowledge of the terrain to quickly deploy his thousands of troops around the little exile force. Within hours, it was clear the effort was failing fast. Castro's air force, though equipped only with a few old U.S. planes inherited from the previous regime, gave a remarkably good account of itself, sinking two of the freighters carrying all of the brigade's reserve ammunition and most of its communications equipment. Though the force managed to hang on for another few days, it was clear that only a full-scale U.S. invasion could conceivably salvage the situation.

In Washington, Kennedy sought to project an atmosphere of normality. He even attended a white-tie state dinner on the first night of the operation, which resulted in the ridiculous spectacle of men in formal evening dress running around White House corridors, speaking in hushed tones. As the dimensions of the disaster became clearer, Kennedy kept his cool in public. Privately, he was devastated, slipping out into the Rose Garden to weep in the early hours of April 18.

➠ *He worried too much about the political fallout.* For the most part, Kennedy seemed more concerned with political rather than military matters over the next few days. He especially sought to assuage the political leaders of the Cuban exile community so that they would not attack him in the press. (He had them secretly brought to the White House for an Oval Office meeting.)

Accounts of Kennedy's handling of the affair make for painful reading. Despite his previous insistence that there was to be no involvement of U.S. troops, he ultimately authorized U.S. Navy fighters to escort the remains of the exile air force in a last-ditch bombing mission over the besieged beach—but he ordered the markings painted out on the U.S. aircraft first. Incredibly, as late as April 19, he was still anxious to keep the "noise" level down. In any event, the mission ended when the navy fighters failed to rendezvous with the Cuban exile planes. Someone had forgotten there was a one-hour time difference between the Bay of Pigs and the Cuban airfield in Nicaragua. It was one final blunder in an affair littered with them.

Learning from Mistakes

Although leaders cannot avoid making mistakes and misjudgments, they can admit them and learn from them. Figuring out what went wrong and then applying this lesson in the future can enable a leader to achieve success down the road.

Acknowledge the Mistakes. "How could I have been so stupid?" became Kennedy's mantra over the next few weeks. Much to his own amazement, however, Kennedy was able to defuse much of the domestic political fallout by accepting personal responsibility. "Victory has a hundred fathers, but defeat is an orphan," he said. "I am the responsible officer of the government." His approval rating soared almost overnight to an incredible 83 percent.

Identify What Went Wrong. Sometimes this means asking someone who was not involved in the final decision. It was Eisenhower who put his finger on

one of the main flaws in the run-up to the invasion. JFK invited his prede-
cessor to lunch at Camp David shortly after the disaster, and the old man
gave the young man a talking-to that, it is probably safe to say, Kennedy had
never before experienced.

"Mr. President, before you approved this plan," Eisenhower asked, "did
you have everybody in front of you debating the thing so you got the pros
and cons yourself and then made the decision, or did you see these people
one at a time?"

Of course, there had been no such meeting. The concern for security and
the general atmosphere of administrative disorganization in the early days of
the Kennedy White House, combined with Kennedy's own lack of executive experience at this point in his presidency, had conspired to prevent it. It
was part of a whole catalog of mistakes.

Kennedy may have "taken responsibility" for the disaster, but that did not
mean there would be no consequences for those he believed had misled him.
In a meeting with Bissell, the deputy CIA director, shortly after the brigade's
remnants had been captured, the Anglophile Kennedy used a British political
analogy to explain the situation. "In a parliamentary system, I would resign,"
the president said. "In our system, the president can't and doesn't. So you
and Allen [Dulles] must go."

There were other changes in the wake of the failure. Administrative procedures in the White House and State Department were tightened up, and
National Security Adviser Bundy was given more authority to decide what
did and didn't come to Kennedy's attention. But the biggest lesson Kennedy
took away from the episode was that he needed more frank and reliable
advice.

Choose More Reliable Advisers. Principally, that meant his brother, Robert.
RFK had been informed of the Cuban affair only a week before it was
launched, and so he had no role in its planning and execution. Now, in
addition to his position as attorney general, he would sit in on important
meetings as something of a "surrogate president," with no one's best interest
but his brother's at heart. Bobby's new role would reach full flower a year
and a half later, during the Cuban missile crisis.

Speechwriter Ted Sorensen's role was widened to include foreign as well
as domestic policy. Maxwell Taylor, a career army officer and World War II

hero who had resigned as army chief of staff over differences with Eisenhower, was brought in, first as an informal adviser and later as chairman of the Joint Chiefs of Staff.

In general, Kennedy became much more hard-nosed with regard to the advice he was getting from outside of this tight circle, especially on foreign and defense policy. Another foreign policy crisis was brewing in Laos, a small, landlocked country athwart Vietnam in Southeast Asia. The Pentagon was eager to throw in U.S. combat forces. General Lyman Lemnitzer, the chairman of the Joint Chiefs, told Kennedy that a U.S. Army division— about 12,000 men—could be on the ground in Laos in twelve days.

"How will they get in there?" Kennedy asked.

"They can land at two airports," Lemnitzer responded, indicating their location on a map.

"How many can land at those airports?" Kennedy persisted.

"If you can have perfect conditions, you can land a thousand a day."

"How many communist troops are in the area?" Kennedy asked.

"We would guess three thousand."

"How long will it take them to bring up more?"

"They can bring up five, six thousand, eight thousand, in four days."

"What's going to happen," an annoyed Kennedy asked, "if on the third day you've landed three thousand—and then they bomb the airport? And then they bring up five or six thousand more men? What's going to happen? Or if you land two thousand, and then they bomb the airport?"

Lemnitzer's answers didn't satisfy Kennedy. "We would have troops in Laos right now if it weren't for the Bay of Pigs," he told Sorensen later.

Attempt to Make Amends. Kennedy was able eventually to make political lemonade of sorts out of the lemons of the Bay of Pigs. He felt a responsibility for the brigade's members languishing in Castro's prisons. He was able eventually to negotiate their release in exchange for drugs, farm equipment, and other goods Castro wanted. Rather bravely, and against the advice of many of his aides, who feared booing or worse, he agreed to appear at the Miami Orange Bowl in December 1962 to welcome the surviving members of Brigade 2506 home. The appearance, with Jacqueline Kennedy addressing the crowd in fluent Spanish, was a triumph.

Evaluate Your Plan Objectively. If Kennedy became more cautious elsewhere in the aftermath of the Bay of Pigs, he became more reckless still in the case of Cuba. Unfortunately, he just wasn't able to be objective about the Bay of Pigs or Cuba and, as a result, he became even more determined to get rid of the communist regime there. A study group he put together immediately after the Bay of Pigs to "give special attention to the lessons that can be learned from recent events in Cuba," soon morphed into a brainstorming session on finding ways to destroy the Castro regime. At a National Security Council meeting less than a month after the Bay of Pigs, Kennedy and his aides reiterated that "U.S. policy should be aimed at the downfall of Castro."

Putting pressure on the Cuban regime was not in itself a bad idea. Castro had made it plain before Kennedy took office that he was no friend of the United States. He had never won a free election and showed no sign of wanting to hold one. Worse, from the perspective of the United States, he openly bragged of his willingness and desire to "export" his form of government throughout the Western Hemisphere. Castro's increasing closeness to the Soviet Union made that potentially more than an idle threat and offered the Kremlin a secure base of operations in the Western Hemisphere. Keeping the Cuban dictator preoccupied at home, therefore, was a way of keeping him from making trouble elsewhere. In some ways, the Kennedy effort against Castro prefigured the so-called Reagan Doctrine of two decades later, in which the United States armed and trained guerillas opposed to Soviet-backed regimes in Afghanistan, Nicaragua, and elsewhere.

Don't Get Caught Up in Personal Vendettas. But Operation Mongoose, as Kennedy's effort against Cuba came to be known, was conceived not primarily as an instrument for bringing freedom to the Cuban people, but as vengeance against a man who was perceived as having humiliated the Kennedys. ("Don't get mad, get even," was a favorite Kennedy maxim.) Constant pressure, coordinated directly out of the White House by Robert Kennedy, was brought to bear on the CIA, the Pentagon, and other government agencies to "do something" about Castro and his regime. The tactics varied from support for small-scale infiltrations of the island by Cuban exile commandos intent on sabotage and disruption, to the assassination of Castro himself.

The obsession with "getting rid of" Castro (it seems inconceivable that both John and Robert Kennedy did not know that this meant assassination) may have blinded the two brothers to the fact that they were confusing means with ends. Leaving aside the morality and legality of killing a foreign head of state, John F. Kennedy's own interest in history should have told him that he was making the same mistake as turn-of-the-century anarchists, who wrongly believed that assassinating members of European royal families—as well as U.S. President William McKinley—would bring about social changes the anarchists thought desirable. It was by no means certain that the death of one man, however important, would necessarily lead to the desired regime change. Lenin's death, after all, did not mean the end of communism in Russia. Nor did Stalin's nearly three decades later.

In the early 1960s, Castro's right-hand man, Ernesto "Che" Guevara, or Castro's brother Raul, could likely have filled Castro's empty boots quite adequately. If anything, killing Castro might have strengthened the communist regime's hold on power if it were shown—or even widely suspected—that the United States was responsible. The image and reputation of the United States would have suffered as a result. Also, the U.S. government's involvement with organized crime figures in order to bring about the death of Castro—when it was, at the same time, arresting and prosecuting gangsters in the United States—sent mixed signals (to the gangsters themselves and the nation at large) when the plots were revealed years later.

Probably the biggest oversight caused by this myopic focus on eliminating Castro was that the Kennedys apparently gave little or no thought to the potential Soviet and Cuban reaction to Operation Mongoose. Nikita Khrushchev's family members and aides subsequently revealed that the ongoing operations against Cuba after the Bay of Pigs convinced the Soviet leader that another invasion of Cuba was likely, and that it would be far more serious and therefore more likely to succeed. Although this was probably not the primary reason for the Cuban missile crisis of 1962—Khrushchev was worried about closing his own "missile gap"—it likely was a contributing factor.

When you are evaluating your mistakes, make sure you are being objective about it. If making the mistake only made you blindly determined to achieve where you had failed, you may just end up making a bigger blunder.

The Vienna Summit: Getting Off on the Wrong Foot

Kennedy was especially haunted by the possibility that a "miscalculation" on either his own part or Khrushchev's could lead to nuclear war. JFK's June

1961 meeting with Khrushchev in Vienna, for example, was itself a miscalculation that had important effects on the rest of his presidency. Initially inclined to put off any meeting with the Soviet chieftain (Kennedy had, after all, criticized Eisenhower for what he termed excessive reliance on "summitry"), he changed his mind after becoming president. Perhaps he was influenced by Winston Churchill's unsuccessful urging of an early summit on Eisenhower in order to "take the measure" of the men in the Kremlin.

JFK should have heeded his gut instincts. Coming less than two months after the Bay of Pigs calamity, the timing almost automatically placed Kennedy on the defensive. The knowledge that Kennedy would be under pressure from back home to be "tough" with the Russian probably made Khrushchev even more determined than usual not to appear soft. For his part, Khrushchev was under pressure because of the rising tide of refugees fleeing into West Berlin, as well as popular discontent at home for more consumer goods and political freedoms. From the start, therefore, the Vienna meeting was unlikely to be a love fest; it is, in fact, illustrative of at least two mistakes and misjudgments on Kennedy's part:

1. *He was inadequately prepared.* On the surface, Kennedy prepared well for the summit, but only on the surface. He got the standard State Department and CIA briefings about the mercurial Russian, and he spoke with the reigning experts on Soviet affairs in the United States: George Kennan, Charles "Chip" Bohlen, and W. Averell Harriman. These men, however, had invested their careers in improving relations with the Soviet Union, so adopting a tough line with Khrushchev was unlikely to find favor with them. Harriman in particular offered what turned out to be disastrous advice. "Have fun," he told Kennedy.

   There were serious omissions. Kennedy apparently did not consult with former President Dwight Eisenhower or Vice President Richard Nixon, both of whom had met with Khrushchev and would have offered a perspective different from Harriman and company. There was also no presummit effort to arrive at agreements in advance. The agenda was only lightly outlined.

2. *He misjudged Khrushchev.* Kennedy went into the meeting under the impression he could converse with Khrushchev "politician to politician," ignoring the fact that Khrushchev was not a conventional politi-

cal leader by Western standards. As tough as the Kennedy political operation was, it didn't compare with the hard, bloody school in which the Russian had been formed. Kennedy had gotten to where he was by persuading large numbers of voters to put their fate in his hands. Persuasion wasn't high on Khrushchev's list of priorities. He had reached his position by outmaneuvering, threatening, and, ultimately, eliminating his rivals.

The meeting got off to a bad start and never recovered. Khrushchev immediately took the initiative, reacting badly to Kennedy's warnings about "miscalculations" that could lead to nuclear war. He apparently thought the American president was patronizing him. He berated Kennedy for past American support for colonial regimes and labeled efforts to export communism to other nations as "sacred." Kennedy's pleas for maintaining the status quo between the superpowers were read by Khrushchev as efforts to stand athwart the tide of history.

Kennedy's efforts to lightly brush aside Khrushchev's arguments on these points (he was trying to "have fun") had the effect of pouring gasoline on the fire, because the Soviet chieftain thought he was being belittled. Kennedy made no effort to defend Western capitalism as a superior form of societal organization (maybe having Joe Sr. as a father did not help in this regard), thus allowing Khrushchev to seize the moral high ground. Kennedy was thus put on the defensive and never recovered.

Not even a one-on-one meeting with the Soviet leader at the very end of the summit seemed to soften the Russian's hard-line insistence that he would sign a separate peace treaty that December with the puppet Soviet regime in East Germany. Theoretically, such a move could sever the rights of the Western powers in Berlin and bring the United States and the USSR to the brink of war. "It will be a cold winter" were the president's parting words to Khrushchev.

Kennedy returned from the summit "shattered," in Harriman's grim estimation. The boyish charm that had melted the heart of the Groton headmaster when the Muckers Club was unmasked and that had carried Kennedy through most of his public life had finally met its match in Khrushchev.

Immediately after the two-day meeting concluded, Kennedy commented that the summit was the "roughest thing in my life."

The blow to Kennedy's pride was substantial. Some veterans of the Kennedy White House recalled later that the most unsettling period of the administration was not the Cuban missile crisis, but the weeks following the return from Vienna. The president moved through his daily routine in something like a daze, muttering that he had allowed Khrushchev to treat him "like a boy." It is also not clear what side effects the president could have been experiencing as a result of the various pain-killing medications that New York–based "Dr. Feelgood," Max Jacobson, had injected in Vienna.

Learning for the Future

Still, Kennedy drew some important lessons from Vienna in the days and months ahead. He kept open the lines of communication, both official and unofficial, between the White House and the Kremlin (with Robert Kennedy becoming a kind of unofficial go-between with the Soviet embassy). A part of him would always have a certain sympathy for Khrushchev, despite their miscommunication, since Khrushchev was the only other person in the world who could understand the burdens Kennedy carried when it came to the peace of the world. When the Cuban missile crisis came along, Kennedy was alone among his advisers in holding the door open to allow his opponent an honorable retreat. "I don't want to put him in a corner," he said. "We don't want to push him into a precipitous action."

Misjudging the Civil Rights Movement

A photograph of a smoldering Greyhound tour bus—the company's optimistic slogan, "Leave the driving to us!" looking oddly out of place on the blazing vehicle's side panel—ran on the front pages of American newspapers on May 15, 1961. Kennedy biographer Richard Reeves wrote that when Kennedy saw the photograph he "realized there was a revolution going on in America."

It was a revolution Kennedy himself had a role in sparking, though it took him some time to realize it. His call to the youth of the nation to enter public service—"ask not what your country can do for you; ask what you can do for your country"—was interpreted by many as a call to end one of the great stains on the American record: legalized segregation.

Securing equal rights and equal treatment for America's black population—then colloquially known as "Negroes"—was an emotional and moral cause for a substantial number of Americans as John F. Kennedy assumed the presidency. Appealing to emotion and morality, however, was not the way to get the attention of JFK. Kennedy was a supreme rationalist, which led him to misjudge the civil rights movement in several ways:

➡ *He underestimated the need for change.* One of the most important things a leader needs to do is to take the pulse of the people he's leading. If you are out of touch with your constituency, you will be unable to inspire them in good times, or control them in bad.

Kennedy underestimated the importance of civil rights as an issue at first. "In 1953, John Kennedy was mildly and quietly in favor of civil rights legislation as a political necessity consistent with his moral instincts," wrote Kennedy aide Theodore Sorensen in his memoirs. "In 1963, he was deeply and fervently committed to the cause of human rights as a moral necessity inconsistent with his political instincts.

"Kennedy was not converted to this cause by the eloquence of some persuasive preacher or motivated by his own membership in a minority group," Sorensen explains. "John Kennedy's convictions on equal rights—like his convictions on nearly all other subjects—were reached gradually, logically, and coolly, ultimately involving a dedication of the heart even stronger than that of the mind."

Sorensen's insight that Kennedy's views on civil rights had little to do with his own background is telling—and it contrasts with what some others have written. Joe Sr. never wearied of railing against the supposedly pervasive anti-Irish and anti-Catholic discrimination in Boston. Such experiences did not, however, automatically translate into sympathy for others facing similar barriers, as Joe Sr.'s ill-disguised racial and ethnic prejudices demonstrated.

➡ *He wouldn't put the issue high on his list.* During his careers in the U.S. House of Representatives and the Senate, Kennedy seems to have spared little thought for the special plight of American blacks. To the extent he discussed African-Americans at all, it was simply as a political constituency. Though there were relatively few blacks in Massachusetts, he wanted their votes, just as his grandfather Honey Fitz had done. That blacks south of the Mason-Dixon Line were denied that privilege did not loom large in his consciousness.

With Kennedy, though, his misjudging of the importance of this issue ran a bit deeper than merely "out of sight, out of mind." Never averse to a good time, the new congressman found himself immediately drawn to the company of Southern Democrats, who were among the most indefatigable raconteurs on Capitol Hill. His best friend in the House and later the Senate was Florida's George Smathers, a supporter of segregation. When Kennedy made his unsuccessful bid for vice president at the 1956 Democratic convention, some of his strongest support came from the Southern delegations. It's hard not to believe that Kennedy's personal friendships with numerous Southern lawmakers contributed to his public reticence on the issue.

None of this meant that Kennedy was a closet segregationist. His opinions, rather, were reflective of many Northerners at the time. In general, he supported the aspirations of blacks for full citizenship. He voted to ban the poll taxes that were used to keep blacks from voting in the South, as well as for a federal antilynching law and the Fair Employment Practice Commission. He also voted for the mild 1957 Civil Rights Act, the first such legislation since the 1870s. He viewed the complex web of social taboos that governed race relations in the South with bafflement. He thought racial discrimination a bizarre waste of time and resources and, ultimately, a drag on the country's ability to present itself to the rest of the world as a beacon of freedom opposing Soviet and Chinese communist tyranny.

The brutal realities of power relationships in the Democratic party and in Washington also governed how Kennedy approached civil rights as he began thinking about running for president. For most of the twentieth century, successful Democratic presidents had united Northern intellectuals, union members, and urban ethnics into a coalition with white Southern segregationists to oppose Northern and Midwestern financial interests and small-town dwellers. Underlying that alliance was the unspoken agreement on the part of presidents Woodrow Wilson, Franklin D. Roosevelt, and Harry S Truman that nothing be done that would disturb Southern "domestic arrangements" (i.e., segregation).

The essentially one-party politics of the American South also gave Southern members of Congress exceptional electoral longevity that ensured they were in major leadership positions on key committees. As Kennedy took office, Virginian Howard Smith chaired the House Rules Committee and Mississippian James O. Eastland oversaw the Senate Judiciary Committee—two panels that had been the graveyard of almost all previous attempts at passing meaningful civil rights legislation. Even J. William Fulbright of Arkansas, who served as chairman of the Senate Foreign Relations Committee and was about as liberal-minded a Southern Democrat as there was to be found on Capitol Hill, was a down-the-line supporter of legalized segregation.

➡ *He feared communist affiliation.* Another problem for Kennedy—and much of the American public—in pursuing civil rights was the distinctly left-of-center cast of much of the civil rights movement itself. Communists and those sympathetic to communist causes had long been prominent in the movement. Robert Kennedy thought Martin Luther King Jr.'s ties to people with communist backgrounds so potentially damaging that he authorized the infamous FBI wiretaps against King, which continued until 1965.

➡ *He compromised in order to get the support he needed in the South.* To even secure his party's nomination for president, Kennedy had made some bows toward segregationist sentiment. He criticized Eisenhower's decision to use federal troops to integrate Central High School in Little Rock, Arkansas. (That was why, during his own administration, he used U.S. marshals rather than soldiers whenever possible.) As president, he appointed some federal judges who were clearly segregationists, and in the South, he appointed none who could be called racially liberal.

Kennedy thought that he had to have the support of the white South (or at least not their active opposition) if he was going to have a prayer of passing health insurance for the elderly, a higher minimum wage, an economic program to jump-start the stagnant economy, not to mention the bigger defense and foreign aid budgets Kennedy wanted on the foreign policy side. Charging ahead on civil rights legislation, Kennedy believed, would only jeopardize his entire agenda, which would ultimately hurt blacks.

"[A] lot of talk and no results will only make them madder," Kennedy explained to aide Theodore Sorensen after a disappointed civil rights delegation had left his office. "If we drive . . . moderate Southerners to the wall with a lot of civil rights demands that can't pass anyway, then what happens to the Negro on minimum wages, housing, and the rest?"

The problem with all this *realpolitik,* however, was that JFK created a very different impression during the 1960 campaign, raising the expectations of the burgeoning civil rights movement. He insisted, for example, on including the strongest-ever plank in favor of civil rights in the 1960 Democratic platform. He told the chairman of the Southern Christian Leadership Conference, Martin Luther King Jr. (who was unimpressed when he first met Kennedy in mid-1960), that the sit-in movement at segregated Southern lunch counters, which began in February 1960, had caused him to "reevaluate his thinking and he had become more committed to a strong presidency on civil rights."

That was what people had in mind when they heard him say at the outset of his campaign:

> In the decade that lies ahead—in the challenging revolutionary sixties—the American presidency will demand more than ringing manifestoes issued from the rear of the battle. It will demand that the president place himself in the very thick of the fight, that he care passionately about the fate of the people he leads, that he be willing to serve them, at the risk of incurring their momentary displeasure.

He underlined his apparent commitment to civil rights shortly before the election, when King was imprisoned in Georgia on a trumped-up charge. The civil rights leader's wife, Coretta, was justifiably frantic for his safety, fearing her husband would be murdered behind bars. Civil rights leaders reached out to both presidential campaigns, pleading for some public expression of concern that might stay a villainous hand.

Richard Nixon, who was quietly a member of the National Association for the Advancement of Colored People (NAACP) and had met King before Kennedy, was also pro–civil rights. He considered the request, but ultimately decided the best course was to keep quiet. Kennedy came close to making the same decision, but was prevailed upon to change his mind by Sargent Shriver, his brother-in-law, and Harris Wofford, a Notre Dame law professor who was his informal adviser on civil rights matters. "It's the right thing to do," Kennedy said as he picked up the phone to call Mrs. King.

Nevertheless, Kennedy did not mention the subject of civil rights in his ringing inaugural address. His campaign promise to end "with the stroke of a pen" racial discrimination in federally funded housing projects was quietly put on the back burner. JFK eventually signed the order, without fanfare, after the 1962 midterm elections.

One action Kennedy took early in his presidency was backing the effort by House liberals to expand the size of the House Rules Committee and end its role as a reliable roadblock to civil rights and other liberal legislation. The addition of three new members, two Democrats and one Republican, would give liberals a majority on the panel. Kennedy backed the effort strongly, and with the support of the dying Speaker of the House Sam Rayburn, it passed 217–212. Later, the administration also supported congressional passage of the Twenty-Fourth Amendment, abolishing poll taxes that were used to prevent blacks from voting. (It was ratified in 1964 during the Johnson administration.) An amendment that would have banned literacy tests, however, failed.

➡ *He let the revolution start without him.* But there was something out there that was beyond the control of John F. Kennedy or anyone else: a demographic revolution. A large cohort of young people, born during World War II and just after it, was beginning to reach maturity and political awareness in the early 1960s. The burst of "Kennedymania" that was seen during the 1960 campaign was among the first signs of it. These were the "freedom riders" and the people doing the sit-ins. They identified with John F. Kennedy, and the advent of his presidency filled them with hope.

This fact sometimes seemed lost on the Kennedys themselves. In contrast with his later image as a civil rights crusader, Bobby Kennedy made some incredibly callous statements with regard to civil rights early in the administration. He freely admitted he didn't "stay awake nights" worrying about civil rights before he entered office. "Mississippi will work itself out," he said privately. "Maybe it's going to take a decade and maybe a lot of people are going to be killed in the meantime."

His brother sometimes wasn't much better. "Can't you get your goddamned friends off those buses?" Kennedy snapped to Wofford as Southern segregationists bombed and shot up interstate buses carrying the freedom riders. The man who had fired the imagination of a generation of young people was dismayed to see his rhetoric becoming a double-edged sword for the White House. "Where are they getting these ideas?" Kennedy wondered aloud to a black political leader as idealistic civil rights workers flooded the South. "From you," he replied.

His half measures were inadequate. Kennedy decided to play it safe and ask for no new civil rights legislation at the beginning of his administration. In consultation with his brother, the new president moved to use current laws aimed at securing black voting rights in the South. Once sufficient numbers of black voters were enrolled, the Kennedy brothers reasoned, the civil rights problem would cure itself by forcing Southern lawmakers to contend with black voting strength.

"[Y]ou register these people to vote and Jim Eastland [the Mississippi senator] will change his mind," Kennedy told King. "Or there will be somebody replacing him."

The Justice Department thus stepped up the filing of voting rights suits. Staffing the civil rights division with bright, ambitious young Ivy Leaguers, the Kennedy administration filed fifty-seven voting rights suits, compared with just six under Eisenhower. And thirty of those suits were in Mississippi, with one in James O. Eastland's own Sunflower County.

Yet, although the Kennedy strategy may have looked workable on paper, it failed in the real world. Voting rights suits were complex and difficult to bring. (The evidence typically ran more than a thousand pages.) And while the lawsuits wound their sinuous way through the courts, black tenant farmers who bravely stepped forward to register to vote often found themselves thrown off their land and denied welfare payments, if they weren't assaulted or murdered. The FBI, under the iron rule of J. Edgar Hoover, claimed to have no jurisdiction over voting rights cases and thus made no effort to protect civil rights workers or those they were trying to register to vote. The Kennedy approach thus did not hold great promise.

When pressed to do more, Kennedy often cited obstacles that he said prevented him from doing what civil rights leaders wanted. He said he didn't have the authority to act; there were still problems with federalism, and so on. As time went on, civil rights advocates became increasingly cynical about such claims, saying they sounded more like excuses than reasons.

➡ *He overrelied on symbolic gestures.* Where the Kennedy administration excelled on the civil rights front was in the not unimportant realm of symbolic action, and he provided enough of that to keep most black leaders convinced he was on their side. When Kennedy noticed not a single black face in the U.S. Coast Guard Academy contingent marching in his inaugural parade, Kennedy directed speechwriter Richard Goodwin to call the Coast Guard commandant and tell him to ensure that it didn't happen again. Kennedy also created the President's Committee on Equal Employment Opportunity, which he pressured a reluctant Lyndon Johnson to chair.

Kennedy also appointed some fifty blacks to high administration posts, including his deputy press secretary, Andrew Hatcher, and deputy assistant secretary of state Carl Rowan. He also appointed five black federal judges, more than any other president, including Thurgood Marshall, the NAACP attorney who successfully argued the landmark Supreme Court school desegregation case *Brown* v. *Board of Education*. Kennedy also regularly invited prominent blacks to White House social events (although he refused to be photographed with Sammy Davis Jr. and his Swedish-born wife).

Important as such gestures were, however, they were not what the civil rights movement was ultimately seeking. It wanted voting rights, the right to serve on juries, the right to make and enforce contracts—in short, the full panoply of rights that white Americans took for granted. In theory, Kennedy wanted those things as well, but there seemed to be so much else that was more important: Khrushchev, Castro, averting nuclear war, the space race, and the stalled economy. Civil rights would just have to wait its turn.

"When I believe we can usefully move ahead in the field of legislation," Kennedy said at a news conference, "when I feel there is a necessity for congressional action, *with a chance of getting that action* [italics added], then I will recommend it."

➡ *He emboldened segregationists with his ambiguous stance.* Events, however, would not wait on John F. Kennedy's schedule. As he stuck doggedly to his legalistic course of action—the voting rights cases, the enforcement of federal court orders, and endeavors to maintain law and order—Southern segregationists increasingly met civil rights efforts with violence and terrorism.

Kennedy didn't take into account that his go-slow approach might be interpreted as irresolution by civil rights opponents and would thus embolden them. As a result, the administration repeatedly found itself thrown into crisis management mode as domestic violence exploded on a scale not seen since at least the 1930s and perhaps the Reconstruction.

On September 25, 1961, for example, Herbert Lee, a Mississippi farmer who was involved in voting rights activism, was shot and killed in Liberty, Mississippi. His white killer was acquitted. Two weeks later, 116 high school students were sent to jail for participating in a protest march. While the march proceeded, one white civil rights worker, Bob Zellner, endured a savage beating by members of an angry mob of several hundred whites as police stood by and FBI agents took notes. There would be many such incidents—and far worse—in the years to come.

Kennedy's response to the rising disorder was to issue public appeals for calm and adherence to the rule of law, while urging his brother to redouble his efforts to secure black voting rights. But he still seemed to view the entire issue fundamentally as a distraction. When told that some African diplomats driving from the United Nations in New York to Washington, D.C. had been refused service at a Maryland restaurant, his response was annoyed puzzlement over why they were driving in the first place. "When I travel between New York and Washington," he said, "I fly."

The battle—literal and figurative—to admit James Meredith to the Oxford campus of the University of Mississippi in September 1962 seems to represent something of a turning point for Kennedy. For a man who so valued his oratorical abilities, the abject failure of his nationally televised address on the eve of the crisis to have any positive impact whatsoever on events in Oxford shocked Kennedy. It began dawning on him that he had underestimated the magnitude of the task facing both him and the nation in this sphere.

Still, Mississippi wasn't quite enough to get his undivided attention. A month later came the Cuban missile crisis, and Kennedy was able to put civil rights on the shelf once again in favor of foreign policy, his favorite subject.

➡ *He ceded the initiative until the tide turned.* JFK's disengagement from the issue resulted in his committing the cardinal leadership sin of ceding the initiative. So far, it had been the segregationists who had taken advantage of that reality. As 1963 dawned, however, it would be the turn of the civil rights movement.

Birmingham, Alabama, was known as probably the most segregated city in the country and home to the nation's most violent Ku Klux Klan chapter, which had been active since World War II. Its all-white police force, under the control of Eugene "Bull" Connor, was known for its callousness and brutality toward blacks. Martin Luther King Jr. and Wyatt Tee Walker knew that if they could help break segregation in Birmingham, they could break it anywhere. Their explicit aim was to create a crisis, to provoke a violent reaction on Connor's part that would shock and educate world opinion in general and American opinion in particular. More specifically, one particular American: John F. Kennedy. "The key to everything," King observed, "is federal commitment."

Kennedy got the message King was hoping for, and it was televised. Thousands of black schoolchildren took to the streets of Birmingham. After an initial period of restraint, in which Connor refused to take the bait, Connor eventually responded with nightsticks, police dogs, and most memorably, fire hoses. The sight of young children being knocked to the ground by huge streams of water finally got many Americans to sit up and take notice of what was happening in their own country. It got John Kennedy's attention. The pictures, he told his aides, made him sick. Later, he commented that Bull Connor had done more for civil rights than any American since Lincoln.

Kennedy Gets Strongly Involved

John Kennedy may have been slow to awaken to the growing revolution in America. But once he saw his mistake in misjudging the civil rights movement, he jumped in and took a strong stand. His own response to this miscalculation is a classic three-step strategy for confronting, handling, and overcoming mistakes:

1. *Recognize there is a problem.* Kennedy's thinking in the realm of civil rights advanced dramatically in early 1963, as he realized how badly he had misjudged the overall situation. In February, he cautiously asked Congress for a bill to guarantee voting rights, but he soon came to realize that stronger medicine would be needed. The white Southerners, JFK told his staff, were "hopeless, they'll never reform. . . . The people of the South have done nothing for integration for a hundred years, and when an outsider intervenes, they tell him to get out; they'll take care of it themselves, which they won't."

   Also, from a political standpoint, Kennedy finally recognized that appeasing the South's political class simply wasn't getting him anywhere. Kennedy's low profile on civil rights seemed to make Southern committee chairmen no more receptive to the rest of his agenda, while white liberals and northern blacks were becoming increasingly alienated.

   Whether a more aggressive stance by Kennedy on civil rights earlier in his administration might have had an impact on the ground in the South must forever remain open to conjecture. Where it might have paid dividends, however, was on Capitol Hill. Withholding federal funds from Mississippi because of its denial of voting rights, as some of Kennedy's advisers suggested and he rejected, certainly would have gotten the attention of Senator Eastland. As it was, the likes of Eastland saw no reason to cooperate on the rest of the Kennedy agenda if they perceived no penalty for defying him on civil rights.

Yet, as with much of Kennedy's public career, it was the foreign policy dimension that was probably the decisive factor. The sight of American citizens being beaten and brutalized in the streets of their own cities for attempting to exercise their rights was an intolerable image for America to present to the world at the height of the Cold War. ("And what about the blacks in the South?" was a standard Soviet propaganda reply to American criticisms of the Soviet Union's human rights record.) In testimony before Senator Eastland's Judiciary Committee, Robert Kennedy pointedly asked if it was possible to consider a black man from Mississippi a citizen for purposes of the draft, then, when it came to voting, to consider him a citizen of Mississippi, so the federal government was powerless to help him.

2. *Be visible when addressing the problem.* The noncrisis at the University of Alabama over the admission of its first black students gave Kennedy the high-ground opening that he was seeking. When Alabama Governor George C. Wallace's threat to "stand in the schoolhouse door" and go to jail, rather than admit the students, was revealed to be empty bluster, the way was cleared for Kennedy to propose comprehensive civil rights legislation. Martin Luther King called the president's June 11, 1963, speech "eloquent" and "profound." Roy Wilkins said it was "the message I had been waiting to hear," and that he "fell asleep that night feeling new confidence."

3. *Acknowledge the mistake.* Seen from today's perspective, where legal racial equality in America is taken as a given, it may seem hard to credit Kennedy for his achievement with that speech. In retrospect, the struggle for racial equality seems to have an inevitability about it, such that it couldn't have turned out any other way. That just isn't true. It is commonplace to, somewhat patronizingly, credit John F. Kennedy, as well as Abraham Lincoln, with "growing in office" on racial issues. This ignores the fact that other men in the same position did not "grow" in office at all on this subject. Woodrow Wilson, for example, betrayed no evidence of changing his retrograde racial views one iota,

in spite of experiencing the first large-scale twentieth-century race riots during his time in office.

The great insight, of course, was King's: White America had to be convinced of the need for action. Birmingham, and then the great March on Washington in August 1963, helped achieve that. But that would have been in vain had John F. Kennedy not been *prepared* to admit he had misread the situation initially—and been willing to change his mind.

As a leader, don't be afraid to acknowledge a mistake. You need to be objective and flexible enough to change your focus to address crises.

How to Make the Most of Mistakes

➡ *Admit failures.* Mistakes and misjudgments are unavoidable; what counts is how you react to them. Many leaders don't want to lose face by admitting failures. But sometimes the admission is a necessary first step to addressing an issue. Kennedy's acknowledgment of his personal responsibility for the Bay of Pigs fiasco kept the political fallout to a minimum.

➡ *Right the mistake, and avoid similar ones.* Don't focus on the fact that you made a mistake. Try instead to focus on avoiding similar mistakes and rectifying the one you made. Kennedy's turnaround on civil rights was heralded by his June 11, 1963, speech to the nation. He didn't dwell on the mistakes of the past or his own misreading of the situation. As their leader, he called upon Americans to follow him in righting a longtime wrong.

➡ *Remain objective.* Don't let recovering from a setback become a personal vendetta; when things get personal, they get messy. You have to maintain enough distance to be objective and make the right decision. Kennedy allowed his intense dislike of Castro to cloud his judgment in relation to Cuba and its head of state. However, he recognized a certain kinship between himself and Khrushchev despite their strong differences of opinion. This helped him to defuse the Cuban missile crisis by giving the Russian leader a bit of leeway rather than backing him into a corner.

→ *Avoid tunnel vision.* What you think is most important may not in fact be what is most important. To avoid tunnel vision, you should make sure you do enough research into what the problem is. Check with all parties concerned. Get good advisers, and include opinions from people who have handled different situations. By continually checking your opinions against those around you, you can determine whether you are addressing the right issue in the right way. Many successful companies use 360-degree feedback for their leaders. This review process allows people in all positions—those working under the leader, on par with the leader, and above the leader in the hierarchy—to give the top executive feedback. It is a quick and effective way to determine whether you are meeting the needs of your organization.

CHAPTER 11

Crisis Management:
Be the Coolest Man in the Room

"He was so completely convinced of the rightness of his course that there was no evidence whatsoever of strain or of nervousness or of tension. . . . [T]his, in itself, was tremendously inspiring because when you are in a period of real crisis you look, then, to your leadership. And if your leader is nervous and upset and tense, this translates itself to everyone else and you in time translate that feeling to other people."

—REPRESENTATIVE HALE BOGGS,
ON THE EXPERIENCE OF BEING BRIEFED BY
JOHN F. KENNEDY DURING THE CUBAN MISSILE CRISIS

There is probably no aspect of leadership more important than the ability to manage a crisis. When crises arise, as they always will, leaders must stay focused on the main task at hand. You can't allow yourself to get distracted by side issues. You must project calm in the face of the crisis, so your people will be calm, too. That way you'll get valuable input and feedback from your advisers, although you must sift through sometimes-contradictory advice to reach your final decisions. And once you've come to a decision on how to handle the crisis, you must be firm and confident in your course of action.

An Early Lesson in Crisis Management

At around 9 P.M. on September 3, 1939, just nine hours after young John F. Kennedy had watched Britain declare war on Germany from the Stranger's Gallery of the House of Commons, the German submarine *U-30,* lurking off the western coast of Scotland, was stalking a British merchant vessel. Since the British ship was steering a zigzag course and was running with her lights out, Oberleutnant Lemp, the *U-30*'s commander, assumed she must be a troop ship or an armed merchant cruiser.

Lemp loaded torpedoes and fired. The SS *Athenia,* a passenger liner carrying more than 1,100 passengers from Liverpool to Montreal, was hit. The death toll was 112, including 28 Americans. The event eerily echoed the sinking of the *Lusitania* in the First World War.

The remaining passengers and crew, which included about 200 Americans, were rescued by British warships and brought to Glasgow. The U.S. ambassador to Great Britain, Joseph P. Kennedy, dispatched his son Jack, who was about to return to begin his last year at Harvard, to Scotland to see to the survivors' needs.

Jack visited the injured in hospitals and met with the rest of the survivors in a large hotel. He assured them that the embassy would provide money for replacement clothes and luggage and arrange passage for them on a ship flying an American flag. Kennedy assumed that the Germans would not attack an American ship because the United States was so far neutral in the conflict.

The passengers were having none of it. "We defiantly refuse to go until we have a convoy," a female passenger declared, loudly seconded by her fellow passengers. "You have seen what they will do to us."

Jack said he would pass the passengers' demands on to his father. Joe Sr., however, dismissed them. He was a diplomat. He wasn't in the business of organizing convoys. The *Athenia* survivors would be placed aboard an American-flagged ship to be taken home and that was the end of that.

Jack Kennedy had experienced his first public crisis. In the end, not everyone was happy, but all turned out reasonably well. This would become a pattern for Kennedy's public career, especially his crisis-packed presidency. Here's a closer look at some of the ways Kennedy handled crises.

The PT-109: Staying Cool and Moving Forward

The PT (or patrol torpedo) boat was not one of the more inspired ideas of the Second World War. Admiral John Bulkley, their major booster, convinced the navy brass in Washington, D.C. that the PTs could sink virtually the entire Japanese navy on their own, and he got funding for large numbers of the fast, small boats.

The reality was somewhat different. The plywood hulls of the PTs couldn't withstand even the smallest-caliber bullets. Their main armament, the Mark VIII torpedo, was unreliable. Most had no radar and their radios had a nasty habit of conking out at the worst possible moment. Their balky engines were powered not by diesel fuel, but high-octane gasoline, which meant the boats went up like a torch when hit. (After the war, Jack Kennedy had an opportunity to inspect a captured E-boat, the German equivalent of the PT, and pronounced it much superior.)

The bravery of their crews went a long way toward making up for the PTs' deficiencies. It was the prospect of action and danger in the South Pacific that drew Jack to service in the U.S. Navy and then the PT boats. Using his father's connections, he wangled a commission in the United States Naval Reserve, which allowed him to enter the service without a physical examination, which he likely would have failed.

But a crack JFK made about how getting himself killed for the "grand old flag" might be good for the political career of his older brother, Joe Jr., caused his family much distress. Thus, Joe Sr. seems to have exerted his considerable influence to keep his second son stateside, and Jack found himself driving a desk in Washington, D.C. Idle hands are the devil's workshop, and Jack was soon involved with a woman named Inga Arvad. She may not have been a Nazi spy, but she certainly had a murky past and was no fit company for the son of Ambassador Joseph P. Kennedy. Jack was soon whisked off to a navy base in South Carolina.

Jack had to pull some serious strings of his own in order to get out to the war zone. If his father wouldn't help, maybe his grandfather would. John "Honey Fitz" Fitzgerald intervened with Massachusetts Senator David Walsh, the chairman of the Naval Affairs Committee, to get Jack the coveted PT boat assignment. Despite the use of such influence, Jack wasn't a poor choice as a small boat commander. He had been sailing off Hyannis since he was a child, after all, and was thus familiar with boat handling, winds, tides, currents, and the like. He was also a strong swimmer, in spite of his back problems.

On the night of August 1, 1943, the PT-109 was one of fifteen PT boats sent out into the Blackett Strait west of New Georgia Island in the heart of the Solomon Islands war zone. Their mission was to intercept a force of Japanese ships that had managed to get past a U.S. destroyer screen. Two weeks earlier, Jack's boat had narrowly avoided being hit by bombs dropped from a Japanese plane, and two of his crewmen were wounded. But the attack scheduled for the night of August 1 was to be their first real baptism of fire.

For most of the PT crews that night, the action proved anything but. The navy's official history describes it as "the most confused and least effective attack the PTs had been in." Lacking in coordination (only a handful of the boats had radar), barely half the PTs fired their weapons, and none scored any hits. The Japanese ships, nicknamed the "Tokyo Express" by the Americans, roared on to their destination.

Following this action, many of the torpedo boats called it a night and withdrew. Lieutenant (junior grade) Kennedy's PT-109 and two other boats, however, never got the word. Jack, at the helm of the PT-109 and wearing a life jacket, ordered the ship to run muffled at six knots on one engine. Still concerned about Japanese planes and troops on nearby islands, he was trying to run as quiet as possible. The rest of his crew had their eyes peeled in the blackness, looking for any sign of movement.

The Japanese destroyers that had gotten past the other PTs earlier that night had delivered their supplies and reinforcements. They were now heading back whence they came—and straight at the PT-109.

"Ship at two o'clock!" shouted Howard Marney, the starboard machine gunner. At first, Kennedy's crew thought it might be one of the other two PT boats still in the strait with them, which delayed their reaction slightly. When it became apparent it was not, Kennedy turned the helm hard and ordered full power, but before the two idle engines could spring to life, the bow of the Japanese destroyer *Amagiri* slammed into the 109's starboard side, just fore of the torpedo tube. Two of Kennedy's men, Harold Kirksey and Marney, who had shouted the first warning, were killed instantly. As he was thrown about, Kennedy recalled thinking to himself, "This is how it feels to be killed."

The PT-109 was not split in half, as some accounts maintain. The boat appears to have remained largely intact, though its heavy engines caused the stern to sink below the surface after the collision. The flammable gasoline ignited, causing a fire that seemed certain to burn to death those who weren't killed immediately. But it seems the powerful wake of the *Amagiri* sucked most of the fuel away from the area, inadvertently saving the survivors. The Japanese paid no attention.

Most of the PT-109 survivors managed to stay close to the wreckage, but several had been thrown some distance away. Charles Harris was from Boston and was a good swimmer, but he bashed a knee in the incident and was also wearing a now-waterlogged sweater under his life jacket. Kennedy helped him aboard, clowning with him to keep up his spirits, saying, "For a guy from Boston, you're putting on a great exhibition." In no mood for jokes, Harris cursed at Kennedy.

The other man, forty-one-year-old Patrick "Pappy" McMahon, was by far the oldest member of the crew. (He even had a son in the navy.) He was hampered from getting back to the 109 because he was badly burned in the explosion. Stripping off his shoes and pants, Kennedy swam out to retrieve McMahon, taking the strap of the burned man's life jacket in his teeth and towing him back to the wreckage.

Kennedy's relationship with his crew now faced its most severe test. Fortunately, he had put the months before the collision to good use forging the men of the 109 into a good crew. In spite of his bad back and numerous health maladies, Jack Kennedy never shirked his share of the dirty work, stripping to the waist to help the crew scrape barnacles off the hull and doing other heavy maintenance work in the brutal South Pacific sun. He rarely, if ever, stood on rank. (Many were unaware until later that he was Ambassador Kennedy's son.) In this respect, he was unlike his elder brother, Joe Jr., who was very rank conscious and generally unpopular with many of his enlisted men.

The issue was what to do now. It does not appear to be true that the crew of the PT-109 was given up for dead almost immediately, according to the best detailed account of the incident, Joan and Clay Blair's *The Search for JFK*. An air search was mounted (though it does not appear to have been very thorough). More significantly, an Australian Navy "coast watcher" named Arthur Evans was informed to keep an eye out for the PT-109 survivors. Evans alerted a network of local natives on the surrounding islands about the lost PT boat; his actions would prove crucial to the rescue of the survivors.

For the moment, the survivors continued clinging to the wreckage, hoping to be spotted by a passing PT boat. Unfortunately, Jack did not fire a flare gun he had on board for fear it would give away their position to the enemy. This was an omission that proved costly, since a flare sent up soon after the accident would likely have resulted in the crew's fairly quick recovery, when other PTs were still in the area.

As it was, Kennedy and his men stayed with the wreck of the 109 until midday the next day. With the hulk filling slowly with water and threatening to founder, they had to find another refuge. The nearby island of Kolombangara had 1,000 Japanese troops on it and was clearly out of the question.

The official navy report recounts what happened next:

> Kennedy decided to swim for a small island barely visible (actually three miles) to the southeast. Five hours later, all eleven survivors had made it to the island after having spent a total of fifteen hours in the water. Kennedy had given McMahon a life jacket and had towed him all three miles with the strap of the device in his teeth. After finding no food or water on the island, Kennedy concluded that he should swim the route the PT boats took through Ferguson Passage in hopes of sighting another ship. After Kennedy had no luck, [Ensign George H. R.] Ross also made an attempt, but saw no one and returned to the island. Ross and Kennedy had spotted another slightly larger island with coconuts to eat and all the men swam there with Kennedy again towing McMahon. Now at their fourth day, Kennedy and Ross made it to Nauru Island and found several natives. Kennedy cut a message on a coconut that read "11 alive native knows posit & reef Nauru Island Kennedy." He purportedly handed the coconut to one of the natives and said, "Rendova, Rendova!" indicating that the coconut should be taken to the PT base on Rendova.

> Kennedy and Ross again attempted to look for boats that night

with no luck. The next morning the natives returned with food and supplies, as well as a letter from the coast-watcher commander of the New Zealand camp, Lieutenant Arthur Reginald Evans. The message indicated that the natives should return with the American commander, and Kennedy complied immediately. He was greeted warmly and then taken to meet PT-157, which returned to the island and finally rescued the survivors on 8 August.

In their book, the Blairs dispute many of the details in the official navy account. But the clinical prose of the navy report (written by Byron "Whizzer" White, whom Kennedy would later appoint to the Supreme Court) to some extent actually understates Kennedy's heroism. Jack had managed to salvage the PT-109's lantern and he took it with him when he swam out into the Ferguson Passage in hopes of flagging down a passing PT. He was extremely fortunate he did not see anything, for any PT boat probably would have blown him out of the water long before he got close enough to tell his story.

Like everything to do with the Kennedys, the PT-109 story has attracted conspiracy theorists. (White's subsequent appointment to the Supreme Court, for example, is sometimes cited as a "payoff" for covering up Kennedy's supposed negligence and/or incompetence in the incident, although there is no evidence for this claim.) An undoubtedly jealous Joe Jr. made it clear in a letter to Jack that he didn't think much of his abilities as a skipper.

Claims that Kennedy was delinquent in his duty or deserved court-martial for what occurred don't stand up to scrutiny. If Jack made mistakes that night in the Blackett Strait, he was not the only one, and his mistakes were not the most serious. His heroism was attested to by the surviving crew members—not years later, but in the moments immediately following their rescue, in the accounts they gave to two reporters.

The PT-109 became the cornerstone of the Kennedy legend, of course, almost as much a part of presidential folklore as George Washington crossing the Delaware or Abraham Lincoln splitting rails. Joe Sr. arranged for *The New Yorker* magazine and later *Reader's Digest* to do stories on his son's exploits—stories that were reprinted in the millions of copies during Jack's subsequent campaigns. (The PT-109 narrative was powerful; it certainly is no coincidence that when young John F. Kerry entered the navy during

Vietnam, he was attracted to service in the Swift boats, that war's equivalent of the PTs.)

The main lesson to be taken away from this incident is that throughout the crisis, Kennedy stayed cool. There were moments when he and his men might have been better served if he had thought more carefully before acting (his swim into the Ferguson Passage is a good example). But he was always moving forward, always looking for another opportunity. He never stopped trying and he never gave up hope.

Another important aspect of the story is Kennedy's low-key treatment of it afterward. Although urged by his aides to play up the incident in his campaigns, Kennedy himself rarely mentioned the PT-109 unless he was prompted. ("It was involuntary" was his response to a high school student's question about how he became a war hero. "They sank my boat.") And on those occasions when the incident was raised, he gave all the credit to his men and paid tribute to Kirksey and Marney. He knew that boasting of his heroism would not only appear immodest, it would also appear indecent, given the deaths of these two men.

Lesson: Braggarts aren't popular, and if you really are a hero, let other people tell the story.

The Berlin Crisis: Knowing When to Step Back

If one place deserved the title "crossroads of the Cold War," it was Berlin in 1960. When the victorious Allies decided to divide Germany into zones of occupation in the wake of World War II, they also decided to divide the historic German capital. Unfortunately, the city was isolated more than 100 miles inside the Soviet zone of occupation. The Western sectors, under the control of U.S., British, and French military authorities, was an island of freedom in a communist sea.

Thus, there was always a steady flow of refugees from East to West. But as the West German "economic miracle" took off in the mid-1950s, the contrast between the sectors became more and more stark, and the movement increased accordingly. Defecting to the West was often no more complicated than taking a subway ride.

By the summer of 1961, 30,000 East Germans a month were making the trip, overwhelming the city's refugee reception center. Worse, from the point of view of East German boss Walter Ulbricht (and, of course, Nikita Khrushchev), the people who were leaving were among East Germany's best and brightest: doctors, teachers, engineers, chemists, and the like. If the flow continued unabated, the only people left in East Germany would be the hard-core communist party members, the elderly, the infirm, and those without the wit or resolve to better their circumstances. It went without saying that it would be impossible to build a viable society on so shoddy a foundation.

This subject was clearly on Khrushchev's mind at the Vienna summit with JFK in June 1961. He handed Kennedy an *aide memoir* stating that within six months, the Soviet Union intended to sign a separate peace treaty with East Germany, officially ending World War II. Such an agreement would, at least in theory, terminate the West's rights in the divided city. The Western Allies would thus be illegally occupying the territory of a sovereign state and subject to eviction—by military force, if necessary.

Kennedy made clear in the strongest possible terms to Khrushchev that he would not be driven out of West Berlin. Better than anyone, Kennedy knew that leaving the city would ultimately mean leaving West Germany and Western Europe altogether. Upon his return from Vienna, Kennedy began reviewing his options—political, diplomatic, and military—for the confrontation that clearly could not be far off.

The circumstances were sobering. Kennedy consulted the Allies and found that France was opposed to any concessions to the Soviets over Berlin. The British were more frightened of a war over Berlin, but preferred that the Americans take the lead to negotiate some sort of deal. Between this divided counsel and Khrushchev's bellicosity, Kennedy had few attractive options when he appeared on television to address the nation on July 25, 1961.

The president placed the onus for any conflict on the Soviets (the "choice of peace or war is largely theirs, not ours"). He also emphasized the military buildup he had requested prior to departing for Europe two months earlier. He leavened the message by expressing a willingness to negotiate but left any solutions vague. This was done in part to avoid upsetting the Allies, and in part because the State Department couldn't come up with any alternative that might not look like surrender.

Khrushchev dismissed Kennedy's speech as posturing and bluff, though it was generally well received both at home and abroad. (A major miscalculation was Kennedy's call for a reinvigorated civil defense program and backyard bomb shelters; this set off a totally pointless debate about whether it was moral to shoot your neighbors if they wanted to enter your bomb shelter. Kennedy subsequently played down the civil defense angle as a result.)

One aspect of Kennedy's speech did not, however, receive the attention it deserved, except in the realm of its intended audience. Throughout the speech, Kennedy emphasized Allied rights in *West* Berlin. James P. O'Donnell, a former *Newsweek* correspondent who was a childhood friend of Kennedy's and who was now working for him in the State Department, was one of the few who noticed it before the speech was given. He urged that the word *west* be excised to emphasize that Kennedy was defending Allied rights in the city as a whole. The advice was rejected. Although O'Donnell was technically correct, JFK knew that few Americans would risk war over mostly theoretical Allied rights in East Berlin.

For three weeks after Kennedy's address, the status quo bumped along uneasily. Then, shortly after midnight on Sunday, August 13, 1961, trucks laden with barbed wire and building materials appeared on the eastern side of the Soviet zone. Careful to avoid actually stepping across the line, members of the East German Workers Defense Committees (communist party members all) began building obstructions to crossing between East and West. Subway and rail stations that crossed the two sectors were closed. People who tried to cross, in either direction, were turned back.

"I think they're going to build a *wall*," was the amazed response of CBS News reporter Daniel Schorr as he witnessed the odd goings-on in the Soviet sector.

That was just what they proceeded to do. Over the next weeks and months, what the East Germans dubbed the "anti-fascist protection barrier" grew from coils of barbed wire to a twelve-foot high brick-and-mortar obstruction that would be lighted and guarded twenty-four hours a day by troops with orders to shoot to kill anyone attempting to cross from the East to the West. The Berlin Wall would stand for twenty-nine years.

Like the Japanese at Pearl Harbor, the Soviets had saved their move for a Sunday morning, when few policy makers would be at their desks or even in town. Kennedy was vacationing at Hyannis Port when he got the news of events in Berlin. Some of his advisers urged an immediate return to Washington, but Kennedy chose to stay where he was, even being photographed going for an afternoon sail. Later, Kennedy ordered the U.S. garrison in the city beefed up and he dispatched Vice President Lyndon Johnson and retired General Lucius Clay—the hero of the 1948 Berlin airlift—to the city as a show of support to the West Berliners.

Although he could not dare admit it publicly, the wall suited JFK just fine. "A wall is better than a war," he said later.

He caught considerable flak for this decision, both from the Republican conservatives in Washington and from the Socialist mayor of West Berlin, Willy Brandt. The American public as a whole, however, was relieved that they no longer had to worry about whether to shoot neighbors trying to enter their bomb shelters. They backed Kennedy's policy of defending freedom where it existed, but not putting the peace at risk simply to make a point.

And although Khrushchev and Ulbricht may have thought they had solved a problem with their wall, they created another one. The Berlin Wall proved a propaganda defeat of major proportions for the Soviet Union and would serve as an ongoing embarrassment for the remaining life of that regime. It was this weakness that Kennedy exploited to the hilt with his "Ich bin ein Berliner" speech of June 1963.

The Cuban Missile Crisis

The Cuban missile crisis of October 1962 has been exhaustively chronicled in numerous books and articles (not to mention two motion pictures). There have even been conferences of the surviving participants (except for the Cubans) from which unique insights have been gleaned into the thinking on both sides.

This book is not the place for a detailed reconstruction of the events in the Cuban missile crisis. There has been a great deal of second-guessing of JFK's management of the crisis in the years since, including charges that he brought it on himself and that the settlement of the crisis was far more favorable to the Soviet Union than the United States. These controversies will rage on. What matters, however, is what Kennedy knew at the time and what he did with that information. Seen in context, Kennedy's courage, patience, coolness, and determination defused one of the greatest threats to world peace of the nuclear age.

It is more instructive here to examine how Kennedy handled the crisis, rather than the actual chronology of the crisis itself.

Putting First Things First

The missiles were discovered definitively on October 14, 1962, by a U-2 spy plane flown by Air Force Major Richard "Dutch" Heyser. Although National Security Adviser McGeorge Bundy had the news by evening on October 15, he chose not to inform Kennedy until the morning, allowing the president to get a good night's sleep before what was likely to be a difficult ordeal.

"We've got big trouble," the president told his brother by telephone the next morning from his White House bedroom. "Get over here." Robert Kennedy arrived and was shown the reconnaissance photographs Heyser had taken. He cursed the Soviets, who had promised, via RFK's unofficial Soviet embassy contact Georgi Bolshakov, among others, that they would introduce no offensive weapons into Cuba.

The president's first decision was to maintain absolute security over the information. All was to appear as normal in the White House. For that reason, he did not schedule an immediate meeting of his top national security officials but instead chose to keep his morning appointments. The first crisis meeting would therefore not take place until 11:45 A.M.

The makeup of that meeting reflected Kennedy's desire for a looser, less formal meeting process than the structured procedures of the Eisenhower years. Ever mindful of being "boxed in" by the experts, as he had been at the Bay of Pigs, he wanted to cast the net wider than the advice available from those in formal positions of responsibility. Thus, what became known as the ExComm, or Executive Committee of the National Security Council, also included Treasury Secretary C. Douglas Dillon, former Secretary of State Dean Acheson, the attorney general (brother Bobby), speechwriter and policy maven Theodore Sorensen, and Appointments Secretary Kenneth O'Donnell. Acheson, Sorensen, and O'Donnell were there especially to "watch the president's back" and ensure that he was not put in an untenable position politically.

The first item of business at that first meeting was to ensure that the United States was indeed facing a major threat. The reconnaissance photos were anything but a model of clarity. Although they were clearly labeled—"missile erector," "missile fueling truck," etc.—the objects to which these labels referred appeared to untrained eyes as little more than smudges. Kennedy closely questioned the experts on what appeared on the pictures and how they could be certain of what they showed.

The photographs did not show the presence of nuclear warheads, but that they were present, somewhere, no one doubted. The major question was when the missiles would be ready to fire. This was unanswerable, given the lack of knowledge about whether all the parts the Soviets needed were present on the island and how hard they were working. After an awkward silence, CIA Deputy Director Marshall Carter spoke up and said a week, maybe two.

Determining What Course of Action Should Be Taken

Satisfied that the missiles were indeed being installed, the question now facing the small group gathered in the Cabinet Room at that first meeting was awesome. What action could be taken to remove the weapons threat that would not provoke the Soviet Union to fire the missiles and possibly start a world war?

From this overarching question flowed all manner of subissues. Would America's European allies, who viewed Washington's obsession with Fidel Castro with bemused detachment if not bafflement, back the United States in the crisis? What about Latin America? Would Khrushchev demand concessions in Berlin or elsewhere in exchange for removing the missiles in Cuba? Could the lid of secrecy be kept in place and for how long?

The discussion was freewheeling and ultimately resolved itself into looking at four main options: 1) a surgical strike on the missile sites; 2) a wider attack on Soviet military sites in Cuba; 3) an attack on and general invasion of Cuba; 4) a blockade of Cuba and diplomatic negotiations.

Although the last option, a blockade, was eventually followed, early opinion leaned heavily toward some kind of military action. Interestingly, it was Robert F. Kennedy—the man who had been most hawkish on the issue of "doing something" about Castro and Cuba over the previous year and a half, as well as at the early afternoon meeting—who put the brakes on the idea at a later evening meeting. As the discussion of the details of an air strike unfolded, RFK passed a note to Ted Sorensen saying, "I now know how Tojo felt planning Pearl Harbor." This made a deep impression on the president, pushing him toward seeking some kind of peaceful resolution.

Establishing a Process

That first meeting would become a template for those that would follow over the succeeding twelve days. Together, and in smaller subgroups, the ExComm advisers would examine the evidence before them, debate the information it presented, and deliberate about the options available. Robert F. Kennedy later likened it to "talk, debate, argue, disagree, and then debate some more [which] was essential in choosing our ultimate course."

For the five days before Kennedy's speech to the nation revealing the crisis, the ExComm members met secretly in the Cabinet Room, the Oval Office, and a conference room at the State Department. (Occasionally, to preserve secrecy, meetings were held in the public rooms of the White House, such as the Yellow Oval Room.) The attendance list was ever-changing. The more visible members of the ExComm, such as Vice President Lyndon Johnson, had public engagements that could not be changed lest suspicions be aroused, so they could not attend all meetings.

The overall atmosphere continued to be free-form, with deputies encouraged to challenge their chiefs. Robert Kennedy and Defense Secretary Robert McNamara emerged as the leading personalities of the crisis, along with the president. Bobby encouraged JFK to stay away from some meetings so that some members of the ExComm would feel more comfortable speaking their minds. While RFK served as the de facto ExComm chairman (Secretary of State Dean Rusk shied away from the role), he saw his place as that of a prober and a skeptic, particularly with regard to proposed military solutions. He hadn't forgotten the blithe assurances of success about the Bay of Pigs that the president had received from the Joint Chiefs of Staff.

That didn't mean RFK consciously sought to dominate the discussions, however. He often went long periods without saying anything, and even sometimes sat in a chair against the wall instead of at the table, so as not to be too intimidating a presence. Ultimately, RFK emerged in the uncharacteristic role of a stabilizing influence and the voice of common sense, as Undersecretary of State George Ball put it.

As needed, outside experts were brought in or consulted. Kennedy spoke with British Prime Minister Harold Macmillan several times by telephone, and with Truman administration defense official Robert Lovett in New York. Also valuable were Llewellyn "Tommy" Thompson, the former ambassador to the Soviet Union, and UN Ambassador Adlai Stevenson.

Not everyone was sold on the way the ExComm operated, of course. Dean Acheson, the former secretary of state who had grown progressively more hawkish as the distance grew from his time in office under President Harry Truman, thought it largely a waste of time. (Kennedy found a better role for Acheson by dispatching him to Paris to secure the support of the prickly and unpredictable Charles de Gaulle.) But, over the nearly two weeks of the crisis, the ExComm members—under Kennedy's relatively light but sure hand—systematically worked their way through the options until they arrived at the one President Kennedy himself had favored from the beginning: a blockade of Cuba (which was labeled a "quarantine" for legalistic reasons), along with a parallel diplomatic track to seek the missile's removal.

Staying on the Initiative

Kennedy has come under retrospective criticism for his decision to make the crisis public with his October 22 speech appealing to Khrushchev to remove the missiles. Why didn't he quietly inform Khrushchev of his knowledge of the missiles and seek to work out a behind-the-scenes diplomatic settlement, rather than make public a crisis that nearly led to nuclear war?

Such criticism ignores the fact that Kennedy *had* been engaged in "back channel" negotiations with the Soviets as well as public discussions before the discovery of the missiles, and he had been lied to repeatedly. (Kennedy met with Foreign Minister Andrei Gromyko in the early days of the crisis—when it was still secret—and the Russian continued to insist that there were no missiles in Cuba. The president said later it was all he could do to restrain himself from pulling out the U-2 photos.) Khrushchev's credibility was not high with JFK in October 1962.

Also, if the president had revealed his knowledge of the missiles secretly to Gromyko, the initiative would have passed to Khrushchev. The Soviet leader could then have delayed responding until the missiles were operational. He could publicly announce the presence of the missiles and declare that as two sovereign states, the Soviet Union and Cuba could engage in any agreements they liked. He could also have pointed to the presence of similar U.S. missiles on the periphery of the Soviet Union, especially in Turkey, and placed Kennedy on the defensive internationally. (Kennedy had ordered the removal of the obsolete, inaccurate, and unreliable Jupiter missiles from Turkey several times, but both the U.S. Air Force and the State Department had dragged their collective feet. They didn't want to upset the Turks, who had lobbied Eisenhower hard for the missiles.)

The secret emplacement of nuclear missiles in Cuba unquestionably represented a shift in the global balance of power. Virtually all of America's nuclear early-warning systems were pointed north, toward the expected route of a Soviet missile attack over the North Pole. Soviet weapons in Cuba would render that entire system obsolete, as well as cut warning time down to only minutes. Furthermore, Castro could have used the missiles, at least implicitly, to threaten his neighbors. If the president had allowed the missiles to stay in Cuba, Robert Kennedy told his brother, "You would have been impeached."

By making the crisis public, Kennedy kept the Soviet leader reacting to him, rather than Kennedy having to react to Khrushchev. When your opponent is in such a position, he has less time and mental energy to plan his own countermoves.

Reacting to New Developments

One aspect of the crisis that was not ignored by the members of the Ex-Comm was the moral dimension. Robert Kennedy made the point emphatically at a meeting on October 18, in which he elaborated on the Pearl Harbor analogy. Any air strike or invasion would kill thousands of Cubans. "My brother is not going to be the Tojo of the 1960s," the attorney general said. Acheson was enraged by the comment, but Kennedy responded that a surprise attack on a small nation would do tremendous damage to American standing throughout the world, especially with small nations.

This moved the discussion more in the direction of a quarantine, which was Kennedy's favored approach. It was argued that the blockade would not get the missiles out of Cuba, but it would at least prevent any more missiles (or warheads) from entering. Also, an air strike would lead to unpredictable escalation. Kennedy had read Barbara Tuchman's best-seller *The Guns of August,* which detailed the outbreak of World War I, and he feared the confrontation would spiral out of control in a similar manner. Deputy Defense Secretary Roswell Gilpatric summed it up as an issue of "whether the president would start out with limited or unlimited action, and he thought it should be limited action." An air strike or invasion could still be undertaken later, if necessary.

It is important to note that this did not represent a consensus view of the ExComm. Acheson, along with Maxwell Taylor (the chairman of the Joint Chiefs of Staff), Paul Nitze (the State Department policy-planning chief), and others remained in favor of a military solution. And although Robert McNamara has sought in the years since to present himself as favoring a peaceful solution almost from the beginning, he was more inclined toward a military solution as the crisis went on. (A formal vote of the ExComm found eleven advisers in favor of quarantine and six voting for an air strike.)

Keeping Your Cool (Most of the Time)

The situation in Cuba and the world was not static during the crisis. Two incidents in particular carried special dangers. It is to Kennedy's credit that he did not escalate them.

The first was when an American U-2 spy plane flying over the Arctic wandered off course and encountered some Soviet fighter planes. "This means war with the Soviet Union!" exclaimed McNamara. Kennedy's response was exasperation rather than belligerence. "There's always some SOB who doesn't get the message," he said.

The second was more serious. Kennedy had ordered reconnaissance of Cuba to continue throughout the crisis, in spite of the danger from Soviet-built surface-to-air missiles (SAMs). On October 27, a U-2 piloted by Major Rudolph Anderson was struck by a SAM, killing Anderson instantly. Advocates of a strike against Cuba were greatly strengthened, arguing Khrushchev himself had ordered the shootdown as a show of defiance. (Years later, it was revealed that a Soviet general had defied orders and fired the missile.)

Kennedy, however, rejected the calls for, at the very least, attacking the offending missile site. He knew that accidents happen, especially in tense situations. "It isn't the first step that concerns me," he told his advisers, "but both sides escalating to the fourth and fifth step—and we don't want to go to the sixth because there is no one around to do so."

Kennedy kept his fabled cool for most of the crisis, although there were occasional outbursts. When a congressman walked out of a State Department briefing and gave secret information to the press, Kennedy was furious. He went so far as to track down the State Department briefing officer, Thomas Hughes, who, at that moment, was waiting for a plane at an airport.

"The president is calling American Airlines passenger Mr. Hughes," was the head-turning announcement that came over the airport public address system. Puzzled, Hughes picked up the phone to hear the familiar Boston accent at the other end demanding, "What the hell is going on?"

Putting Yourself in the Other Person's Place

Throughout the crisis, Kennedy was almost alone in keeping Khrushchev's interests at the forefront of the discussion. Perhaps the source of this empathy was that Kennedy recognized that only the Soviet leader truly shared with him the responsibility for not blowing up the world. Wherever it came from, this was a tremendously mature and insightful judgment, given the bullying and disrespectful way Khrushchev had treated him at Vienna sixteen months earlier.

"I don't want to put him in a corner," Kennedy said at various points in the crisis when an aide suggested strong action.

For his part, Khrushchev seemed to find it hard to do the same thing, lamenting at one point, "How can I deal with a man younger than my own son?"

Almost from the beginning of the crisis, the Jupiter missiles on Turkey's border with the Soviet Union had hovered like Banquo's ghost over the proceedings in the ExComm. Early on, Kennedy noted that a trade of the Cuban missiles for the missiles in Turkey would be a "good deal," and he didn't see how he could justify turning down such a trade if one were to be offered.

That, in the end, is exactly what happened. The crisis was ultimately re-solved through a combination of overt pressure and covert diplomacy. On

Friday, October 26, Soviet Premier Nikita Khrushchev sent Kennedy a telegram offering to remove his missiles if the United States promised never to invade Cuba. Kennedy was set to agree. But then on Saturday, October 27, Khrushchev sent another telegram upping the stakes, saying he'd remove his missiles from Cuba if the United States took its own nuclear missiles out of Turkey.

For two decades, Kennedy's aides and friendly historians have propagated the myth that the president accepted the first telegram and simply ignored the second. However, in 1982, on the twentieth anniversary of the crisis, a group of these aides—including Robert McNamara—revealed that, in fact, Kennedy acceded to the missile trade, that he told only a handful of advisers about the deal, and that he even told the Soviets that the deal would be off if they publicized it.

In 1987, the John F. Kennedy Library in Boston started to release tape recordings of the ExComm sessions, the meetings that Kennedy held with his advisers during the missile crisis. The tapes not only confirmed the revelation about the missile trade but also revealed that nearly all of Kennedy's aides were vociferously opposed to the deal at the time.

Exactly why Khrushchev accepted the deal has never been entirely clear. Castro urged him to fire the missiles on October 26, a request that no doubt had a sobering effect on the Russian. The crisis was also damaging Soviet relations with the emerging Third World, with a number of African and Asian nations unexpectedly criticizing the Soviet leader.

What Kennedy would have done if Khrushchev had not offered the deal, or had rejected it when Kennedy accepted it, is unclear. Pressure for a military solution would have been strong, but the available evidence seems to suggest that he would have continued to try the diplomatic route. He might have tightened the blockade further to include goods for military *use,* for example, such as oil and gasoline, as opposed to simply military equipment. He also had a backup plan in place to ask United Nations Secretary-General U Thant to intervene, if necessary.

History has borne out Kennedy's decision not to strike first. It has since been revealed that there were indeed nearly a hundred Soviet nuclear warheads on the island and that the Soviet general in command had received authorization to "use his discretion" on firing them in the event that contact with Moscow failed. An invasion of Cuba might have gotten rid of Castro, but if Miami or Atlanta had been incinerated in the process, it seems unlikely that most Americans would have considered that a fair trade.

Although he was careful to avoid gloating in public, Kennedy knew he had scored a great triumph. Obviously evoking the memory of Lincoln at the end of the Civil War, he cracked, "Perhaps this is the night I should go to the theater."

Although he was justifiably elated at the outcome, Kennedy wasn't fooled about the applicability of the solution to the Cuban missile crisis to other situations. Shortly after it ended, he invited historian Arthur Schlesinger into his office (Schlesinger was writing an official history of the administration) and dictated his reasons for believing the United States had prevailed in the crisis. Among them were that the United States possessed overwhelming military superiority, both generally and locally; that no vital Soviet interest was at stake in Cuba; and that Khrushchev did not have a case he could plausibly sustain before the world.

"He worried that people would take the wrong lessons away from the crisis," Schlesinger wrote in his notes. Kennedy's concern proved valid in Vietnam, when many of the participants in the crisis misapplied its lessons of graduated pressure (i.e., "escalation") to an inappropriate situation.

How to Manage Crises

➡ *Don't ignore a crisis.* Crises are inevitable and they don't just go away. You must learn how to manage them. In the mid-1990s, a Web site popped up that parodied the Muppet Bert from *Sesame Street*. It was called "Bert Is Evil" and had doctored photographs showing Bert with Adolf Hitler, the KKK, and Osama bin Laden. At the time, the Sesame Workshop (the producer of television's *Sesame Street*) didn't do much to fight these images; then, in 2001, after the attacks of September 11, the image of Bert with Osama was used in anti-American posters at a violent protest in Bangladesh. Naturally, this was picked up by the media and widely publicized. Had Sesame Workshop fought to have the pictures removed from the Web site earlier, it could have avoided this negative exposure. Now, the company has a plan to fight such abuse and more actively protects its image. If the *Sesame Street* producers had taken decisive action at the time, they not only would have discouraged other offenders, but would have had a legal basis to demonstrate that such misuse is commercially damaging for them. Don't ignore a crisis. Develop a plan to attack it and prevent it from happening again.

➡ *Learn to make educated decisions.* The advice you receive is likely to be divided; consensus in crisis situations is rare, so don't wait for it. The bigger the decision, the less likely you are to get everyone to agree. The U.S. president has the power to mobilize troops in a national crisis. To wait for consensus in Congress might be too late to handle an immediate threat. Weigh the pros and cons of each choice and make an educated decision. That's why you are the leader.

➡ *Don't be rattled or swayed by new developments.* Don't allow unexpected developments to divert you from your main course unless there is good reason. Outside events can occur because of stupidity or carelessness as easily as by design. Make sure you thoroughly evaluate "evidence" before making any decisions.

➡ *Above all, keep your cool.* If you show indecision or fear, that will inevitably communicate itself to those you are trying to lead. One of today's best-known leaders, former New York Mayor Rudolph Giuliani, makes a point of saying that the key to crisis management is to get calmer as the situation escalates. That way you can think clearly and make better decisions than if you let yourself become distracted. In addition, it is hoped that those around you will follow your lead.

CHAPTER 12

Faults and Failings:
How JFK Nearly Destroyed Himself

"In short, there's simply not
A more congenial spot
For happily-ever-aftering than here
In Camelot"

—FROM *CAMELOT,* THE MUSICAL,
BY FREDERICK LOWE AND ALAN JAY LERNER

Leaders are accountable to many people; it's part of the burden of leadership. Your subordinates, your bosses, your peers, your suppliers, your customers, and the public at large must all have varying degrees of faith in you. This doesn't mean you have to be perfect—nobody is. And it doesn't mean that you aren't entitled to your private life—of course you are. But you're headed for a fall if you conceal secrets so shocking that if they came out, they could ruin you and your organization.

It is a myth that anyone referred to the Kennedy administration as Camelot during Kennedy's lifetime. (Kennedy, who attended prep school with lyricist Alan Jay Lerner, likely would have snorted with derision if anyone had done so.) The legend actually dates from a postassassination interview that Jacqueline Kennedy gave to journalist Theodore H. White that ran in *Life* magazine. She recalled that her husband loved the Lerner and Lowe musical *Camelot,* and that the final verse to the song of the same name, quoted on the previous page, was his favorite. The metaphor of the handsome young President Kennedy as King Arthur, Jackie as Guinevere, and Kennedy's aides as the Knights of the Round Table proved irresistible to a public still in shock and deeply grieving Kennedy's loss.

Those who describe the Kennedy family as "American royalty" are closer to the mark than they perhaps realize. (Who are royalty but the lucky descendants of some exceptionally ambitious and ruthless ancestor like Joe Kennedy Sr.?) Likewise, the Camelot metaphor reveals more than those who believe in it think it does. The story of Camelot, after all, is not a lighthearted romp. It is in fact a rather dark story of egoism, adultery, and betrayal.

At the end of T. H. White's novel *The Once and Future King,* on which the musical *Camelot* is based, jealousies destroy King Arthur and the idyllic world of his court. The revelation of Kennedy's faults and failings, which began with the publication of Judith Campbell Exner's autobiography containing her claims of affairs with both Kennedy and mob boss Sam Giancana, destroyed many Americans' image of Kennedy's Camelot.

Our faults are often related, underpinning and reinforcing one another. The wellspring of Kennedy's faults lay in his excessive comfort with secrets and lies. Let's take a closer look at how this tendency intertwined with his character and the events of his life, and how you can avoid the same pitfalls.

Kennedy's Sexual Promiscuity: The Alpha Male Unbounded

When scholars and historians began debating "the Kennedy legacy" back in the 1960s, it is safe to say that no one thought about the possibility that his very name would one day become a byword for sexual incontinence.

But that is today's reality. (When Geoffrey Perret, who wrote the first one-volume biography of Kennedy, told people what he was working on, he said the first question he typically got was not related to the Cuban missile crisis or some other public event, but rather, "What are you going to say about all those girls?".) John F. Kennedy's sexual promiscuity is now as firmly entrenched in American political legend and folklore as George Washington's chopping down the cherry tree and Ulysses S. Grant's drinking—and with considerably greater basis in fact than either of those stories.

JFK was scarcely alone in having extramarital affairs in the circles he moved in, of course. Among powerful men in Washington, New York, or Hollywood, having girlfriends on the side aroused no more comment among one's peers than a trip to the golf course. Perret describes this as classic "alpha male" behavior. (Borrowed from the animal kingdom, the term "alpha male" denotes the male individual in charge of all other males in the group, such as in a wolf pack. The term is often applied to hypercompetitive men with a drive to dominate others.) Not that all males behave promiscuously, of course, or even all alpha males, but such behavior among rich and/or powerful men in all cultures is hardly uncommon.

But it is the sheer scale of Kennedy's womanizing, rather than the mere fact of it, that inspires something approaching awe in the observer. It seems never to have occurred to young JFK, starting in his midteens, that he might be engaging in reckless, let alone immoral, behavior. His only concern appears to have been whether he had contracted venereal disease. On several occasions, it appears nearly certain that abortions were quietly procured, usually with the aid of a devoted Kennedy hanger-on named Edward Moore.

Certainly, Jack didn't have much of an example when it came to sexual misbehavior. His father carried on numerous affairs, most notoriously with actress Gloria Swanson (and he bragged about others that he probably didn't have). JFK's mother seems to have been firmly in the grip of the idea that sex was purely procreative in nature. She moved out of Joe Sr.'s bedroom shortly after Teddy was born and seems not to have given the subject much thought ever afterward.

Joe Sr. seems to have encouraged sexual adventuring on the part of his sons as part of their growing-up process. If he ever upbraided them or expressed his disapproval in any way, it is unrecorded. This hands-off approach had predictable consequences. Among the Kennedy sons, Robert alone seems to have treated his wedding vows with more than passing seriousness.

Even while in the hospital as a teen, Jack wrote (frequently obscene) letters to friends bragging about conquests among the nursing staff. Although some of this was no doubt adolescent braggadocio, there is good reason to believe that much of it was true. This behavior continued into his adult life, with scarcely a break except for those periods when he was isolated in the

South Pacific during World War II or completely incapacitated by back or other ailments. He complained to Prime Minister Harold Macmillan of Great Britain (a friend and distant relation to the Kennedys) that he got headaches if he didn't have sex at least every two or three days.

Like his widely varied stable of friends and acquaintances, Jack's lovers ranged from European aristocrats to Hollywood stars, such as Marilyn Monroe and Greta Garbo, to prostitutes procured off of Washington's streets by willing aides and Secret Service agents. When no one else was available, there were always members of the White House staff, including two members of the secretarial pool who were called upon so regularly that the other members of the staff dubbed them "Fiddle and Faddle." Even the family members of close friends were not off-limits: one of Kennedy's ongoing liaisons at the time of his death was Mary Pinchot Meyer, sister-in-law of Kennedy's journalist chum Benjamin Bradlee.

"We're a bunch of virgins, married virgins" was the reaction of one stunned White House staffer to Kennedy's philandering. "And he's like God, f—— anybody he wants anytime he feels like it."

The mind reels at the chances Kennedy was taking. The blackmail potential alone was enormous. JFK's relationship with Monroe—originally facilitated by brother-in-law Peter Lawford—threatened to become public as the increasingly unstable and drug-dependent actress spiraled toward breakdown and suicide in the summer of 1962. People with good reason to hate and fear the Kennedys, such as Teamster boss Jimmy Hoffa and mobsters Santos Trafficante and Carlos Marcello, could have made grim use of such information.

Then there was the national security angle. One of Kennedy's conquests was Ellen Romesch, a shadowy woman of East German origin who ran a business providing "favors" for politicians and lobbyists. She had had an affair with a Soviet diplomat, and when her friendship with the president was revealed, she was swiftly deported.

Why didn't the press reveal such goings-on? There were several reasons. At the time, American society was far more reticent about discussing sex than it has subsequently become. Such things were perceived as "none of our business." The prevailing mood in this regard is captured nicely in the novel *Seven Days in May,* which was coauthored by JFK's friend Fletcher Knebel. In it, an American president refuses on principle to blackmail a Mac-

Arthur-like general with love letters the general has penned to his mistress, even though the general is threatening to overthrow the president and seize control of the American government.

Another reason for press reticence was more practical: the threat of litigation. Until the 1964 *New York Times* v. *Sullivan* case made it next to impossible for well-known public figures to sue successfully for libel, the press could generally write about such shenanigans only if they were aired in open court (which is one reason divorce cases were so extensively and luridly covered in the press in those days).

Still, it's not as if there was *no* coverage. Gossip columnists repeatedly described the dalliances of "a high government official," and as the time of his death approached, there were signs that the press was becoming bolder and less inhibited. "Good night, Mrs. Kennedy, *wherever* you are" was a talk show host's veiled means of referring to the state of the president's marriage. Although historians often debate what might have happened in Vietnam if Kennedy had lived, very few consider that other counterfactuals are possible as well, such as a major sex scandal that almost certainly would have ended Kennedy's reelection hopes and his career in the bargain.

After all, exactly that had happened to Kennedy's friend Harold Macmillan in the last summer of Kennedy's life. Just a month before Kennedy's death, Macmillan was forced to resign as Britain's prime minister due largely to the fallout from the scandal surrounding the admission by Macmillan's war secretary, John Profumo, that contrary to his earlier denials, he had indeed had an affair with a high-class prostitute named Christine Keeler. What made this politically fatal to Macmillan was that Keeler had also had an affair with a Soviet intelligence agent. Shades of Ellen Romesch. Kennedy was well versed on the scandal, but he seems not to have for a moment considered that something similar could happen to him. He made no changes in his own behavior.

Although many have spun elaborate psychological reasons for Kennedy's recklessness in this realm, there really isn't much of a mystery. On the few occasions when some particularly bold individuals worked up the nerve to ask Kennedy about his philandering, he was surprisingly blasé about the matter. This was simply how powerful men behaved, he said. His extensive reading of history, particularly British and European history, which he preferred to American history, confirmed him in this belief.

The Kennedy Marriage: A Glorified Sham

The greatest casualty of this philosophy was, of course, his marriage to Jacqueline Lee Bouvier. Although the union of "Jack and Jackie" was presented to the public as idyllic, it is now clear that they were fundamentally incompatible as a married couple. Her refined tastes in music, fashion, food, and art meshed poorly with his more plebeian outlook. His intense interest in politics was more than matched by her utter indifference. And although she was inured to male sexual infidelity by the example of her father, John "Black Jack" Bouvier, and his treatment of her mother, Janet Auchincloss, even Jackie seems to have been taken aback by her husband's serial adultery. "I love Jack," she burst out to some friends during an exceptionally difficult period, "but he's impossible!"

The two adjusted to this situation in various ways. They spent long periods of time apart, and neither seemed to pine for the other's company during these bouts of separation. Around the White House, Jackie would sulk by refusing to perform her duties as First Lady (a title she loathed), often begging off because of supposed ailments. (The White House press operation frequently had to scramble when the "ill" Mrs. Kennedy would be spotted water skiing or horseback riding soon after one of these cancellations.) She would pass assignments she thought unpleasant or boring off onto Lady Bird Johnson. Jackie would also go on shopping sprees in New York and Paris, sticking a none-too-happy Jack with the bills.

Sometimes, her myopia with regard to political issues could lead to embarrassment. When Martin Luther King Jr. visited the White House in the midst of a civil rights crisis, Jackie spoke to him at length about antique furnishings. After she had moved on, the mystified King turned to one of Kennedy's aides and said, "Well, well, wasn't that something?"

They each doted on their children, of course, but even there, differences flared. Jackie was determined to give them as "normal" an upbringing as possible and sought to keep the press away from Caroline and John Jr. The president, attuned to the political advantages of a young, vibrant family, wanted photographers and reporters to document their every move.

Where the marriage was an undeniable success, however, was in the support Jacqueline gave Kennedy in setting the high tone of the administration. Although initially unenthusiastic (he worried about a public perception of high living), he quickly warmed to the idea of redecorating the White House when the popularity of the idea became evident.

Jackie's natural charm and grace, plus her facility with languages, proved tremendous assets to her husband, especially when dealing with such prickly foreign leaders as Charles de Gaulle and Nikita Khrushchev. (She even acted as an unofficial interpreter between the French president and her husband, handling adroitly complex issues of foreign and defense policy.) Her beauty, relative youth, and aristocratic bearing—especially when compared with her three immediate predecessors—seemed to send crowds into paroxysms of ecstasy whenever and wherever she appeared, whether in the United States or abroad.

The two grew temporarily closer after the death of their infant son Patrick in August 1963, and Kennedy sent her a passionate love letter on their tenth wedding anniversary a month later. But Kennedy was soon back to his old ways. In October 1963, she was the source of rare public embarrassment for him when she was photographed wearing a bikini aboard the yacht of Greek shipping magnate Aristotle Onassis. Kennedy ordered her to come home immediately, but she insisted on taking her time. Shortly before they departed for Dallas (the first time she had accompanied him on a political trip during his presidency), the couple were overheard quarreling before a public event.

In short, far from being made in heaven, the Kennedy marriage occupied the outer suburbs of hell. From a public relations/career standpoint, it must be judged an outstanding success. At the same time, however, both parties, as well as those around them, paid a steep personal price for maintaining the façade. Kennedy friends and associates were unavoidably drawn into the deception—part of the "price of admission" to the magic inner circle, as Richard Reeves put it. These people found themselves lying to others, and not infrequently, themselves, about what they were actually doing. Inevitably, Kennedy's moral corruption was not simply "his own business." It corrupted all those who came within range of him.

Kennedy's Health: A Seriously Sick Man

The photographs of John F. Kennedy and his family sailing, swimming, and playing touch football on the lawn at Hyannis are as indelibly inscribed on our collective memory as just about any images in American history. To be sure, the Kennedys have always been a very physically active clan, but part of it was calculated: the concealment of the fact that John F. Kennedy had serious physical problems that might have confined him to a wheelchair or perhaps even killed him before too terribly long.

His youthful health problems with his back, his bowels, and Addison's disease have been well documented. But the watchword of the Kennedy administration was "vig-uh," so the need to maintain the image of an active, youthful president was essential. This need led Kennedy into the hands of some very dubious characters indeed.

Most of the trouble was caused by Kennedy's unstable back, which generally ached at the best of times and throbbed excruciatingly at the worst. Planting a tree while on a state visit to Canada early in his term, he threw out his back so badly his doctor wanted to have him carried off *Air Force One* in Washington. Kennedy adamantly refused, imagining the pictures that would reach the newspapers. But he was forced to deplane using crutches, and with the help of a cargo lift that obviated his need to use the stairs. He sometimes got around the White House with the aid of crutches discreetly secreted throughout the executive mansion. He also wore a nonmetallic back brace. On one occasion, CBS newsman Robert Pierpoint spotted Kennedy in a wheelchair during a trip to Florida.

It must be said that Kennedy bore the pain stoically, never complaining publicly and—only very rarely—privately. Anyone who has ever suffered from chronic pain, however, knows how desperate the desire for relief can be. His initial White House physician was Dr. Janet Travell, a specialist in muscular disorders, but all Travell really did was inject his back muscles with nerve-deadening procaine. But Kennedy's body soon became tolerant of the drug and Travell was forced to inject him with greater frequency (as often as six or seven times per day) and with higher doses, to less effect.

In the celebrity circles in which Kennedy moved, the use and abuse of chemical stimulants was far more widespread and tolerated than in American society at large. Frank Sinatra apparently introduced Kennedy to Dr. Max Jacobson, a New York–based physician who counted stars such as Eddie Fisher, Alan Jay Lerner, Truman Capote, as well as Sinatra among his "patients." In fact, Jacobson was, as the tabloids later dubbed him, a "Dr. Feelgood." (He ultimately lost his license to practice medicine.) Jacobson shot

his clients up with amphetamines ("speed") and other wild concoctions that
made them feel better for a time. Known as Miracle Max, he began treating
Kennedy during the 1960 campaign and continued to do so during Kennedy's presidency. That was bad enough, but worse was the fact that Kennedy
kept this information from his other physicians.

The German-born Jacobson soon became a fixture around the White
House, even accompanying Kennedy to the disastrous Vienna summit with
Nikita Khrushchev and injecting him right before his first meeting with the
Soviet dictator. Did the injection prevent Kennedy from performing at his
best? That is only speculation, but Kennedy's uncharacteristically tongue-
tied performance lends credence to the theory.

There were people around Kennedy who tried to pry him away from
Jacobson, notably his brother Bobby. But Jack would have none of it. Kennedy kept seeing Jacobson, sometimes as often as twice a week, until his
death.

All of this was concealed from the public, of course. (Whenever Kennedy's back problems became too severe to be hidden, they were simply as-
cribed to "an old war injury.") In fact, his vertebrae were steadily deteriorat-
ing, and it is possible that had he lived and been reelected, he might have
been confined to a wheelchair by the time he left office in 1968.

By no means were Kennedy's back problems his only maladies. He suffered from a variety of allergies for which he received regular injections. He
became increasingly intolerant of milk as time went on and also had to re-
strict his alcohol intake. To top it all off, his vision became steadily less acute
(he wore large, horn-rimmed reading glasses in private) and was even par-
tially deaf in his right ear.

There is certainly something admirable about Kennedy's ability to face up
to the challenges of the presidency with an utter absence of whining about
his hard luck at having such a weak body. At the same time, a president who
needs to be high on various narcotics administered by a quack in order to
function hardly inspires confidence. Some have pointed out that Franklin D.
Roosevelt disguised his disabilities, but that hardly clinches the argument.
More than a few historians think the dying FDR was at a disadvantage near
the end of his life in negotiations with Joseph Stalin. Kennedy should have
been more forthcoming about his health problems and let the American
people decide.

Kennedy and the Problem of Integrity

In his speech to the Massachusetts state legislature before his inauguration as president, Kennedy said he expected to be judged by what he termed "the high court of history" by several criteria:

> For of those to whom much is given, much is required. And when at some future date the high court of history sits in judgment on each one of us—recording whether in our brief span of service we fulfilled our responsibilities to the state—our success or failure, in whatever office we may hold, will be measured by the answers to four questions:
>
> First, were we truly men of courage—with the courage to stand up to one's enemies—and the courage to stand up, when necessary, to one's own associates—the courage to resist public pressure, as well as private greed?
>
> Secondly, were we truly men of judgment—with perceptive judgment of the future as well as the past—of our own mistakes as well as the mistakes of others—with enough wisdom to know what we did not know, and enough candor to admit it?
>
> Third, were we truly men of integrity—men who never ran out on either the principles in which we believed or the people who believed in us—men whom neither financial gain nor political ambition could ever divert from the fulfillment of our sacred trust?
>
> Finally, were we truly men of dedication—with an honor mortgaged to no single individual or group, and compromised by no private obligation or aim, but devoted solely to serving the public good and the national interest?

Kennedy was certainly a man of considerable courage and judgment, who was willing to stand up to both his foes and friends when the occasion demanded. That he was dedicated to certain overarching principles in his public life there can be no doubt. But was he a man of "integrity"?

By his own lights, in any case, he was. Note how Kennedy in the speech defines "integrity." It means never running out on one's political principles for reasons of financial gain or political ambition. That Kennedy would have done anything in his public life for reasons of financial gain is inconceivable, given his family's great wealth. And beyond the normal trimming and compromises of political life, he threw over no major political principles or stands in order to advance his career.

To Kennedy, in other words, integrity meant only *public* integrity. His private life simply did not enter into the equation. That a man who wrote and spoke so eloquently and with such passion about integrity, and how "a good conscience" was "our only sure reward," could be so cavalier about his private behavior still puzzles those who thought they knew him.

All human beings are not quite what they appear to be, of course. Many people often conceal secrets even from those closest to them. That doesn't make it right, of course, but it is often true.

In the case of a wealthy, powerful public man (or woman), it is certainly possible to conceal, at least for a time, very damaging information about oneself. Kennedy was hardly the only person to do this. Woodrow Wilson was able to prevent the public from knowing the full extent of his being disabled by a stroke in 1919 and 1920, with his wife effectively functioning as president for much of that time. Grover Cleveland concealed an operation for cancer of the jaw while he was in office.

It is probably not necessary, however, to be quite so secretive about health issues, especially in this era of "full disclosure." President Ronald Reagan provides the best example. He underwent operations to remove cancerous lesions several times during his presidency, each time making the announcement publicly and dealing with the consequences, which were few. Reagan's openness in dealing with his polypectomy is credited with bringing the issue of proper screening for colon cancer to national attention. When he was diagnosed with Alzheimer's disease after leaving office, he admitted it and turned the occasion into a heartfelt "farewell" to the American people, an address that was recalled fondly years later at his funeral.

Sickness may be beyond one's control, but loutish behavior is not. Kennedy's lack of sexual self-control may have been forgivable in a hormone-addled teenager, but certainly not in the leader of the free world.

Generally speaking, secrets and lies are impossible to maintain forever. The "high court of history," by which Kennedy set such store, has a way of smoking them out. And when it does, the results often are not pretty. One explanation for the wild swings in opinion about Kennedy's historical reputation—which are probably greater than that of any other president—may be that many people cannot reconcile the high ideals and noble intentions of his public utterances with the moral squalor of his private behavior.

John F. Kennedy overcame obstacles and beat the odds in many respects in order to have a significant and consequential public career. As president, he got most of his major public decisions right, and one of them—his commitment to equal rights for black Americans—was historic by any standard. Sadly, that accomplishment is now marred in the public mind by the truth of the life he led behind closed doors. And that, rather than any sense of unfulfilled promise, remains the real tragedy of John F. Kennedy's life and leadership.

How to Avoid Embarrassment—Tips for Leaders

➠ *Avoid putting yourself in compromising situations.* That way, you won't get caught. Despite a far more lenient attitude toward sexual issues than was present in Kennedy's time, Bill Clinton's second term as president was severely compromised (and nearly ended) by his dalliance with a young intern in the Oval Office. Because he was unable to control his baser instincts, Clinton played right into the hands of his critics and opponents. The ramifications of such a revelation in regard to JFK would have been disastrous to Kennedy himself, his presidency, and the country as a whole.

➠ *Don't be phony.* Project an image of who you really are, not a false image of what people want to believe. For the most part, people have an amazing capacity for acceptance, but they don't like to be fooled. In the late 1950s, however, the disclosure that some of the country's beloved television quiz shows of the time were fixed caused a major public scandal. It took many years for the TV networks to dare to put game shows on the air again, and then they adopted entirely different formats from the previously popular question–and–answer program.

➠ *Try to be as open as possible, within reason.* Of course, you're entitled to your privacy, no matter how public a figure you may be. But concealing important information concerning your health, your finances, or your connections, for example, can lead to major problems. The more you try to keep secret, the more shocking the revelations will be if they come out.

➠ *Don't expect other people to cover up for you.* Living a lie puts a lot of pressure on those around you. A leader who asks others to lie and keep secrets for him risks losing the respect of his people. Leadership is hard enough without trying to lead people who resent you. The spate of tell-all books by insiders over the last twenty years or so (ironically, unlike in Kennedy's time, when such tattling was considered poor form) reveals how quick underlings are to "spill the beans" on their bosses.

Bibliography

Ballard, Robert D. *Collision with History: The Search for John F. Kennedy's PT 109*. Washington, DC: National Geographic Press, 2002.

Barber, James David. *The Presidential Character: Predicting Performance in the White House*. Englewood Cliffs, NJ: Prentice-Hall, 1972.

Berry, Joseph P. *John F. Kennedy and the Media: The First Television President*. Lanham, MD: University Press of America, 1987.

Beschloss, Michael R. *The Crisis Years: Kennedy and Khrushchev, 1960–1963*. New York: HarperCollins, 1991.

Bishop, Jim. *A Day in the Life of President Kennedy*. New York: Bantam Books, 1964.

Blair, Joan, and Clay Blair, Jr. *The Search for JFK*. New York: Putnam, 1974.

Bradlee, Benjamin. *Conversations with Kennedy*. New York: W.W. Norton & Co., 1975.

Buckingham, Marcus, and Curt Coffman. *First, Break All the Rules: What the World's Greatest Managers Do Differently*. New York: Simon & Schuster, 1999.

Burns, James MacGregor. *John Kennedy: A Political Profile*. New York: Harcourt Brace, 1960.

Claflin, Edward B. *JFK Wants to Know: Memos from the President's Office, 1961–1963*. New York: William B. Morrow & Co., 1991.

Clarke, Thurston. *Ask Not: The Inauguration of John F. Kennedy and the Speech That Changed America*. New York: Henry Holt & Co., 2004.

Collier, Peter, and David Horowitz. *The Kennedys: An American Drama*. New York: Summit Books, 1984.

Dallek, Robert. *An Unfinished Life: John F. Kennedy, 1917–1963*. Boston: Little, Brown, 2003.

Giglio, James N. *The Presidency of John F. Kennedy*. Lawrence, KS: University Press of Kansas, 1992.

Goldzwig, Steven R., and George N. Dionisopoulos. *"In a Perilous Hour": The Public Address of John F. Kennedy*. Westport, CT: Greenwood Press, 1995.

Hamilton, Nigel. *JFK: Reckless Youth*. New York: Random House, 1992.

Hayward, Steven F. *Churchill on Leadership: Executive Success in the Face of Adversity*. Sacramento, CA: Prima/Forum, 1998.

Henggeler, Paul R. *The Kennedy Persuasion: The Politics of Style Since JFK*. Chicago: Ivan R. Dee, 1995.

Kennedy, John F. *Profiles in Courage*. New York: HarperCollins, 2003.

———. *The Strategy of Peace*. New York: Harper & Brothers, 1960.

———. *The Uncommon Wisdom of John F. Kennedy: A Portrait in His Own Words*. Edited by Bill Adler and Tom Folsom. New York: Rugged Land, 2003.

————. *Why England Slept*. Westport, CT: Greenwood Press, 1981.

Kennedy, Robert F. *Thirteen Days: A Memoir of the Cuban Missile Crisis*. New York: W.W. Norton & Co., 1999.

Leamer, Laurence. *The Kennedy Men: 1901–1963*. New York: William B. Morrow & Co., 2001.

Lincoln, Evelyn. *My Twelve Years with John F. Kennedy*. New York: McKay, 1965.

Matthews, Christopher. *Kennedy and Nixon: The Rivalry That Shaped Postwar America*. New York: Simon & Schuster, 1996.

Newell, Waller R. *The Code of Man: Love, Courage, Pride, Family, Country*. New York: Regan Books/HarperCollins, 2003.

O'Donnell, Kenneth P., and David F. Powers, with Joe McCarthy. *"Johnny, We Hardly Knew Ye": Memories of John Fitzgerald Kennedy*. New York: Pocket Books, 1972.

Paper, Lewis J. *The Promise and the Performance: The Leadership of John F. Kennedy*. New York: Crown, 1975.

Parmet, Herbert S. *Jack: The Struggles of John F. Kennedy*. New York: Dial Press, 1980.

————. *JFK: The Presidency of John F. Kennedy*. New York: Doubleday, 1984.

Perret, Geoffrey. *Jack: A Life Like No Other*. New York: Random House, 2001.

Postrel, Virginia. *The Substance of Style: How the Rise of Aesthetic Value Is Remaking Commerce, Culture, and Consciousness*. New York: HarperCollins, 2003.

Reeves, Richard. *President Kennedy: Profile of Power*. New York: Simon & Schuster, 1993.

Reeves, Thomas C. *A Question of Character: A Life of John F. Kennedy*. New York: The Free Press, 1991.

Renehan, Edward J., Jr. *The Kennedys at War: 1937–1945*. New York: Doubleday, 2002.

Roberts, Andrew. *Hitler and Churchill: Secrets of Leadership*. London: Weidenfeld & Nicolson, 2003.

Salinger, Pierre. *John F. Kennedy, Commander in Chief: A Profile in Leadership*. New York: Viking, 1997.

————. *With Kennedy*. New York: Doubleday, 1966.

Schlesinger, Arthur, Jr. *A Thousand Days: John F. Kennedy in the White House*. Boston: Houghton-Mifflin, 1965.

Silvestri, Vito N. *Becoming JFK: A Profile in Communication*. Westport, CT: Praeger, 2000.

Sorensen, Theodore C. *Kennedy*. New York: Harper & Row, 1965.

————. *"Let the Word Go Forth": The Speeches, Statements, and Writings of John F. Kennedy, 1947 to 1963*. New York: Dell Books, 1991.

Strock, James M. *Reagan on Leadership: Executive Lessons from the Great Communicator*. Sacramento, CA: Prima/Forum, 1998.

————. *Theodore Roosevelt on Leadership: Executive Lessons from the Bully Pulpit*. Sacramento, CA: Prima/Forum, 2003.

Walsh, Kenneth T. *Air Force One: A History of the Presidents and Their Planes*. New York: Hyperion, 2003.

Wanniski, Jude. *The Way the World Works: How Economies Fail and Succeed*. New York: Basic Books, 1978.

White, Mark J., ed. *Kennedy: The New Frontier Revisited*. New York: New York University Press, 1998.

Index